THE
LONGEST
WAR

Published 2024
Printed in the United States of America
Print ISBN: 978-1-64742-688-0
E-ISBN: 978-1-64742-689-7
Library of Congress Control Number: 2023923261

For information, address:
She Writes Press
1569 Solano Ave #546
Berkeley, CA 94707

Interior Design by Tabitha Lahr

She Writes Press is a division of SparkPoint Studio, LLC.

"The Uses of Sorrow" by Mary Oliver
Reprinted by the permission of The Charlotte Sheedy Literary Agency as agent for the author. Copyright © 2006 by Mary Oliver with permission of Bill Reichblum

Names and identifying characteristics have been changed to protect the privacy of certain individuals.

THE

a psychotherapist's

LONGEST

experience of divorce, custody,

WAR

and power

CATHERINE HARRINGTON, PhD

SHE WRITES PRESS

Dedicated to

all mothers and fathers everywhere.

CONTENTS

PREFACE

....

The specific spark for writing about this part of my life came from an Overeaters Anonymous meeting. I was a speaker only once, and I went for broke: I confessed I did not have custody of my sons. In that era, a mother without custody was assumed to be unfit—either a drug addict, too ambitious, or mentally unstable. Until then, I had hidden my shame and, when possible, stayed vague; my story seemed too complicated to explain to non-veterans.

After the OA meeting, four women came up to me to say they, too, did not have custody of their children and they never talked about it to anyone. We each carried the shame of the culture as a private burden. That incident was the first time I realized I had company, and gave me the idea to write my story.

I lived through these years in a fog of war, putting one foot in front of the other, fighting for my survival. Like many people who have survived trauma, I had fragments of facts and recollections but no sense of the whole. I had outrage and pain, but no ability to describe a coherent sequence of events. All I had were anecdotes that existed almost in isolation. Mostly, what I had was a physical sense of dread, fear, and seemingly unending tears.

I needed to understand what had happened. How did a marriage that began with such hope go awry? How did we bring this on ourselves? Who did what? How did it escalate to such catastrophic proportions? Could I have prevented any of it? Tempered it? Changed it?

There are no villains in this memoir, even though at one time I believed there were. We are all flawed people, using each other to smooth our rough edges, like pebbles in a stream. In the great mystery of life, very little is personal, yet each of us is responsible.

I waited nearly twenty years from our last court hearing before starting to write this story in 1999, but I quickly learned that twenty years was not enough. I was still too raw, and at every writing session, I dissolved in tears. The trauma of the years-long custody fight not only replicated but also reinforced the trauma of my childhood. For decades, both remained undigested in my body.

Three months into my initial writing, I had a dream, which condensed and illustrated my experience of having custody of my sons taken from me.

> There is a big room, like a school gymnasium, with a lot of people in it. Two children are brought to the door and invited in. Everyone at the entry treats them well and makes it seem like this is a wonderful place to be, but I know it is all fake. The children are told how they will be fed and have a lot of things to play with. But I know the truth . . . once they are inside, they will be ignored and be starved to death. I know that this is really a maximum-security prison.

I put the memoir aside. I needed to find my fragmented selves, my little ones and my young-mother ones, and bring them all to safety and wholeness. To do that, I needed professional help. I sought out and found skilled and compassionate practitioners to accompany me as I opened Pandora's box and digested my untold fear, grief, and fury. Eighteen years after my first attempts at writing, I dove in again in 2017 and spent five years researching, writing, revising, and healing.

Preparing for publication opened more layers of previously dormant distress. Emotional PTSD flashbacks put me in a tizzy, and my usual clear thinking became anxious, circular, and filled with doubt. I needed more rounds of help, more evolution, and as always, more tears.

I have needed a quarter of a century to get this book written, edited, and published. I hereby declare this story documented, integrated, and still evolving.

PROLOGUE

....

December 1941

I—a gestating fetus—am marinating in bourbon and smoke. Old Crow and Lucky Strike are my mother's brands of choice. Maybe it is the fact of me that pushes her to drink. I am an unplanned third pregnancy soon after my two older sisters. My father's sperm penetrating my mother's egg destined her to three children under the age of three. More Old Crow, please.

I feel the tremor of Pearl Harbor even though I am only a dividing zygote. How could I not? The world changed on its axis. Twenty-five hundred dead, twelve hundred wounded, all in one day. No barrier can protect me from that kind of shock; it shapes who my mother is, and who I am becoming.

The anxiety of war seeps into my cells. The menfolk disappear to faraway places—places with no meaning in the Aggies town of Fort Collins, Colorado. Places whose names might have meant adventure in another era now only ring of dread and danger. *Rangoon* means one more young farmer felled.

The women carry on. They run the farms, using ever-younger hands who should be in school. The women feed their babies but worry where the food will come from. The Longmont farm women—my mother's in-laws—reach out to her, but prickly and haughty, she rejects their embrace. She doesn't need solace. My father, a one-eyed surgeon, cannot go off to war. His homebound presence reassures her of her superiority.

At twenty-three, she'd married the most desirable bachelor in Fort Collins—a thirty-five-year-old doctor—and she expected a life of ease.

The stability my mother imagined evaporates as I grow in her twenty-seven-year-old belly.

The war permeates mundane chores of daily life. Like all householders, she saves scraps of aluminum foil. The Japanese air invasion might begin at any minute so at night, we pull the drapes, turn off lights, and hide inside our houses. Any light escaping to the skies might reveal our whereabouts to the enemy, an enemy who, by its very otherness, invades the amygdala—lurking, growing in everyone's imagination. Neither the shining sun nor a carpet of snow on the fallow fields brings relief from the oppressive blanket of shapeless fear.

A new surge of cortisol surrounds my fragile heart when my mother learns of her father's death, seven weeks before I'm due. The adrenaline makes me uncomfortable, restless, and agitated. It does not abate. I am the reason she is unable to travel to his funeral to say goodbye. She fulfills her obligations while her hormones run wildly inside us, igniting only the first of her resentments that will last my lifetime.

I want out of this toxic stew of hormones, cigarettes, and whiskey. I push my way out six weeks early, only fourteen months after my older sister made her way into the world. The only preparation made for me had already been made for the two previous births; we each were to have been named John Alsop Cooper Jr., after my mother's brother, whose name she selfishly snatched from her barren sister-in-law before my aunt could use it for her own adopted son. I breathe in my mother's disappointment at my gender. I know it is my job to soothe her, to make her happy. I spend my life trying. Instead of "John," I am given my mother's name as my first name, but I am called by my middle name "Kay," named after the wife of my father's good friend, a woman my mother doesn't like.

I find life outside the womb no better than life inside. My existence seems to be a curse; my father's father dies six weeks after my birth. My introduction to life: I am guilty for being a girl, I absorb their grief over losing their parents, and I ingest the fear of bombs from the sky.

What in other families might be a bright spot turns deadly for me: my father likes me.

On first holding me, he says, "She's a cuddler. We can stop now."

My need to cuddle sets me up for a lifetime of triangles, exclusion, and pain. I did not know then that because my father likes me, my mother will dislike me. He will invest fantasies in me that should be placed in her. Her jealousy will worm into me, making me hide my light, fearful that any escaping beam may bring on the enemy air invasion.

At six weeks old, my sensitive eyes are not made for the bright, August sunshine. Frantic, my arms and legs flail, not by any agency on my part, but as a release from tormenting hunger. While I'm in the side yard, my mother has entrusted my care to Putsch, our Dalmatian, who will not let anyone near me, including the mailman.

My mother, who herself has only a tenuous hold on life, imposes order on her distressed world by putting me on a feeding schedule. To ease her life and to make me independent, she puts me outside and props my bottle so she can be productive at more pressing chores. For me, that means starvation. I can't stay latched on. My head jerks from side to side in frustration. I am not capable of coordinating a purposeful movement.

No one wants to feed, comfort, or hold me.

I need more. More food. More touch. More loving sounds to surround me. I need a face to gaze into mine. I need a world where someone other than Putsch believes I am more than a bother.

I always need more.

My not-yet-developed eyes open to search for a face that will help me regulate my nervous system. Only Putsch is there.

Even though braying with colic, I feel like a ghost child.

As I grow, my mother and father continue teaching me to disrespect and to be angry at my body.

When I'm little, my father and his brother, Uncle Don, play catch with me in the back yard. Every few successful catches, my father takes a step backward, lengthening the distance between himself and my uncle. In the home movies, they're smiling, obviously enjoying themselves. Two or three people stand around, watching.

Uncle Don tosses me to my father, the tight ball of my infant body making an arc over the eight feet between them. My father reaches out toward me, his hands grasping my body. His hands know about catching—he was "Twinkletoes Harrington," the star quarterback on the 1924 state championship University of Colorado football team. Once I'm in his hands, he lowers his arms to soften the impact of my momentum.

He laughs at his success and skill and at the same time, takes a step back, increasing both the challenge and the risk of dropping me. He then tosses me back to Uncle Don.

As the space between them lengthens, the trajectory of my body lowers. They can't throw me as high if they have to throw me a greater distance. Each step back increases the force they must use to make me—their ball—reach its goal.

The women, seemingly passive, look on. No one dares to question the men who bring home the bacon. No one dares to question the wisdom of throwing an infant around. No one knows to think about the consequences to the baby's brain, jiggling in the brain cavity and then suddenly being thrust against the side of the hard skull. Maybe they think I like it.

The silent home movies offer no audible clues.

My father and his brother make my mother the object of a cruel game; they can delight in her anxiety and yet also, by making her a witness and therefore a participant, make her collude in using her newborn as a football.

It was unthinkable that she could stop the game.

CHAPTER 1

....

March 1972

A virgin when I married, I never imagined I would be fleeing to my former gynecologist to get an IUD inserted. I never imagined I'd have the need for an IUD, since my husband had a vasectomy two years ago. After eight years of marriage, I never imagined I would contemplate cheating on him, preparing to commit adultery. I was not a cheating kind of girl.

But as I drove for over an hour to my appointment through the East Bay tunnel, over the Bay Bridge, through San Francisco, down Highway 101, to Palo Alto—all those congested miles alone with my thoughts—I had to confront this new reality, this challenge to my good girl identity: I was planning to sleep with someone else. I wanted to be desired, to be touched, to talk to someone who was interested in talking to me. I was twenty-nine, healthy, smart, and lonely. I had sons—five and three years old. I left them with a babysitter so I could undertake this nefarious deed. I did *not* want to get pregnant from an affair.

I made the appointment with the doctor I no longer had a relationship with. If I had made this request of my current gynecologist, I'd have to confront my shame every time I went for a Pap smear. I hoped sixty miles would put distance between me and this act, allowing my decision to exist in a parallel life.

At the doctor's office, I put away my early memories of Walter, my husband.

Dr. Baker greeted me warmly. He had delivered my older son five years ago, and I had great affection for him.

"I want to get an IUD inserted." I was nervous, and my voice sounded small, tight, like a little girl.

"Why? Have you stopped using birth control pills?"

"Yes."

"Were they not working for you?"

"They were okay, but I don't want to take pills every day." I offered up a bogus reason, withholding my duplicity.

"Well. There have been some difficulties with the IUD."

"I know, but I had one before and it worked well for me." I decided I must be direct. "My husband had a vasectomy two years ago. I'm planning to have sex with another man, and I don't want to get pregnant."

Dr. Baker frowned. "Does he know you're doing this?" A reasonable question, given that it was 1971, the beginning era of the open marriage.

"No."

"Do you plan to tell him?"

"No."

He stared at me. I stared back, defiantly, reminding myself I was an adult, free to make my own decisions. I was swimming upstream against everything I'd ever been taught about morality, but I was also trying to be a responsible adult and not get pregnant.

"Well. I certainly do not approve of what you are doing. I'm not willing to insert an IUD under these circumstances. I recommend that you go home and think about this. You'll be much happier if you change your mind."

My paper gown fluttered from the air current as he closed the door behind him.

Dismissed. Upbraided, as if he were the priest protecting the catechism, preventing me from becoming a fallen woman.

It was ironic that my intended lover was a priest-to-be.

I wanted to be transported invisibly out of the doctor's office to avoid seeing or talking to anyone. I feared they'd be able to see through my clothes, to the scarlet "A" Dr. Baker had just pronounced. Slut. Besmirched. Sullying my marriage vows.

Against my will, a tear trickled down my cheek. I *knew* what I was planning was wrong. And I knew I was going ahead with it anyway.

I stopped to pay the receptionist.

"Dr. Baker said there's no charge for the visit." I was grateful for not having to pay money, a transaction I would have to hide from Walt.

When I got in the car, I sobbed, unable to hold back tears of frustration and fear. I was trapped in a high-status marriage that was killing me. Someone else was interested in me. A kind man, a spiritual man of God had offered to touch me.

Three months before I sought out an IUD, I had coffee with Paul, a fellow master's of social work student. We'd been in classes together for four months and occasionally had coffee together.

On our last coffee date, Paul had said to me, "I would like to sleep with you." My head jerked up from the menu. I stared at him. The January wind gusted outside.

"Twice. No more. Just twice."

The blood drained from my face. I was stunned. We were both married to other people. Paul was the theologian in our cohort at school, a deacon in the Episcopal Church working toward his ordination as a priest. Who was this handsome, irreverent man sitting across from me, calmly proposing adultery?

Any frisson between us had been totally unspoken before this moment. I stared at him with a tumult of emotions. I was excited, but I was also a good girl—a married girl, with two young children.

3

But, unlike my husband, Paul was interested in what I thought. He listened to me. He was radical and athletic; he had a beard and a spiritual life.

"I don't want to have an affair. I just want to sleep with you twice."

The whole thing startled me. We were at the coffee house with no name, near the corner of Hearst and Euclid. The high ceilings, spare tables, and uncomfortable wooden chairs made the place feel European. I looked at Paul, swallowed, looked away, swallowed again.

"Why twice?" I finally managed to squeak out.

"I just want things to be even with my wife. She slept with a man twice the year after we were married."

I glanced at Paul, then looked down at my coffee.

"I've been looking for someone for two years. You're the first person I've found that I want to sleep with."

I looked directly at him. He looked mischievous, then teased, "Besides, I like your breasts."

I stared at him, glad no one was sitting near us.

"Well . . ." I did not look at him in horror and say, "No. Absolutely not." I was astonished—and excited—to find my good girl wavering on the edge of a precipice. I considered his offer for weeks; both thrilled and terrified of sex with Paul, I was in the purgatory of indecision. I admired him. I was titillated by him. I was excited to be desired.

Coffee with Paul was no longer innocent. The genie had escaped.

Paul's confidence had always fascinated me. He was never cowed by authority the way I was. When he told me about his escapades during the Free Speech Movement, I was thrilled. Still tightly bound by my mother's rules—no white shoes in winter, always wear gloves when going downtown—I lived vicariously through his stories of challenging institutional authority.

My parasympathetic nervous system appeared to have taken over. My thinking abilities became unbundled from the autonomic responses of my body. My heartbeat quickened, my breath became shallower, and blood rushed to my face. My prefrontal neocortex had resigned its executive functions of logical thinking and clear decision-making.

When the coffee arrived, Paul rearranged the silverware to make space for the cups and pastry we were sharing. My hand lingered on the table near his, hoping his finger would lightly brush mine. My hunger to be wanted, to be seen, was dangerously unfulfilled. I yearned for physical connection, no matter how slight.

His hand quietly reached out to envelop mine, a proprietary assertion that he had permission to take hold of my hand, to cross the physical boundary that the law and the Bible admonished was wrong.

I let my hand rest under his. No protest rose from my nervous system. The new excitement of being alive was growing neurons in my cells, building synapses inside my body, just as the synapses of the world outside my body were disintegrating.

I stayed suspended in the moment, hardly breathing. Deep inside my body, I knew I was irrevocably moving toward touch, toward life, toward what had been absent for eight years of marriage. His palm sent warmth throughout my body. His masculine assertion of privilege, his assumption of my acquiescence excited me.

Paul and I had coffee again, and again. We touched, we talked, we debated the morality and immorality of our impending decision. We talked about psychopathology, about R. D. Laing and the genesis of schizophrenia. We sought the privacy of my car, finally daring to kiss, and kiss, then kiss some more.

My duplicity put the foundation of my life at risk—Walt would divorce me immediately—but that didn't stop my foolhardy movement toward Paul. I made the appointment for the IUD.

My double life started building itself, brick by brick.

CHAPTER 2

....

August 1964

At the precipice of marriage to Walt, I was ready to be initiated, ready to invite penetration. Chaste for the three years we had spent apart, but aroused by Walt's hands all over me, I wanted more.

The first time Walt and I petted was after several months of dating, when we were in his family's mothballed vacation home in Ben Lomond in the Santa Cruz mountains. The place had a musty, dense air—a spookiness waiting to envelop guilty trespassers. We hadn't planned on taking my blouse off—it just happened, startling both of us. We were like two eight-year-olds who had done something deliciously naughty, and this hot, secret knowledge formed a new bond.

Now, three years later, in anticipation of our marriage in three weeks, I'd already started the newly developed birth control pill. I was safely infertile. With his erection pressing against me, I knew he wanted more, too. Still a virgin, I offered myself to him.

"Let's make love."

The couch in his parents' sitting room looked out over the whole Bay Area, with Alcatraz directly westward. Further west, two red beacons marking the Golden Gate Bridge blinked in unison. His parents were soundly asleep upstairs.

He kissed me again, arousing me further, and I felt safe to give in to our desires.

"Let's make love," I whispered again, my passion allowing the girl who was raised to be meek and virginal to melt away.

"I think we should wait," he replied, continuing to kiss me.

"Why?" I whispered as he burrowed into my neck.

"It's only a few weeks."

I pulled my head back and looked directly at him. I hesitated.

"I want to wait," he answered definitively, as if this decision were a law school case. He then presented the final, conclusive evidence. "I think you'd feel better, too."

We continued kissing, but shame tugged at me and pulled me into a dark cave. I was embarrassed to have been so forward and to have offered myself to him. I was humiliated that he rejected me. I felt vulnerable and alone, with no safety net. I felt no anger, only shame.

I didn't know it yet, but we had just agreed on the rules for our marriage: he knew best. He was authorized to declare what I felt, just as my mother always had.

By choosing to marry immediately after graduating, I had transferred my care directly from my parents to Walt, without awareness of doing so. Instead of finding a job and renting an apartment as my girlfriends were, I squandered my opportunity to test my wings in the wider world.

Plenty of red flags alerted me to difficulties connecting with Walt, even before we married. But I was intimidated by both Walt and my mother. Yes, I had clues but not clues I could see. As I drove from the doctor's, I remembered another drive through Rocky Mountain National Park, when Walt came for my sister Laurel's wedding, three years after we'd become a couple. He was visiting me after I had been in Spain for a year with Sarah, my other sister, when I was a sophomore in college.

7

The only way for Walt and me to have private time together was to take a drive.

I'd been home only two weeks. In Spain, I'd discovered Spaniards lived in the present tense, always ready to make daily life festive. They were open, big-hearted, free. My tight corset of obligation began loosening there. I became fluent in Spanish, slowly melting into the language a looser, happier, more musical me, less worried about being proper. I fell in step with the sensuality of drinking sangria, eating turron at Christmas, and savoring roasted chestnuts from street vendor braziers.

I scarcely knew Walt, but the idea of him tethered me to safety. Through our letters, we consolidated our commitment to each other. After a year's absence, I was filled with excitement to see Walter, tell him all about my Spanish adventures, hear about his first year at Harvard Law School, and dream about our life together.

But the light-hearted love chatter I had imagined didn't materialize. Being alone in the car with him turned out to be excruciating. We had nothing to say to each other. My body hugged the passenger door. Every topic that came into my mind escaped into the ether.

The silence grew oppressive, constricting my innards like a washrag twisted dry. I knew it was the girl's job to keep a conversation going. I tried my best, but I failed. I wanted time to swallow me up, spit me out.

When Walt and I had met, he was a senior and I was a freshman. He was "chief of staff" to the student body president and wielded power in university decisions. I was turned on by his knowledge even though the way he paraded it made me feel inferior. I'd had many beaus, but I had not put any on a pedestal the way I did Walt. I was still starstruck by Walt as he competently maneuvered the curvy road across the Continental Divide.

After a year of longing, I'd imagined we would touch, talk tenderly, and risk whispering tentative ideas about our future together. Once face to face with him, I was too tightly bound to initiate such intimacy. Some lurking part of me did not trust Walt to welcome my overtures.

Never having met him, my mother wanted me to marry Walt, and thus, marry into his wealthy family. Although my mother's family was of modest means, her maternal side had descended from Governor Spotswood, the last colonial governor of Virginia[1]; my mother believed herself to be part of the upper-upper crust. She coveted status and already savored her reflected glory through my marriage. She pushed for my engagement; it didn't matter that I was still a teenager.

Walt's now-sober alcoholic mother wanted me to marry her son, even though he, too, was young and inexperienced. She told my mother she didn't know what she would do if I didn't marry him; she expected an engagement this week.

I wanted to marry Walt because maybe . . . at last . . . I could please my mother. Maybe I would finally matter.

When Walt finally met my parents, the tension was palpable. I knew my mother found him arrogant. I swallowed the friction radiating from her silent, strained body. Attuned to her moods as if I were a taut guitar string, I automatically resonated to her overtones. She didn't need to telegraph her dissatisfaction. I already knew.

Seeing Walt through her eyes, I noticed, yet tried ignoring, how he hogged centerstage playing the guitar, instead of ceding the spotlight to my sister, the bride, and her musician groom. I sank in my chair when his attempts at humor fell flat. I quelled my own queasiness at his sarcasm, pretending to myself that he was clever instead of insensitive.

No nuance escaped me. Vigilance was the air I breathed, always trying to calm whatever ephemeral ember might float through the air, hoping I could snuff it out before it sparked into a conflagration.

I reassured myself I'd feel closer to Walt once we had the chance for privacy. I imagined having endless things to say to each other. I'd jabber on about my year in Spain, the Fallas in Valencia, the El Greco Museum in Toledo. I'd hear every detail of his life at Harvard Law, his eating club, Dean Griswold.

Instead, I was tongue-tied. When I started to talk, I dried up like a prune. I wanted to tell him about La Peña del Buen Humor, the singing group in Totana that changed my life. They composed a song about my sister and me, then played it on the local radio station as we drove our green VW bug out of town, departing forever from that cherished, life-giving group.

It didn't help that I still thought in Spanish. For ten months, I'd lived outside the steel-inspired rules of the Denver Country Club, and once I was back, I missed the people, the language, the music, and the laughter that flowed so easily in Spain. I missed the vibrancy that grew inside the Spanish-speaking me. I wanted to be in Spain, not the proper corset of my upbringing.

The year apart allowed me to create an imaginary husband-to-be, then hang it in Walt's closet. I ignored the glaring mismatch between my well-developed fantasy and reality. I followed the programming injected into my fascia and nervous system as a child. Walt was a perfect match to my hardwired code.

I was totally unaware that I had no agency. I believed I was choosing.

I wanted to feel close to my intended. I wanted to tell Walt how stiff I felt, but my words evaporated while still on my tongue. In the August heat, he silently stared straight ahead, driving. Not knowing what else to do, I stared straight ahead, too, looking through the increasingly insect-covered windshield.

The hot air blew in through the window. I'd given up trying to keep the hair out of my eyes or trying to bridge the chasm between us.

I tried again to make conversation. "There's timberline."

CHAPTER 3

·····················

July 1955

When I was thirteen years old, we temporarily lived in Oahu, Hawaii, where my father filled in during the transition between outgoing and arriving plantation doctors. I'd started menstruating, and I was mortally self-conscious about my developing breasts, already bigger than my sisters'.

I wanted my breasts to disappear. All I knew about them was that no one should touch them and sometimes they hurt. I shared my first kiss with the son of family friends on a moonlit beach in Hawaii—a thoroughly romantic initiation but it was only a kiss.

I felt awkward about my body. My dad wanted to photograph me in a bathing suit while standing in a tree. I was too young to recognize that my father's admiration of my nubile body—and that taking pinup pictures of me—would cause problems with my mother. I knew I didn't like doing it, but I was thrilled to have his attention. He didn't take pictures of my sisters.

"Put your arm under the branch to hold it up a little bit."

To help me get up into the tree, my father had stirrup-cupped his hands for me to use. I clambered up, pretending my rump did not pass in front of his face.

I adjusted the branch. It was spindly with long, openly spaced needles.

He snapped a picture, then moved back a few steps; I knew enough about photography to know he was reframing the picture. He did another reading with his light meter, then fiddled with his camera. He changed the f-stop, the calculation of which remained a mystery to me even though he had tried to teach me many times. I was the only girl interested in learning photography.

He took another picture. "Now hold that twig in your hands."

I was already standing with my weight on one leg, the other knee bent, forcing my hip upward. The bark pierced the thin soles of my ballet slippers.

"Hold it lower."

I readjusted my hands.

"Now look down."

Obediently, I look down.

He took another picture. He was an orthopedic surgeon and a hobbyist photographer.

I felt fat. My mother regularly told me I had ungainly hips. I tugged at the bottom of my swimsuit, hoping to camouflage my hips, imagining 1/4 inch lower would make them seem smaller. I nearly lost my balance.

"Hold still."

I froze. I knew film was expensive and precious. I had a Brownie camera and liked taking pictures, too. My mother complained about the cost, so I used my babysitting money.

He took another picture.

Two weeks later, I saw the pictures. I didn't understand why I didn't like them. I didn't understand why my father showed them to his friends. I didn't understand why my mother quietly pursed her lips disapprovingly.

At fourteen, the rich boys from the country club who had never noticed me before started asking me out on dates. My mother also noticed me.

12

She said, "You're going to be large busted. Your breasts will sag, so you'll need special orthopedic bras. I've found a store, but they're expensive."

I felt both special and guilty.

"The appointment is on Thursday afternoon."

I was anxious all week, but said nothing to anyone, even my sisters.

When we entered the orthopedic corsetiere, I was discouraged when I saw my future in the old, buxom women customers. Mrs. Szabo, the owner, was an imposing, matronly figure with a thick Hungarian accent.

My mother, as always, took over as my brain, voice, and mouthpiece, and she and Mrs. Szabo talked about my breasts as if I weren't there. My breasts, Exhibit A, were like a carburetor to a mechanic.

Once I was naked from the waist up, Mrs. Szabo clinically surveyed my chest from all angles and selected a variety of bras for me to try. Each pushed me flat, as if it were a straightjacket for wayward breasts.

Mrs. Szabo announced her verdict. "This fits her best."

I had not said a word since entering the shop.

"Will this prevent sagging?" my mother asked.

"Vell, it is this vay." She turned to me, looked me in the eye, and instructed me with severity. "You must not take these bras off except to bathe. You must sleep in them. Do you understand?"

I nodded. I promised myself I would be a responsible owner and wear the bras all the time.

Once I got the new bras, I inspected myself in the bathroom mirror. The bra smushed me up against myself, making me satisfyingly flat.

Throughout adolescence, I tried hiding my breasts, as if I had done something wrong, like fertilizing them too much. For fourteen years, throughout marriage and the bearing of two children, I wore my orthopedic bras morning and night. Thoroughly brainwashed, I bound my own breasts.

CHAPTER 4

....

September 1964

My wedding was my mother's creation. The balcony at the top of the curving staircase at the Denver Country Club provided the perfect Scarlett O'Hara setting from which to throw the wedding bouquet. My green alligator purse and shoes were the pièce de résistance as guests pelted Walt and me with rose petals when we left our wedding reception on September 1, 1964. I was the picture of a young matron, replete with hat, gloves, and a two-piece wool suit whose straight skirt emphasized my nemesis—my hips.

Walt blessed the heckling crowd, "*Pax Nobiscum*," with his palm extended toward them, two fingers raised in a pope-like gesture.

My mother's recent brain surgery for an aneurysm had prompted us to consider downsizing the wedding, but her doctor strongly advised us to go ahead. "She's living for that wedding."

While Walt's father, recovering from eye surgery, wore an eye patch, my mother wore a bad wig.

Post-wedding, Walt and I played the life of grown-ups. My salary as a high school Spanish teacher supported us. Walt used his stock dividends to pay for business school at Stanford. Fully aware of my role as a housewife, I taught myself to cook, making elaborate meals each night. Weekends, I cleaned, shopped, and cooked, often preparing dinner parties for six. Entertaining was an unquestioned part of my role.

In spring, I stopped the Pill. Within four months, I was pregnant.

I quit my job. Walt left business school and started work at a law firm; we bought a house in the East Bay, moved in a sweltering heat wave, and got a dog. Suddenly, I was isolated, with no friends, no job, and no focus except furnishing the house, a job I found intimidating and irritating for it required skills I didn't possess and knowledge that didn't interest me.

One afternoon, a sociology student doing a study about gender roles knocked at our door. This concept had never occurred to me before. I was lonely and scared. I ate compulsively and donned a false front to other people. So, I prolonged my talk with this student. I felt like asking her to move in, just to have good company.

When I am seven, if I promised to be careful, I am allowed to use the phonograph with certain 78 rpm records. The only one I listen to is, "The Little Tune That Ran Away." It resonates with me; I am that tune. I am not valued, and I am played badly. I, too, want to run away.

Seven months into my pregnancy, two months after Walter and I had moved into a new house, I came home from grocery shopping on a crisp October day to find that Mun, our new Brittany spaniel puppy, was missing. Dropping the bagged groceries in the kitchen, I ran up the hillside in our backyard, searching for him.

I laboriously climbed to the back fence where a gate opened to a wide field, often populated by cattle. I walked through the field. No cows to be seen; no Mun either. At thirty-two weeks, the baby wasn't big, but my center of gravity was off, so I carefully picked my way back down the hill to the house.

My guilt blossomed. I must have overlooked something or done something wrong for Mun to have escaped. I got more frantic by the minute. I called Walt to share my distress, but he was in a meeting. I walked up and down the street, searching for the dog.

I repeated the trek up the hill, then back down, worrying he might have entered the large pipe funneling the creek into the sewer. Could the puppy have drowned? I ignored my need to rest and hiked back up the hill.

Three hours later, the phone rang. A neighbor I knew only slightly asked if I'd lost a puppy. They had him! I was so relieved, I almost started crying.

Mun had spent the last hours entertaining their five children. My fear for Mun was misplaced, but my self-blame did not abate. Walt later deduced the gap under the gate he had built allowed Mun's escape, but the grooves of guilt were too deeply wired in me to allow myself any redemption.

Only three years old—my very first memory—I am flooded with guilt and shame.

Rosella—our beloved maid, cook, house manager, and mother substitute—had visited her family elsewhere. My mother, one sister, and I pick her up at Union Pacific Station when she arrives in Denver.

Excited that she's returned, I run to her embrace. I'm the first girl to reach her.

"I only have one rose, and I promised I would give it to the first girl I saw."

As she hands me the rose, I bloom inside, filled by her love. I admire the rose and savor being special, casting aside any self-doubt by holding on to the visible evidence. I proudly show my mother my new treasure.

"I was the first girl she saw!" I nearly burst at the seams.

With my sister in tears at her side, my mother grimaces at me. "That's not fair. You have to share the rose with Sarah."

*Like milk in coffee, shame and guilt merge, flooding
my red blood cells and stopping any joy from circulating in
my system. Tricked and dejected, I am ashamed of myself
for wanting, I hand over the rose, choking back my own
tears. I learn it is not okay to desire.*

The next afternoon, my contractions start six weeks early.
I held my secret fear deep in my heart. *Did I start a false labor
by my overexertion?*

The doctor told me to come to the hospital, just to be safe. I
called Walt in San Francisco; we decided to meet at his parents'
house in Oakland. I drove there through contractions.

Walt's father greeted me with, "This baby can't be born today.
This weekend is the opening of duck season!"

John's announcement was unnecessary; I knew Friday opened
duck season, which dictated the rhythm of our lives every fall.
Opening weekend was a long-standing tradition in the Morgan
family. I didn't know how to answer John, so I stayed quiet. Walt
said nothing.

Walt and I drove to the hospital in Palo Alto. He had not yet
seen me with my "cramps" but quickly figured things out as we
drove. If I held on until a slow count of twenty-two, the contraction would subside.

I gripped the ribbing of the '64 Impala convertible when a
contraction hit, transmuting my silent screams into the metal. I
hung on, counting thirteen . . . fourteen . . . trying to breathe . . .
sixteen . . . seventeen.

Walt spoke words of encouragement. "Only five more counts
to go."

I endured until twenty-two. If the pattern held, I would have
ten minutes of relief until the next round of agony.

It was Tuesday, 6:10 p.m. on October 18. The baby's due
date of December 6 should not have interfered with duck

season. I tried being chipper and conversational in my allotted gap of ten minutes.

"At this rate, we only have five more to go till we get there. I can do that."

Silence.

"It's lucky the contractions weren't this painful when I was driving to Oakland to meet you." I tried entertaining him.

"Yeah," he replied.

At the hospital, it became clear these contractions were not going away. Dr. Baker arrived, examined me, and gave orders to have me prepped. Good girl to the end, I was socially correct and pleasant with the nurse as she chatted me up while shaving my pubic hair, giving me news reports from the nether regions about the latest swipe and lack of hair. She stayed cheery as she told me it was going to itch like hell as it grew back in.

"Don't worry, dearie. You can't have sex for a while anyway, and by then it won't bristle as much."

Time moved slowly, and the pain got worse. Natural childbirth was rare in 1966. I was dilated but not much. I wanted drugs. I begged for drugs.

But drugs would slow the labor and could be dangerous to the baby. Finally, around 11 p.m., they gave me an epidural, and I felt nothing below my waist.

"Okay, let's move her," Dr. Baker instructed the nurse.

They lifted me onto a gurney, rolled me into an operating room, and then lifted me onto the operating table. Bright lights filled the room. I felt nothing, but Dr. Baker was active between my legs, giving instructions to nurses. The baby was coming.

We approached midnight. With only three minutes to go, the doctor asked me, "Do you want the birth date to be October 18 or 19? We can probably do it either way."

"I don't know." I sort of liked the even number better. I was scared, not fully present while my body did its thing. I felt nothing, even when he performed an episiotomy.

"The head is crowning. Looks like it's going to be the eighteenth."

The delivery room got quiet as the nurses and doctors concentrated on getting the baby born. They'd called in the pediatric residents to attend to the baby.

"You have a boy."

I waited for the squall. Silence. I held my breath. They were all at my feet. I felt the intensity and concentration emanating from their active hands and brains. No sound. What were they doing? They gave shorthand directions quietly to each other. They were a fluid unit at my crotch, and I no longer existed for them. What was wrong? Why wasn't the baby crying?

CHAPTER 5

....

October 1966

Finally, after what seemed like hours, an infant wailed. I started breathing again. My baby was alive. They put him on my chest. He looked scrunched and round and red. He had a halo of blond angel hair. I was surprised. I hadn't necessarily thought my baby wouldn't have blond hair, but I never thought it would be so white. It startled me. His face was full of cheeks, like Mr. Magoo.

"Because he's so small, we need to take him to the pediatric nursery right away," the doctor gently informed me. "It is not unusual for babies to lose weight after birth, but we want to observe him."

I was ecstatic. He was alive, crying. I would see him soon.

"Do you want him circumcised?"

I looked around in confusion. I had no idea. I was startled by the suddenness of the question and the need for an immediate answer. No one had told me to prepare, and Walt and I never discussed it. I had grown up with girls; Walt had been my only sexual partner. I looked at Walter, uncertain, hesitant. I didn't even really know much of what it meant. I experienced unreality, with no sense of authority over this baby or this decision.

The doctor looked at Walt and Walt answered a definitive, "Yes."

"I'm going to sew you up a little tighter than you were before," the doctor told me as he smiled and winked at Walt. "You'll be sore for a few days."

I felt like a spectator. The power to make decisions about my own baby and my own body swirled in the ether of the room, not available to me.

The four-and-one-half-pound baby was whisked away and put in an incubator in intensive care. I was euphoric . . . and desperately thirsty, but the nurse would not allow me to drink, telling me I would throw up if I drank now. As the anesthetic wore off, the euphoria disappeared, and the pain began. Unlike labor, this was chronic, throbbing pain from the episiotomy. I was unable to get comfortable.

But we had a baby! My thirst and my baby—I could think of nothing else. We didn't have a name for the baby yet; I hadn't realized we'd need one that soon. For weeks, I'd tried getting Walter to focus on the name, but he had ignored the question. I even wrote possible names on 3 x 5 cards, putting up a new card each day on his closet door.

The next day, Walt visited the hospital after work. Painfully, I walked with him down to the intensive care nursery. Our baby required mid-level care . . . not the most serious, but then, not the easiest, either. We peered at our yet-to-be-named baby through the window, this tiny creature in an incubator, and we reassured ourselves he was healthy. We looked at the pale and listless babies in the sickest level and felt safer. Our baby had color and got red when he cried. We glanced at the babies in the regular nursery but moved on quickly; they were too plump for us to tolerate.

The nurses fed our baby every two hours, hoping he would suckle one-and-a-half ounces. I wanted to feed him and hold him, but the nurses said it was too dangerous. With my inexperienced care, he might not get enough nourishment. I acquiesced. I was only allowed to stick my hands into the two holes of the incubator, lift him two inches, and then carefully place him down again.

The gap between what I wanted and what I was allowed made my heart break.

On day two, with pressure from me, we finally named the baby William Alan, matching Walt's initials, but not his name. Walt was W. A. M. III; I was grateful Walt did not insist our baby carry around a "IV" for the rest of his life.

Dr. Baker couldn't explain why Alan came six weeks early— maybe my physical activity the day before searching for our missing puppy or maybe because I, too, was premature. I didn't talk to anybody about the dark fears of my culpability. Walt and I didn't talk about the possibility Alan might not leave the hospital, or that he might never be able to use his newly-minted name.

More robust than this tiny creature I birthed, I got discharged Friday morning, leaving Alan behind.

Walt and I drove home, trying to buoy ourselves with the belief the baby was okay. We didn't have much to say to each other. Walt attempted conversation, musing who would be at the Duck Club this weekend. His monologue faltered. We remained silent, each of us pondering the elephant between us of whether he would go to the opening weekend of duck season in just a few hours.

I finally lanced the tension. "Of course, you should go." Against my own needs, I advocated for him. He would stay home if I asked, but he would resent it, and I would have to continue pretending I was okay and protect him from my fears and my feelings. I didn't know how to ask for comfort; he didn't know how to share the sorrow that our baby might die.

He glanced at me. He knew he shouldn't, but he wanted to accept my blessing to abandon me.

"Yes, go." I sent him off to get drunk, pass out cigars, and be proud of his virility for having sired a son.

Once home, he packed up hesitantly. "Are you sure you're okay?"

We go through the ritual again.

"Yes." *Just get out of here! I need you. I need comfort. I need holding. I need a baby. I need what you don't know how to give me. So go.*

I cried as the door closed. The ragged sobs became yawns. I knew I should eat but didn't know what food was in the house. The phone rang.

My good friend, Barbara, who had a ten-month-old baby girl, welcomed me home.

"You should not be there alone!" She was appalled to find out Walt had gone hunting.

"I'm fine," I insisted. There must have been something in my voice that belied my words.

She announced, without consultation or question, "I am bringing the baby and dinner, and I am going to spend the night with you. I will be there in an hour."

I wept again, grateful for undemanding company, for freely given love.

Over the next few days, the episiotomy bit at me. I hurt when I sat; it was even harder to drive. Even though I had no baby at home, my mother flew out for three days "to help." I didn't know how to do anything but pretend to welcome her and participate in the charade. I asked only one thing of her: to be the driver for the two-hour round trip to the hospital to see Alan.

"I don't like to drive on the bridge," she said.

So, I drove both of us, only to be able to do nothing more than stick my hands into the incubator to pick up the swaddled baby two inches, then put him down. I couldn't hold him or feed him.

"He's too fragile. I'm sorry," the nurse said with sympathy. "You're just not experienced enough."

I didn't know then that my acquiescence would become a major regret. I wished I had demanded to have a skin-to-skin welcoming to Alan's body, a physical connection to my heartbeat, a murmuring nurturance. Nor did I know that moment of concession was only the first enactment of what would become a lifelong dilemma. Did my showing up help him or hurt him? This was the first time I was told I was a danger to my son . . . but not the last.

Not only did I have to drive to see my son, I had to be alone in the car with my mother for two hours. I didn't go the next day. The baby wouldn't know whether I'd been there or not. All I wanted to do was lie down. Instead, bent over and aching, I chopped vegetables, set the table, and then cooked dinner. My crotch throbbed. With her Old Crow, my mother sat in the living room playing tug-of-war with the new puppy.

"*Grrrr*," she growled at him.

The tension from the tug-of-war inside my head was about to explode. My rage nearly pushed me out of the kitchen to shake her the way she was shaking the sock. *Just get dinner served, the dishes cleaned, and you can lie down.*

I was mute. I didn't have the courage to tell her she wasn't helping.

Finally, she flew back home.

We measured the days by the baby's weight loss or gain . . . half ounce by half ounce.

Over three weeks, he added eight ounces to his birth weight. When he had triumphed at getting himself to five pounds, the hospital allowed us to bring him home.

His health was delicate, and his discharge instructions were explicit and grave: Quarantine at home for six weeks, preferably eight; no guests; do not take him out; and limit his exposure to germs and people.

On the way home from the hospital, we stopped by Walt's parents' house, meeting outside in the open air to protect Alan from germs. I extended his small-bundled body to Walt's mother for her to hold.

She recoiled. "Oh no! I couldn't."

I continued holding the infant out for her embrace. She kept her hands at her side as she looked at me. "I'm afraid I might hurt him."

We'd all been afraid that simply being alive might hurt him, but I—twenty-four years old and knowing nothing about taking care of a five-pound baby—held him. "No, it's okay. Take him." I offered her another chance.

Arms limp, she again declined.

"Once we're home, we're in quarantine."

She didn't reach for him. Both men watched, mute and useless. I pulled Alan's weightless body back to me and cradled him. I understood that I, alone, was responsible to keep this fragile preemie alive and breathing.

CHAPTER 6

....

September 1967

Alan did not die. I kept the baby alive and learned to be an adequate mother, but my loneliness did not subside. Drowning in the isolation of suburbia, motherhood, and my marriage, I soothed myself by compulsively eating the teething baby crackers, as if they were meant for me.

Walt's childhood with an absent father, alcoholic mother, and boarding school at age six taught him to build his armor—a necessary and smart thing for him but not helpful to my needs in our marriage. What I experienced as a painful void in our relationship, Walt didn't experience at all. Emotional distance was the norm, a safe state of being for him. The driving force in my life—connection, self-reflection, and self-knowledge—was not present in his ecosystem. Walt not only did not know how to talk about himself or his feelings, he had no active internal life, and no interest in creating one. My introjected mother's choice of my life partner fulfilled her dreams . . . but not mine.

Having learned as a child that anything wrong was my fault, I assumed my dissatisfaction in this marriage meant something was wrong with *me*. *Why am I so unhappy? Why am I bored? Why is alcohol the only way to find each other? Why am I scared to talk to him?*

I had everything I was raised to want: a husband, a lovely house, and a healthy, beautiful child. My husband didn't beat me, he didn't run around with other women, and he earned a good living. What was wrong with me? How could I want more? What *did* I want?

When eleven-month-old Alan was asleep for the night, I pulled Walt to the green couch. I faced him as he sat looking ahead at the burnt-orange chair, part of the contemporary color scheme of green and orange I had created a year ago when furnishing the house.

Sex had become a minefield for me. In women's magazines, I read that sex three to four times a week was normal for a healthy marriage. Sex was not a draw for me. Sex was instrumental for Walt, driving toward a goal with no meandering along the way. I orgasmed only in the privacy of secret masturbation.

But good girl that I was, I did my part to create a healthy marriage. If I got in bed in pajamas, Walt would know I wasn't interested. If I got in bed nude, I risked seeming to signal, only to find out he wasn't interested. We didn't know how to make playful negotiation a possibility. To achieve the three to four nights a week minimum without me having to initiate sex and being rejected, I changed my habits. Every night I got in bed nude. I didn't mind sleeping without pajamas; I did mind the lack of communication in my marriage.

I pulled my thoughts back to the couch and took a breath, trying to inhale enough courage to be able to talk with him about the chasm between us.

"I want you to talk to me, to tell me what you're thinking and feeling."

"I do talk to you."

"I want to know what is happening in your life." I really wanted to talk about us, but that was a request too big to propose. "I want to connect. I have no idea what is happening with you at work, what bothers you, what you're excited about."

"What do you need to know? What brief I'm writing?"

"No. That's not what I mean. I want to know if you like what you're doing, what you're worried about, if you like the people you're working with."

"Well, you know I'm going to New York next week. I've been preparing for that meeting. You know I go in every day and come home every day. I don't know what more you want to know."

I tried conjuring words to explain what I meant.

He continued, "You know the important things. I care about you and Alan, I come home, I don't run around on you. I don't understand what you mean . . . that you don't know what is happening in my life."

"I don't know what you're feeling about anything."

"The day my father married my mother, he told her he would never talk about work at home. And he never did. That doesn't seem like such a bad idea to me."

"But how can I understand what's going on with you if you refuse to talk to me about a major focus of your life?" I was stumped. It *did* seem like a bad idea to wall me off from the juice of his life. But I didn't know how to make him understand. Explaining became a series of twists and turns, a maze that led to dead ends. I started to feel unheard and small.

We'd been having this conversation for almost two years. I felt ignored; he felt confused and irritated by my needs. I married for life. We had a year-old son, and I wanted this marriage to be a good one. I was nervous to propose the idea of going to couples counseling.

"Do you want another drink?"

"Sure. Why not?"

I enjoyed getting a buzz on. In college, Walt taught me to drink, and I was an avid student. I was still not used to the fiery bite of hard liquor but being buzzed felt nice. Plus, I needed the alcoholic bravery before I proposed couples therapy.

He returned with two full glasses of bourbon, just the way my parents liked it—a little club soda and lots of ice. My parents' escape seemed familiar and harmless. Maybe they, too, used bourbon to ease their way to talk to each other. Or maybe my father didn't try talking to my mother; maybe he left her out while he drank and socialized with his golfing buddies at the country club.

CHAPTER 7

....

December 1962

Home for Christmas break my junior year, four months after Walt's first visit and our drive through the Rockies, the air at home vibrated at a disquieting frequency. Something seemed strange. Maybe it was because I was alone with my parents for the first time without my older sisters. My mother was either contradicting me or complaining or was silent and withdrawn.

I called Walt in California to tell him something indefinable was wrong with Mom. He dismissed me.

"You're imagining things."

I agreed with him. I wanted this pit in my stomach to be "imagination."

Since my mother was not around after I talked to Walt, I delivered a drink to my father in his big easy chair. I expected to read my book while he read his paper.

Uncharacteristically, my father started talking. "What did you do today?"

Surprised, I said, "Not much. I saw Rick. We went over to Cherry Creek. I was looking for a present for Mom."

We talked about Mom and presents until the conversation wore itself out.

Trying to be polite, I asked, "Did you play gin rummy at the club?"

"I did, but your mother gets mad at me when I stay late and play."

I said nothing.

"She wants me to come home early. She thinks I should come home after a round of golf. But she doesn't make it very pleasant to come home."

I squirmed in the chair. I did not want to be impolite to my own father, but where was my mother? Could she hear? Paralyzed by fear, alive with fascination, I kept quiet. My father had never taken me into his confidence like that before.

Oh, no. Stop! I want to shout. What if she can hear?

"She always finds something wrong, something to criticize, so it's easier to stay away and play gin rummy, to have a few drinks."

I froze in my chair. By offering a heady brew of confiding in me, it was terrifying . . . awful . . . intoxicating.

"She doesn't want to see how much she nags me, how constantly she feels slighted."

Just then my mother erupted from the hallway into the room. She had been at the doorway, eavesdropping.

Crying, breathing unevenly, she directed her raspy voice at him. "You never pay any attention to me." She gulped for some air, and then mimicked his words sarcastically. "But she doesn't make it very pleasant to come home. I'd rather play gin rummy."

Through her tears, she accused him. "I don't nag you. I ask you to do something, and you ignore me, so I ask you again." Her voice was raggedy, harsh. "If you would listen to me, I wouldn't have to nag you."

Her body lurched. As she leaned against the doorjamb, her voice changed tone and became slurred. "I've taken some sleeping pills." Rather dreamily, looking nowhere in particular, she relaxed with a slight smile on her face. She then collected herself enough to send a bundle of verbal venom across the room. "You won't have to complain about me nagging you anymore." She worked to focus her energy. "You can play all the gin rummy you want!" She stumbled into the hallway and retreated to the bedroom.

Rather slowly, because of his weight and bad hip, my father got up and followed her. My heart raced, and I sat in my chair, immobilized. What if she died? It would be my fault. I could have interrupted my father, but I didn't.

My father returned many minutes later. "She said she only took four pills. I don't think that's enough to have her stomach pumped."

I thought, *How do you know? How can you be sure?* Being mute was the best way to stay safe. *What if she told you she took four, but actually took twenty?* Still in shock, I stared at him.

"It would be better to avoid taking her to the hospital. Even if I didn't take her to Mercy, but to another hospital . . . it would be . . . difficult."

Mercy was his home hospital. *But how can he be so sure she only took four? Isn't his certainty risking her life?* I dared not question him. I forced myself to speak; my voice emerged as a whisper. "Are you sure she only took four?"

The phone rang.

"Harrington residence," he said. After a long pause, he said, "What is her blood pressure? And other vitals?" He nodded. "How long has she been there?" More silence in the room.

"Okay. I'll be down."

Before he was even off the phone, I knew my father was leaving me here alone with my suicidal mother.

"I'm sorry, but I have to go to the hospital. I'm on call. Keep her talking till I get back."

I gulped.

"I won't be long."

I stared at him in disbelief.

"She'll be okay. Just make sure she doesn't fall asleep."

Finally, I was able to speak. "Why can't you ask Gene to go?"

"He's out of town."

"How long will you be?"

"Only an hour or two."

An hour sounded like an eternity. Two sounded even longer.

"If she starts to fall asleep, try to get her up and make her walk if you have to. Just make sure she keeps talking. She'll sound a little drunk, but that will wear off in a few hours." He tried to make his instructions simple.

"Can't you call someone else?"

"If I call someone else . . . well . . . I'd have to explain . . . I think it is better this way. I think she'll be okay."

I must have looked panic-stricken.

"You can call me at Mercy if you need me. They'll page me."

If I need you! What the hell do you mean? I need you now. I need you to stay. I need you to sit by her bedside. She's your wife. You're the grown-up. I'm a kid.

But I said nothing. His final instructions lingered in the air as he walked out the back door to the garage.

Dutifully, I walked to my mother's bedroom. I squished myself next to her on her twin bed, the sliding door of the closet to my right. It felt awkward. We didn't touch in our family. When I was six and sat next to her in the front seat of the car, I had struggled to stay awake. I didn't want to upset her. If my sleepy head fell onto her shoulder, I knew it would have bothered her.

Should I touch her? Should I hold her hand? Would touching her upset her more? I sat stiffly, dutifully, willing myself to be there. My job was to keep my mother alive.

It was not hard to keep her talking. Once started, she wouldn't stop.

"I try to be nice to Daddy, but he would rather play gin rummy than be with me." She guzzled air. "He doesn't talk to me. He doesn't tell me anything. When I ask for help, he ignores me." A new surge of tears began. "You and Sarah get anything you want.

No one ever thinks about me. What about me? You and Sarah spend a year in Spain, but what do I get?"

I stiffened at her bringing her complaints back to me. She had a habit of hurting me. She didn't know how not to.

"I've always wanted a mink coat. Aunt Martha got one. Mary Fixel got one. But no, we spend our money so you and Sarah can go to Spain." She had reverted slightly to the Southern drawl of her Texas childhood. "He doesn't like me to call him at the club, but sometimes I need to tell him something or ask him something. But then he gets mad."

I breathed a little easier; we're back on Dad's shortcomings.

"And today at the drugstore, you got a hairbrush, toothbrush, lotion, and good scissors, but that wasn't enough for you." She's moved to a singsong, taunting voice. "No, that wasn't enough for you. Then you wanted nail clippers. And you bought the really good ones. You want everything, as if it doesn't cost money. You just think money grows on trees."

Then she started over. "You and Sarah went to Spain . . . I never got a mink coat . . . then nail clippers." More tears before shifting back to Dad.

I never knew she resented Sarah and me going to Spain. It was she who had masterminded the whole trip. Her slow, vowel-filled diatribe was ripe with self-pity and hidden wounds. I was both her audience and her prisoner. She continued to berate and abuse me with no responsibility for her actions. I had to stay, encouraging her spewing of a lifetime of hurt.

Finally, I heard the garage door open. My father came into the bedroom and asked how she was.

"She's talked the whole time. She's drowsy and slurring her words, but she's been talking." I needed to escape. "I'm going for a drive."

I grasped onto any reed, any port in a storm. I fled to Walt. Trembling with fear, I dialed Walt's parents' number. I held it together while his mother got him to the phone. Once I heard his voice, I collapsed, weeping tears of release.

"My mother just tried to kill herself."

Speaking the truth out loud startled me, suddenly making it real. All Walt could offer was silence. I watched the mist of my breath in the cold air, hoping for comfort he didn't know how to give.

CHAPTER 8

....

June 1967

When the baby was nearly one and I was lonely, I had tried getting Walt to talk to me, but he didn't understand my need, and I couldn't explain. Months later, I tried once again. I sipped my bourbon and looked directly at Walt, forcing myself to talk. "I would like us to go to couples counseling."

Walt swiveled to face me, startled.

Feminist thinking had barely hatched. Betty Freidan's *The Feminine Mystique* (1963) was just over four years old. The zeitgeist of post-WWII conservatism was shifting to the sexual revolution of the freewheeling '70s. We lived in the fulcrum of this shift, and our marriage was in the balance.

"I would like to go to Muriel's group."

Walt had met Muriel. I had been attending a women's group led by Muriel James, a local psychotherapist and ordained minister. She helped women like myself—well-educated, nonworking mothers with little babies—who were starved for affection and intellectual life. Muriel believed women should be able to develop themselves and have independent thoughts and lives. She had energy, chutzpah, and was the kind of mother I would have liked to have had . . . and to be. She also ran couples groups. Maybe she could help Walt understand me.

I paused to see if I dared continue. "It' s not a lifelong commitment . . . just once a week for eight weeks."

"How would we pay for it?"

I was on a precipice. I was fighting for my own survival. "I want to go because I think we need help. I'm not happy, and I don't know what else to do."

"I understand you're not happy, but I don't know why that means we need to go to couples counseling."

"Because we don't know how to talk to each other."

"What do you mean? We're talking to each other quite successfully right now."

"No. I mean really talk about what's going on between us."

"So, what's going on between us that we can't talk about?"

I didn't think to challenge his circular premise. If we can't talk about it, how was I going to talk about it now? I must not be saying it right. Ghostly trails of my childhood enveloped me. If I could just explain . . . if I could make her understand, if only . . . my mother would love me.

"Emma and Rachel have gone, and they both said it is helpful."

"Helpful for what?"

"I don't know—for their marriages."

"I don't know that we are having problems or need help."

"I think we do, and I would like to go."

"Look," he said with some exasperation. "We're not crazy, you're a good mother, and I do okay financially. I don't see why we need 'therapy.'" He mocked the word *therapy* inserting sarcasm into each elongated syllable.

He returned to his first question. "How are we going to pay for it?"

I hesitated. "If I can figure out a way to pay for it, will you go?"

"I don't see why, but if it's that important to you . . . well . . . I guess so."

I accepted without question Walt's assertion that we didn't have enough money for couples therapy. I didn't know the phrase, "disposable income." I was a homemaker, did not earn money, and knew nothing about our finances. Women had not entered the workforce en masse, and the phrase "stay-at-home mom" had not yet been invented in 1967.

Willful blindness prevented me from understanding we had plenty of money for therapy. The previous year, Walt had bought a purebred, AKC-registered Brittany spaniel puppy, then paid for three months of board and professional training for the dog to become a pheasant-hunting dog. Just like a fish didn't know it lived in water, I was incapable of seeing I had no voice in this parent-child marriage.

Challenging Walt—especially about money—was taboo. So, I hoped I could figure out where I could get some to pay for counseling.

After one of Muriel's speaking engagements, I was in a small group of admirers clustered around her, a little bit out of her view, silent, soaking up her presence and wisdom. I followed the conversation eagerly where others led it, satisfied with any revealed tidbit.

"I'm currently working on a book with Dorothy Jongward explaining Eric Berne's ego states and how they play out. Our hope is that it will help a person direct her own life."

Someone asked when it would be published.

"I don't know," she bemoaned, with exaggerated despair. "Dorothy's niece was helping us type it. She just told us this week that she is quitting because they're moving. I don't know what we're going to do."

Someone else asked, "What are you going to call it?"

"It's had fifteen titles," she laughed. "Probably *Born to Win*. We believe that no one is born a loser, and if people can just understand that the games they play get in their way, they can change them. They'll see that they were born to win."

"Will it tell people how to change their games?"

A demure, doughy, middle-aged woman gazed adoringly at Muriel. The woman looked like she was in charge of keeping the linen ironed at the Episcopal Church, an unlikely one to want to understand, much less change, her game of adoring passivity.

"Oh yes. We're going to have a lot of Gestalt exercises at the end of each chapter, so people can use it as a workbook."

My mind spun. *They need a typist. They need a typist, and I can type.* I took typing in seventh grade. Maybe *I* could be their new typist. I could pay for couples therapy with my typing!

My brainstorm instantly coalesced into a plan. With no time to mull it over, I created the trajectory to get the prize. I pursued Muriel as she walked to her car. Even though I knew her, it felt very bold to encroach on her time, especially when she was leaving. I hesitated. Maybe I should phone her and make an appointment, but I discarded the idea because she's hard to reach. By then she might have found someone else. My chance was right here, right now.

I put my timidity aside and pretended to be robust as I caught up with her in the parking lot.

"Muriel," I called to her. She turned around on hearing her name.

"Oh, hi sweetie. I didn't realize you were there, or I would have said hello to you."

Her generous welcome allowed my blood to return to my head.

"How did you like the talk?"

"I loved it, especially the part about how we can really change our lives if we understand the games we're playing." Then I added, "I overheard that your typist just quit."

"That's right."

"Well . . . I came over . . . to see if I could do the typing? I would love to know more about what you're writing, and maybe we could work something out that would help pay for my husband and me to be in your couples group."

"What an interesting idea. It would be a godsend if you could help type, and then we wouldn't have to waste time trying to find someone. Would you be able to start soon?"

"Sure. I have a baby, as you know, but I could take him to the sitter and come talk to you about what you need, and how we would work it out."

"I'll be home Wednesday morning. Why don't you come by then?"

I walked away exhilarated. I had single-handedly found a way to pay for couples counseling!

We enrolled in Muriel's couples therapy group—four couples with common themes. The men were analytical types; the women wanted more intimacy and companionship. The men felt free to disparage our desires as "touchy-feely."

Muriel started each meeting with a theme, and each of us talked about our experiences with that theme: money, sex, communication, and division of labor. I knew the stakes were high with Walt. If I got openly angry, he would cross-examine me till my arguments made no sense in the world he constructed with his sharp-edged reasoning.

Yet I was there to be open, so I plunged in. "I feel like you are critical of me, without trying to understand. And it makes me angry." I knew I sounded tentative. My voice was small, but at least I was speaking.

"You say that, but you know it's not true."

"It *is* true, and you denying it just makes me angrier."

"Give me an example. Something that I can understand."

"When we were at the pheasant club and climbed the hill, I thought it would be fun to roll down the hill . . . and I did. Later I overheard you complain to Dave that, 'A Morgan doesn't roll down the hill.' As if I had done something wrong."

"I wasn't criticizing you. I was startled that you would do such a thing. And it *did* seem a bit unladylike."

"It sounds critical to me."

I parried. He thrusted.

Muriel mirrored back my "anger" and said that I sounded like a cream puff. Then I became angry at Muriel for what felt like a put-down. But as with my mother, I couldn't be direct, so I seethed, denying to myself that I was as wimpy as a cream puff and wishing Muriel had helped Walt see how he criticized me.

Couples therapy didn't seem to be the refuge and corrective I'd hoped it would be.

When Alan turned one year old, I was asked to be a short-term substitute Spanish teacher at the Acalanes High School district. I found day care for Alan and reviewed conjugations of verbs. I taught Spanish for two months. Alan loved his caretaker, reaching out for her when we arrived. I realized I wanted to work again.

I could speak Spanish . . . but I didn't want to teach it.

For the first time in my life, I grappled with what *I* wanted to do, without my mother choreographing my next move. My mother had organized my year in Spain, which determined my undergraduate major, which led to my teaching career.

The students I taught had confided their personal troubles to me. I realized I wanted to become a psychotherapist. I researched what credentials were needed and decided to pursue a two-year master's program in social work rather than a five-to-eight-year course of study for a PhD in psychology.

As a stepping-stone, I was accepted in a part-time program in psychology aimed at returning women. It included classes one night a week, a group meeting once a week, and a one-day-a-week internship at Napa State Psychiatric Hospital. At Napa, we met with a supervising psychiatrist as a group and rotated assignments through various wards.

Walt agreed to be in charge of Alan one night a week; I arranged alternative care for daytime obligations. At last, I had a toehold in a world where Walt wasn't—a world where, instead of complying, I was expected to expand and learn. I breathed the free air of new world.

CHAPTER 9

....

March 1970

Several months into my training program at Napa State Hospital, the training psychiatrist spoke to me at the end of our group session.

"Kay, will you stay after today? I would like to talk to you."

I was surprised. It was April, the sun was out, and I was due out at the playground to supervise the autistic children. Our student group had been meeting with the supervising psychiatrist for eight months, and he'd never asked to see anyone privately after a meeting. Ever obedient, I agreed.

He did not want to talk about my work.

He did not want to talk about my career.

He wanted to talk about sex.

"I find you very attractive." He smiled coyly. "I would like to meet with you sometime outside of this setting."

I was stunned. I had never been alone with him—only in a group—but he could smell the weak one whom he could cull from the herd. Tongue-tied, I just stared at him, not knowing what to say.

"Maybe we could meet at the Holiday Inn next week after your workday here . . ." He let the proposal hang in the air.

I froze in place. "Well . . ."

"I know you weren't expecting this."

I wasn't attracted to him, but I didn't know how to say no. I knew it was taboo to hurt his feelings. I was raised to take care of the man, especially the doctor. So, I acquiesced. Like a ghost, I left his office and robotically walked to the playground.

My friend saw something was wrong. "What did he want?"

I couldn't tell her what had just transpired.

"He just wanted to check up on how things are going on the autistic ward," I lied, hoping she would believe me. It was the first thing I could think to say.

"You look pale. Are you okay?"

The next week, I couldn't face him. I got a fever and called in sick. The fever went away the next day.

A week later, the night before my day at Napa, the fever returned. Once again, I skipped my day there.

The third week, I knew I could avoid him no longer. I had no memory of how I agreed. I had no memory of how we arranged to meet. I showed up at the Holiday Inn. I didn't want to have sex—yet there I was. How was I going to avoid him, alone in a hotel room, after he rightly assumed I had agreed to a sexual liaison?

He stripped to his underwear.

I stripped to my bra and underwear.

"Come. Sit with me."

He led me to the bed. Gingerly, I sat down. He put his hand across my shoulder. I withdrew, scooching away from him.

"You seem nervous."

Duh! An understatement.

"I am."

"You don't have to be scared. I won't hurt you."

"I've never done this before." He's probably thinking, *That's what they all say.*

He lay on the bed, looking expectantly at me; I sat at the end of the bed, partially turned away.

"We can take it slowly. You don't have to do anything you don't want."

"I've never had sex with anyone but my husband."

His head fell back, and he started laughing. Uncertain what to do, I smiled weakly. "I was a virgin when I married."

He laughed harder. "No one would ever believe we met here and didn't have sex!"

I realized I'd been released. "I'm sorry. I didn't mean—" I fumbled around, not able to look at him.

"This is really a good story!"

"I'm sorry. I've never been unfaithful, and I don't—"

"Nobody is going to believe this."

I was too anxious to get out of there to even be aware he'd already prepared to use me in a story to his buddies. I got dressed and left, not knowing how I would face him the next week.

My compliance with authority shifted from reluctantly agreeing to offer him my body to willingly keeping his secret. The idea of reporting him to an ethics committee never entered my head. I was summoned by the psychiatrist, a power figure, and had no agency to say no.

As I lie on the gurney, the nurse gently leans over my nine-year-old body.

"Sweetie, we need to take off your underpants."

I don't understand why she wants them, and I refuse to relinquish them. I don't realize the doctor will need access to my body for an emergency appendectomy.

Still wearing my underpants, I succumb to the awful-smelling ether.

When I wake, I have a full-belly scar and no appendix.

After surgery, my father touts his prowess to the other docs.

"I raised her right. She kept her pants on."

I am a story he uses to entertain the nurses and his friends at the hospital.

CHAPTER 10

....

February 1968–September 1971

When I was pregnant with our second baby, unbidden, the idea of divorce popped into my head. *It will hurt the baby.* I shut the idea down immediately.

Two years before, after Alan's birth, Walt and I had been prohibited from sex for six weeks. I had wanted to cuddle and be physically close, but Walt wouldn't . . . and I couldn't push. With the second pregnancy, I tried a different approach. I was explicit and repetitive.

"I know we can't have sex for six weeks after the baby is born, but I still want to cuddle."

"Sure."

Walt promised, but I doubted he would follow through.

When Daniel was born, weighing eight pounds, six ounces, I went home with a baby. A big, healthy boy. The daytime was a juggling act—feeding an infant, entertaining a toddler, running a house. At two in the morning, when the quiet surrounded me like a cradle, I was happy. I had no demands but to cuddle and nurse.

Even though Walt agreed to postpartum nonsexual touch, he didn't initiate anything. I would wiggle over to spoon with him in bed, but he'd turn his back to me. I'd put my arm over his side. He was like a board with no welcoming gesture.

"I want to cuddle."

"Okay." He stayed turned away.

With theme and variations, I made overtures. Walt was unresponsive; seemingly, he didn't feel a need to touch me.

"I would like you to reach out and touch me, too."

"I don't want to just act on your command. That's not me."

"I need to be touched."

"I touch you."

"Yes, you kiss me hello and goodbye, but I want more snuggling, talking, holding each other."

"That's not me."

"I need you to be interested in me."

"I *am* interested. I ask you how your day has been, and you tell me."

We went around in circles. Muriel hadn't able to help much. After years of explaining my needs to Walt and feeling shut out, I finally said, "I know myself well enough that if you don't touch me and talk to me, I will end up finding that affection somewhere else."

For me, it was a plea: *Please listen to me.*

The stakes were high. Our marriage was in danger. I was in danger. *I need your help. I need your love and attention.*

Walt heard an ultimatum . . . he thought I was threatening him with an affair if he didn't do what I wanted. Over time, I came to understand he believed that doing what I wanted would compromise his autonomy. We weren't able to understand each other. What I meant and what he heard were two different things. He was furious and angry; I was contrite, apologetic, and frustrated.

The marriage didn't change. I struggled. I shopped. I cooked. We gave dinner parties for his colleagues and friends. I cared for the children. Walt got mad at me for the ring left in the tub, for the stain in the shower. I quietly thought, *He can clean the shower as well as I can,* but I said nothing. I was afraid I wouldn't be able to take back my uncontrolled words. Living in an arid world of criticism and judgment, I felt beaten down and worthless.

When Daniel was two, the word *divorce* paid another visit, niggling around my brain. With no fetus to protect this time, I couldn't banish it. The word *divorce* took up intermittent—but regular—residence.

We'd given up on couples therapy.

Emboldened by having a separate life, I spoke up. "I would like to start individual therapy."

"Why?"

"We've run the course on couples therapy, and I'm still not happy in our marriage."

He was silent.

"You've said it is my problem, so I want to see if I can solve it."

"Well, you know I'm not a fan of therapy."

I was silent, waiting. I cleaned the nonexistent dirt from under my nails.

"It's okay with me so long as it doesn't change anything."

I knew the whole point of therapy was to change oneself, but I promised Walt my therapy would change nothing.

Walter and I had planned on gathering for his mother's birthday dinner. 'Twas not to be. Alice died earlier that morning; her body had been taken to the morgue just a few hours before our dinner. In shock, we decided to come together even though there was no longer a birthday to be celebrated. Walt, his father John, his two sisters, one brother-in-law, and I carried on. The seven of us plus Mary, Alice's friend, made eight.

Alice never wanted to live beyond sixty-five. At the time, I only saw a coincidence that she died on the morning of her sixty-fifth birthday. Walt never mentioned any suspicions to me, and it did not occur to me for another twenty years—only when Walt's niece spoke of it as a factual matter—that Alice committed suicide on her sixty-fifth birthday.

Walt's father had been coping all day by drinking, as did Mary, who had moved in to keep Alice company and "to help." With a gardener, a housekeeper, and a cook, I wasn't clear what "help" was needed. I figured she was Alice's babysitter, who knew how to sniff out hiding places for contraband bottles.

Seated in their elegant home, my in-laws disintegrated before my eyes. Both John, my father-in-law, and Mary, Alice's friend, grew more uninhibited with each drink, till each made accusations about inappropriate behavior of the other.

I hid in the safety of a frozen body, a silent soul. The cook entered with dessert on a silver tray. One by one, she served a neatly shaped sphere of ice cream to each person. We sat in silence.

She left.

Still silent.

Who is going to rescue these people, this conversation?

"Not I," said the little red hen. I'm just an interloper, here by marriage.

Mary nearly fell off her chair. John's face flushed as he poured another drink. No one was babysitting John's drinking. No one dared.

My sister-in-law Dorothy took charge. "Mary, I think it's time for you to go to bed."

Dorothy, too, would be dead in eleven months.

Another suicide.

A month after Walt's mother's death, I pulled into the garage, bringing the car gently to a stop. I didn't want to wake up the boys in their car seats—one a toddler, one a nonmobile baby. Once in the garage, my shoulders slumped. The shopping was done, but the cooking for dinner guests was still before me. I lowered my head onto the steering wheel, feeling its cool smoothness on my skin. I wanted to sit there for an eternity. I wanted to give up—give up what, I wasn't quite clear. I rested another minute till I heard waking sounds from the back seat. I picked up my head and mobilized my body to face the next demand.

With an inhalation of breath, my left hand opened the car door as I grabbed my purse from the passenger's seat. I opened the wayback of the car and stared at the three large bags of groceries as if they were enemies. I heaved them to the ground.

I hesitated. I looked at the now wide-awake toddler and at the sleeping baby. I looked back at the groceries. I calculated my options. If I first took the toddler inside, he's mobile and at risk if left in the house alone. If I left him in the garage, he's also at risk.

I elected to carry the sleeping infant in first, who, unable to move, could safely be left alone. I returned to the garage to find the toddler outside the car, investigating the grocery bags.

I continued to risk leaving him alone while I hauled two of the three bags of groceries indoors. When I returned, my fears had come true. Alan had lifted a bottle out of the bag and was sitting in a pool of spilled milk, next to broken glass, happily splashing the milk with his hand. As he reached for a shard of glass, I leaped toward him, grabbed him under the arms and lifted him to me, simultaneously saving him from slicing his hand while also getting the milk from his pants all over my shirt.

What now? Do I clean up the mess with Alan "helping" while leaving the baby unattended inside? Do I leave the mess and the bag of groceries alone and get everyone inside? But then what? They'll be unsafe inside while I return to the garage.

I needed another adult. I needed a wife. Suddenly I felt the cold wetness of my soiled shirt on my skin. I glanced at my watch. Unless I started cooking, dinner wouldn't be ready in time.

I took both children inside, gave the toddler toys to distract him, ignored the baby's hungry cries, and returned to the garage with a broom, bucket, and paper towel. Not caring about doing a good job, I swept up the glass and sopped up the milk as quickly as I could. I grew an extra arm so I could pick up the bucket, broom, paper towel, and the last bag of groceries. Trying to close the door behind me, I stubbed my toe on the threshold, nearly making a pratfall worthy of the Keystone Cops.

Inside, I found the toddler playing, the baby crying, and no one dead. I got to work, simultaneously unloading the groceries while heating formula for the baby, getting dinner for the toddler, and starting dinner preparation for the guests.

Two hours later, the children were fed, dinner prep was in final stages, and the dining room table was set for six.

Walt arrived. He saw the children in their milk-dried play clothes. "You don't even have them bathed or in their sleepers yet?" He looked around at uncooked vegetables. "Guests are due in twenty minutes."

I turned away from him. "I know." I was curt. My body tightened; my throat contracted. The drama of the garage played in my mind. I considered explaining the life and death choices I made in the last hours, but decided it was too complicated. I checked the oven setting and returned to arranging the peeled vegetables on the roasting pan.

He tried again. "It's late. People are almost here. Why don't you have them ready for bed yet? There won't be time for a bath."

I put the tray of vegetables in the oven, slammed the oven door, and spun to face him directly. I enunciated carefully and clearly, as if talking to a child. "I know."

I picked up the baby and stormed out of the kitchen.

When I'm twelve, my sisters and I bicker in the car till my father loses his patience. He identifies me as the culprit, gives me a quarter, and tells me to get out and take the bus home. Furious at this injustice, I refuse to use his quarter. I've never walked two miles before, and I'm uncertain I can do it, but block by block, my anger propels me.

I walk into the house and slap the quarter on the table. "Here's your quarter," I say and stomp out of the room. My feet are sore, but my pride is intact.

I got the boys ready for bed. I was beaten down. I was privileged, but felt abused, and abused women feel worthless. Did I have *anything* to offer the world? I tried thinking of something I could do that Walt couldn't . . . where he couldn't remind me he was superior and more knowledgeable and I'd failed. I came up empty, defeated, and then—

I can speak Spanish! Walt couldn't.

For the next months, when feeling beleaguered and inadequate, I hung onto that slender thread to prove my worth. *I can speak Spanish!*

The thought became my saving grace.

When the next hurdle came, I didn't wait for a Friday night bourbon buzz. I chose a time the boys were asleep and the dishes done but used no alcohol to screw up my courage. "I want to apply to a master's program. I need another degree if I want to be a therapist."

For my certificate program, Walt had helped out one night a week, but being a full-time master's student was a more demanding request.

"What does that entail?"

"I'm not sure. It depends which program accepts me, if any. I'd have to find childcare, and I'm sure I'd be gone more."

"Who is going to pay for it?"

Always the same question. Money.

"The FIF stock my parents gave me will cover tuition. We'd have to pay for books."

"Well, I guess it's okay with me . . . if you promise to take care of the boys and the house."

Again, I reassured Walt that nothing would change.

He agreed I could apply. It did not feel like a shared decision but rather "permission granted." I felt lucky I didn't have to argue my case further.

I was accepted for the master's in social welfare at UC Berkeley to start in the fall, when Alan was four and Daniel was barely three. I had classes three days a week on campus and an internship two days a week at the Outpatient Psychiatric Clinic at Children's Hospital in San Francisco. I embarked.

I cobbled together the complicated logistics of childcare and did my best to change nothing in Walt's world.

Children's Hospital gave me a hard plastic, permanent name tag embossed with my name. *A permanent nametag!* I stood in the bus line in suburban Lafayette waiting to go to San Francisco. The line was men only, all with jobs. I felt a secret rush. I wanted to burble, "I have a name tag. I have a life, too!"

I juggled kids, the house, shopping, meals, Walt, school, and my internship. I studied. After the children were asleep, I wrote papers. I kept Walt's life stable and undisturbed.

CHAPTER 11

....

April 1972

My mother had given me some cheap emerald chips she got on a trip to Colombia, thinking I might use them in the ceramics I was making. Now, she wanted me to give them back to her. I had already spent two individual therapy sessions on how to respond to her demand. My mother thought gifts, once given, were hers to reclaim. I was learning that gifts, once given, belonged to me.

"How can you do this to me?" My mother's tight voice came through the phone line, straight to my solar plexus.

I knew the drill. I was to give in.

I had dared cross her only twice in my life, both times in high school. The first time, she forbade me from going steady with a boy because his father was not a professional; he was a union foreman at Gates Rubber plant.

"Keep your options open," she had advised, but I went steady anyway.

The second time, she forbade me from running for Head Girl, which was student body girl president.

"You'll get rundown with too much to do."

She didn't want me to shine. Scared to disobey but yearning to run, I waited to file my application till five minutes before the deadline when she couldn't object. Once I won, she appropriated my achievements as her own, crowing to all her friends that I was Head Girl.

On the phone, she repeated, "How can you do this to me?"

My gut tightened, but I was determined to hold my ground.

After years of catering to her and prioritizing her needs, being in therapy had finally given me the gumption to see her demands as unreasonable.

I thought back to when I was a freshman in college. I made the mistake of writing home about how much I missed my high school boyfriend, Rick. Rather than empathizing with me, my mother responded by writing directly to Rick, saying she was sorry that we missed each other; she advised him we should date other people. Even more intrusive, she then phoned Rick's mother and explained to her that our romance was probably a case of "absence makes the heart grow fonder" and not real love. She said we should not waste our college years by yearning for each other.

I was hurt and upset by her behavior, but at that time I didn't see her lack of boundaries as anything but normal; I didn't even know I could have boundaries for her to violate.

Having a therapist mirror my choices changed everything. Only with help did I begin to see my mother's demands—and my husband's—as manipulations. No longer could I easily explain away their war crimes. I was able to shift my perspective.

"Have you used the emerald chips?"

"No. I haven't been making any pottery recently."

"Well, if you haven't used them, I would like them back. I promised to give them to Ruth."

I was startled she had already promised them to someone. My gut tightened. "Well, I might use them. Besides, they're mine."

"But I've already told Ruth she can have them."

I was silent. I appeared as if I were an adult, even though internally, I was a kowtowing, subservient girl hewing the party line. But now I was in graduate school, working, and I had a name tag. Professors and colleagues took me seriously. By osmosis, I was taking baby steps toward taking myself seriously.

"Since you aren't using them, I want to give them to Ruth."

The tongue of fire entered at my belly and diffused through my body, making me shake with fear at what I was doing. I was ready to push open the difficult, creaking door to having a "self." I was deeply aware of the danger my action courted. Terrified, but unwilling to settle for a life of being manipulated, I said, "No. I'm sorry, but I want to keep them."

I held onto the emerald chips—and predictably, my mother was not happy—and went immediately to guilt.

"How can you do this to me? You're not even using them."

Even though I knew I was never going to use them, I said, "I may want to in the future." I gathered more courage and stated the truth. "I'm not doing anything to you. I'm simply wanting to keep the gift you gave me. It isn't yours to give away. You should not have offered the chips to Ruth without asking me."

She was enraged, spit insults at me, and hung up. I trembled but didn't give in.

I had taken a stand! Not bending to my husband's wishes couldn't be far behind.

After I refused returning the emerald chips, my mother wrote to me. "I'm simply asking for the emerald chips. If you're not using them, I don't understand why you won't give them to me, especially since you're embarrassing me in front of my friend."

She continued, cataloging my sins and suggesting she might kill herself.

Being in individual therapy gave me strength. I wrote back. "I do not want you to commit suicide. I love you, and I want you to live. However, I cannot control whether you choose to kill yourself or not. Since it is upsetting to hear about your unhappiness and threats, please, in the future, do not tell me any more about your ideas to commit suicide. I cannot control what you do."

I was shaking and fragile as I stepped out of the ring, but it was exhilarating to declare myself immune to her threats.

CHAPTER 12

....

February–March 1972

For weeks, I had still considered Paul's offer to have sex twice. After Paul's coffee house proposition, we took a video class together, where the professor had challenged all of us in an exercise.

First, we had to pick partners. I actively avoided Paul.

Next, the professor instructed us, "I want each of you to think of something in your life that gives you pleasure—a success, a good memory, something you're happy about. It could be a good client session last week, climbing a tree when you were seven, the birth of a child—anything that makes you excited when you think about it, and that you're willing to talk about."

Silence, as we each considered our topic, then we raised our hands to show we were ready.

"Now, move your chairs to face each other. I want you to tell your partner about this event with all the enthusiasm you feel. Partners, I want you to be bored, get distracted, look at your watch. Then we'll reverse roles."

I told my partner about my year in Spain, about my love of my Spanish mother, my love of the Prado, of Toledo, of the musicians in Totana. It was hard to keep talking when my partner barely looked at me and seemed to barely tolerate my company. My words dribbled away and then dried up. By the end of my story, I felt stupid. My vitality was gone. I wondered why I had thought my year in Spain was interesting to anyone except to me and my sister.

My experience was universal in the class. We all became filled with self-doubt and had trouble continuing. I finished the class with a nagging feeling at the back of my brain.

I didn't have time to delve into the misshapen creature sitting in my amygdala, waiting, waiting. I attended the human development class, took notes, got the assignment, then hurried to the car so I could pick up Alan and Daniel at the babysitter.

The waiting niggle was familiar and known, like homeroom in junior high. While driving home, the misshapen creature forced its way into my awareness. Silence allowed it to take shape, crawling through the smallest of crevices, the fragile openings that appeared in the partnering exercise this morning. I wanted to stay in denial; I did not want to know why the experience in class felt so familiar, but I was unable to keep the truth at bay. My marriage was exactly like the listening exercise we did. I felt ignored and unworthy. I felt stupid.

Maybe the trouble in my marriage was *not* all because of me. Maybe it was partly because of Walt. Maybe his disinterest in me made me feel unworthy and stupid. Maybe, just maybe, it wasn't just me!

I went about my life. I went to class, I organized babysitters, I shopped, did laundry, cooked, started schoolwork at 9:00 p.m. I tried pretending everything at home was okay, and I tried not thinking about Paul constantly. It had been three months of coffee dates and secret kisses. I failed at getting an IUD a few weeks ago; I was ready to try again. I made an appointment with the gynecologist who delivered Daniel, the doctor with whom I had an ongoing relationship. I put the whole sorry story up front, right away.

"I want an IUD," I told him. "I'm planning to have sex with another man. I went to see Dr. Baker, and he refused to give me one."

Dr. Wilson looked at me sympathetically. He had trained under Dr. Baker at Stanford Medical Center. It was Dr. Baker who had referred me to Dr. Wilson four years ago.

"He shouldn't have refused. I'm surprised."

I slumped a little, relieved I didn't have to hold my defiant posture quite so rigidly, and that Dr. Wilson was on my side, even being openly critical of his mentor.

"I'll insert an IUD, if that's what you want. Your periods will be heavier, and there is a small risk it will perforate your uterus. I don't really worry about these things, but I need to tell you. You've had an IUD before, and it was fine, but it's important to be aware of the risks."

Even if *I* was suspect of my own request, he was treating me as an adult who could make her own decisions. He educated me about three different IUDs, their advantages and disadvantages. I asked his opinion and selected the one that made the most sense to me, given his editorial descriptions. He inquired about my marriage, and I told him. He didn't judge me, just wished me well and invited me to come back in a few months to check on the IUD.

I did not want the bill to come to the house, since Walt might find it. As I left, I asked the receptionist, "May I pay now for this office visit?"

She looked befuddled. "It really would be better if we could bill you. That is how we do it."

"But I'd rather pay now."

"It will confuse things." She hesitated. "I guess you could . . . but I don't know how much he's charging you for this visit. I would have to go interrupt him with his current patient." She hesitated again. "Can't we just bill you in the regular way?"

Now it was I who hesitated. I wanted to pay and get it safely done. But clearly it was a problem for her. I didn't want to be pushy and a bother. My childhood training snapped into place: "Thou Shalt Not Disturb the Doctor."

I calculated in my head. The mail usually came in the morning, but always by 3:00 p.m., and Walt didn't get home till 6:00 or 7:00. I could intercept the bill, and then, once I knew how much it was, I could write a check. Walt wouldn't question a check to Dr. Wilson because I went regularly for checkups and Pap smears.

Meekly I agreed, hating myself for the position I was agreeing to, knowing I was creating a crack in the system. What if Walt got the mail before I did?

Externally, I smiled politely; internally, I vowed to be vigilant. I reassured myself it would be okay.

I checked the mail daily. It had been over a week, and still no doctor bill. Focused only on grocery shopping to prepare dinner for guests, I forgot the mail came on Saturdays; I asked Walt to take care of the boys Saturday morning so I could grocery shop unencumbered. Shopping with two toddlers in the cart raised my stress level tenfold. At best, they poked at every item I added to the cart; at worst, they threw newly added items overboard.

Having planned to putter in the garage, Walt agreed. I breathed a sigh of relief.

Diablo Foods was crowded as I threaded my way through the aisles. Walt recently had gotten a raise and increased my allowance for groceries. It was a relief to shop more freely, without continual anxiety about whether we could afford this or that cut of meat. We were planning to barbeque, so I got two market steaks, beautifully marbled with streaks of fat, and as always, more milk, bread, cheese, apple juice, peanut butter, and jam.

I ended up with four huge bags. Walt was in the garage, but he didn't offer to help me. This wasn't unusual, but I sensed a tension in the air. I made one trip from the garage through the family room and into the kitchen. When I came back out, Walt was outside where the boys were playing. I finished bringing in the bags and started to put the groceries away—a task I hated— while also preparing sandwiches. I called out lunch was ready, and the three came in and sat down.

"I got the dill pickles you like." I offered the jar to Walt.

"Thank you."

I poured milk, finished putting away groceries while they ate, and from the kitchen counter, I grabbed a bite of sandwich. They sat at our sturdy 1930's wooden table. Family myth purported Walt had been born on that table. When I expressed my skepticism about this, the story changed—the family owned this table at the time Walt was born. The lacquer was chipped, and the finish on the light wood wasn't very good, but the table was sturdy, and I liked having a family hand-me-down that carried history.

Walt brought the dishes to the sink. Still no talking. I changed Daniel's diapers, got Alan in his nappy underpants, read a story to both of them, and put the boys down for their naps. I went back to the kitchen to finish cleaning up and assess my dinner preparation tasks.

"What is this?" Walt held up an envelope.

My heart thumped; I was sure the blood had drained from my face.

"I don't know. It looks like a bill." I acted nonchalant.

"It is. It's a bill from Dr. Wilson."

I waited, busying myself in the kitchen. At least we're on my turf for this showdown. "Yeah. I saw him recently."

"Why does it say IUD insertion?" He paused. It was sealed, yet, somehow, he knew its contents. As if reading my mind, he explained. "I held it up to the light and read through the envelope." He demonstrated, holding it again up to the light coming through the kitchen window, filtered by the huge, beautiful oak tree in front. "Why does it say IUD insertion?"

"Because I got an IUD put in."

"I've had a vasectomy."

"I know."

"So, what does that mean?" He was withdrawn, cold, and furious.

"It means I had an IUD inserted."

"Why?"

"Because I wanted one."

He walked out of the kitchen.

We didn't talk the rest of the day. We both knew what it meant. Neither of us was willing to name it. His involuted fury was like my mother's; it terrified me.

After three months of moral ambivalence since Paul's proposal, and amid lots of hungry kissing, we were at a Motel 6, near the 580 freeway ramp. It's all we could afford if we wanted to keep the expense hidden from our spouses. When it became clear we'd have sex every chance we could create, I teased Paul about his initial limited invitation of "two times."

Within our limited stolen hours, time expanded as our bodies learned about each other. There was no space between us, no desire to flee. Gone were my inhibitions. I experienced a wildness previously unknown to me, and I wanted that abandon . . . again . . . every day . . . forever.

Hope and vitality returned to my robotic self. I wanted more than a few bourbons on a Friday night. I imagined an alternative to a slow suicide.

Without being aroused, I continued having infrequent sex with Walt. I now knew I *could* be sexually aroused. Nothing was wrong with me. Viscerally, deep in my cells, I knew more was possible.

Paul did not have money, and mine was supervised. We couldn't meet at Motel 6 often, but we managed it whenever we could, usually in the afternoon when babysitters were already hired for my school schedule. I spent less time in the library and more time in bed. Paul and I didn't talk the two days a week I was in San Francisco at my internship. The three days we were at school, we were always in each other's company, unable to get enough.

The weekends became treacherous. Paul and I couldn't talk, yet we couldn't stand not to talk. We discussed our weekend schedules, plotted when it might be safe to connect, and made surreptitious calls to each other at our homes, courting danger.

I carried on. Walt and I presented ourselves to the world as a happy suburban couple. I shopped, cooked, organized dinner parties, and took care of the children. No matter how much I tried acting normal, I was distant and distracted.

Walt didn't appear to notice.

CHAPTER 13

....

January 1972

Less than a year ago I sat through the debacle of the birthday party, the night of Walt's mother's death. Now, Walt's forty-five-year-old sister's dead body was in the next room, and a policeman was questioning me. I'd never seen a dead body close till I saw her body on her bed in Orinda. By the time I got to her house, it was swarming with police, forensic investigators, and soon, the mortuary people, who took her body away. Dorothy's husband, Steve, walked around dazed.

I'd never lied successfully.

"Did she drink?" the policeman asked.

I looked around for help. I was exhausted. Juggling school, an internship, the children, and Walt's demands, I had no reserves.

"Did she drink?" the policeman asked again.

I hesitate. "Yes . . ."

"Regularly?"

"I don't really know."

"To excess?"

"I guess, sometimes." I tried to be evasive while also being truthful. The questions continued, and I squirmed, wondering what it all meant.

Walt overheard and swooped to my side. "She only drank now and then."

I knew she drank heavily, but I stayed mum.

The policeman looked directly at me, sensing a split in our responses. "How much would you say she drinks?"

I punted. "I don't really know. I'm not around her that much." At the time, I was ignorant of what everyone else knew—she combined alcohol with pills.

Later that evening, Walt reprimanded me. "You didn't have to tell the policeman that she drank."

"But she does." I still talked about Dorothy in the present tense.

"Now it's going into the police report, and because they suspect it was a suicide—deliberate or not—the insurance will not pay. Steve and the kids won't get any financial help." He reminded me Steve had lost his job last month.

I made an error that couldn't be unmade. I wanted the floor to open up and swallow me. Without awareness, I accepted the bow-wrapped package of blame Walter laid at my feet. If Dorothy's children became homeless, it would be my fault.

I worried about Dorothy's younger daughter, but I didn't have time to do much for her. My own disintegrating life demanded all my focus.

"**Come on. Get in the car.**" As I hooked each boy into his car seat, I couldn't imagine actively choosing something that would hurt them. How badly would divorce scar them? Irrevocably? Unforgivably? *How selfish of me to even consider choosing myself over them . . . but . . . maybe staying in a loveless marriage would be more damaging to them than divorcing.*

I dropped them off at the sitter's, wondering how a separation might affect them. I didn't want Walt, but I couldn't hurt my children.

As I drove to the bus stop to join the lineup of suburban men, I wondered what it would be like to stand in line as a divorced woman. Could they already see my scarlet letter? Maybe I should stay married. It's safer . . . but I couldn't stop seeing Paul.

Later that evening, I sat at my trusty Olympia typewriter to write a paper for school. Maybe I should just stay married and sneak around. At least that way the boys would be protected.

In my head, the hamster wheel went 'round and 'round . . . and 'round some more. The future with Walt stared me in the face: wealthy, comfortable, predictable, bleak.

The future without Walt was unknown: blank, infused with fog, permeated with fear. Like a moth to the sun, I was a magnet, drawn to the excitement of being alive, wanted, heard, and touched.

Dare I live for myself? Become the black sheep? Not one of the one-hundred-and-six people in my extended family—aunt, cousin, sister, uncle, third cousin once removed—had ever shamed the family with divorce. *Dare I be the pioneer?*

In the '40s, '50s, and '60s, unhappy couples stayed married—but the early '70s? A different story. Open marriage blossomed. The human potential movement was birthing itself. Wanting more from life was suddenly in the zeitgeist. I was part of the loosening of the straitjacket of acceptable choices. I wanted more.

I wanted love. I wanted sex. I wanted talk. I wanted touch. I wanted to feel alive.

Breaking up the family was unthinkable—yet here I was—thinking of it. And that meant I had to think about money. Yet when I focused on money, it skittered away from me like a feral cat, suspicious of being caught. The subject of finances opened a gaping abyss. I knew nothing about our financial situation. I received an allowance, we lived comfortably enough, but I had no voice in how we spent our money.

Walt and I had deftly avoided the topic of money for years. I was raised to be a wife and mother, and the idea of supporting myself was a foreign concept. The future with Walt had sharp outlines; the future without Walt was shrouded in mist. The idea of not having Walt's money deeply scared me.

As I went to my appointment with my supervising psychiatrist, I felt the riptide of Walt's sister's recent death pulling me back into the undertow of the Morgan family. I did not want to abandon Walt's motherless fourteen-year-old niece, whose mother had just killed herself. I was the only functional female left standing in the family. The girl needed me. I couldn't abandon her, but being there for her meant staying married to Walt. Even if I stayed married, I wasn't sure I could help Eleanor. The hamster wheel continued spinning 'round and 'round.

My clinical supervisor had never asked about my personal life in our seven months of weekly appointments, but this time he intuited and asked, "Is there anything going on in your personal life that you want to talk about? You seem a bit distracted."

Without my awareness, my hamster-wheel ruminations must have leaked into my barely born professional identity, presenting themselves to my supervising psychiatrist.

I inhaled. *Should I talk?* I was so tightly wound that, without really choosing, I fell over the precipice. Words tumbled out. "My husband's sister just killed herself—probably accidentally— leaving a fourteen-year-old girl who needs care. His other sister has MS. I'm the sole functioning woman in the family. If I divorce . . ."

I looked away.

"This girl looks up to me. I taught her to swim. I like her. I feel obligated to stay and take care of her."

"It's not your job."

I pulled my gaze back to him. His eyes held me with compassion as he delivered his truth with a certainty I wanted to embrace. "It's not your job."

Shy in this new territory between us, I dropped my eyes to my prepared process notes, which swam before me, my eyes remaining as unfocused as I was.

"She is not your responsibility. If you want to get divorced, that is a decision you must make. You cannot stay married in order to parent this girl."

I looked up at him, at least clear about one thing. "But I don't want to abandon her."

"Remember all of our talks about Jennifer?"

My mind went back a few months. Jennifer, a lost soul, was one of my first clients. I was a newly stable element in her life, yet I was ending her treatment soon, when my internship was ending. Fearing I was damaging her by being yet one more person who abandoned her, I'd been feeling guilty about ending our relationship.

Dr. Persky offered me a wholly different perspective. "Part of life is loss and leaving people. Or having people leave you. If you can talk to her about that with honesty and kindness, you will be offering her a great gift that will help her throughout her life."

Now, thinking about Eleanor, I was aware of the sun shining through his window, making a pool of light on my lap.

"You were terminating with Jennifer and helping her learn about loss. You can do that with this young girl, also, but you cannot stay married in order to rescue her. That is not your job."

I felt as if the pope had given me absolution to divorce. Even if I stayed married, I knew I couldn't really save Eleanor's life, and I just might lose my own.

CHAPTER 14

························

June 1972

For four months, Walt and I lived in a cold war zone. Walt didn't ask about my IUD, nor did I volunteer information. We were formal, tense, and distant with each other.

I couldn't stay in this icy, frozen household. Our marriage felt like deadened steel bars, parallel railroad tracks extending to infinity, never touching. Manufactured laughter, obligatory sex, no spontaneity, no melting of bodies. No matter the financial consequences, I was ready to divorce.

Finally, I called "Uncle."

"We need to talk."

We sat on the couch. He stared straight ahead. I felt as wooden as he looked. I inhaled, glanced at him, and began, knowing there was no going back. "I want a divorce."

It had been just three months since I first slept with Paul—a pretty short time for me to blow up my life and my marriage.

He swiveled and looked at me, his face stunned with disbelief. "That comes as a shock."

Even though I was surprised at his surprise, I stayed silent.

"What do you mean?" He acted confused, as if my simple, declarative sentence were opaque.

"I want a divorce," I repeated, relieved I'd finally declared my intent.

Walt turned away, and a pall descended. We both sat miserably, silently, miles apart in the same room. "What about the boys?"

I'd thought about nothing but the boys.

"It will be hard on them . . . on all of us."

He looked at the floor. "Can't we try again?"

I was weary of trying. I was weary of living. I put my hand on his arm. He glanced at me, and I withdrew my hand. "Walt, for years I've been trying everything thing I know. I dragged you to couples counseling, I tried talking to you, I tried withdrawing, I tried getting mad, I tried not getting mad. I don't know what else there is to try."

"I never believed you were serious. Now that I know you're serious, can we try again?"

I was dumbfounded. For years, I'd been as vulnerable and open with him as I could be.

"It's too late." The words popped out of my mouth, prepared by hours of listening to Carole King's song on the stereo, "It's Too Late."

"Can't we try again?"

"No. I wish I could . . . but I can't." This time, I was the one who turned away.

More silence. Finally, I went to bed—same bedroom, same bed, but no longer the same marriage.

The next morning while the boys ate their breakfast, I heard an unfamiliar noise as I approached the bedroom. I listened, trying to identify it. It stopped. As I walked toward the dresser, I heard it again, coming from the bathroom. I froze.

Walt was in the shower, weeping. He sobbed. I wanted to comfort him. Never in the eleven years of our relationship had I seen him cry, much less release unconstrained sobs from his belly. Not when his mother died, not when his sister died, not when our infant son was hanging onto life.

I wanted to go to him, make the world right again. But there wasn't a way to make the world right unless I was willing to die inside this deadly marriage. He had chosen the privacy of the shower to prevent me from seeing his vulnerability. I knew I couldn't intrude. Besides, there was nothing more to say, no comfort possible. With tears quietly streaming down my cheeks, before he knew I'd heard him, I tiptoed out of the bedroom.

Alone in separate rooms, grief bloomed in each of us.

Deep down, I feared something was wrong with me—I was too needy, I was unreasonable, I was asking for the moon. I had to pull myself together before I saw the boys. Then I remembered: *I didn't think you were serious.*

My heart closed. My tears stopped. Bile rose and crept into my corpuscles, extinguishing any desire to soothe him. I hardened. Suddenly I saw how, just like my mother, he had used me, how he had sucked light from me, refracting it for his own use, leaving too little light for me to feed my own fire.

I'd made my decision. There was no turning back. I wrote to my parents to announce my intention to divorce.

No response. No phone call. No letter. Only deafening silence.

Silence was the kind of punishment that left no mark: severe, destructive, and widely practiced by my mother. The target of her wrath became a nonperson, as if that person had never existed. Banished, shunned, erased, without even a water trail left behind.

I did not want to phone and expose myself to her questions.

My anxiety rose daily, until finally a letter arrived, with my father's physician scrawl on the envelope. Only once in my life had he written me. I held the letter as a precious object, afraid it would evaporate if I touched it the wrong way.

I was scared. What had I done? I knew my mother would be furious and critical. I'd made myself particularly visible now—like a pimple, an unsightly eruption breaking the smooth appearance of our family's well-tended skin.

I looked at the letter, almost pulsating as it sat on the kitchen table. While I fed the boys lunch, it waited like a time bomb.

I waited for the safety of time and privacy. I put the boys down for their naps, then picked up the letter. Curious and fearful, I opened it. "We received your letter. I can't say that I understand your choice, but then, I haven't walked a mile in your shoes. Please let me know if there is anything I can do. If you would like me to come visit, I would, or you are always welcome to come here. Or we could talk by phone or write letters."

I cried. He let me be.

My shoulders relaxed. I didn't have to be vigilant; I didn't have to defend or pretend. My father noticed me and was supporting me, offering to be a father. I wanted to leap at the chance—a chance for him to shift from being a distant, fearsome figure in my life to something softer, a father who was actually aware of me.

I didn't know how I'd go visit him in Denver, but I knew I would. The boys were only three and five, and I would have to get Walt to agree to take care of them for a weekend. I'd also need to make childcare arrangements for Friday and Monday. It was summer, so I didn't have school obligations. The logistics were daunting, but my mind went to work.

I waited for the most benign moment I could find to tell Walt my intentions. The children were in bed. He sat at the kitchen table where the letter had nearly burned a hole, and I was at the sink not facing him. We were both raw. He knew I was having an affair; I knew I wanted a divorce.

I started. "Today I got a letter from my father. He's offered to talk to me, and I want to take advantage of it. I want to go to Denver for a few days." I waited for the non-arriving response. "I could do it over a long weekend and arrange day care for Alan and Daniel on Friday and Monday." I hesitated, fearful to ask anything of him. His back was turned toward me, as it was most of the time.

"I'd like you to take care of the boys on Saturday and Sunday."

He didn't look at me, nor did he respond to the need for childcare. "Who is going to pay for it?"

Money. His only question was about money.

From the opening gate, he set out to use his wealth to intimidate me into submission. He wanted control. If he could withhold, he would. Money became his continuing lever for years to come.

My marriage paralleled my childhood family: a subtle, skillful exercise in power, an exercise in dancing around the truth, in being vigilant to the fluid dynamics of dominance and submission. Protect your territory. If need be, hurt others. In our trio of competitive siblings, my older sisters could out-talk me, out-reason me, out-trick me, and out-ridicule me. Each girl had to fight for herself. There was never enough oxygen to go around.

I evolved into the victim role when growing up. I volunteered for the position in my marriage.

"Who's going to pay for it?" he repeated.

"I don't know."

Silence.

Then more silence.

There was nothing *but* silence in our marriage. I stiffened my spine, dropped my shoulders, and spoke. "I'm going."

My belly was squishy, but I made the words and tone defiant. I was not a natural warrior. I wanted him to understand me. I hoped if I explained well enough, he would. "My father has made a gesture. You know how rare that is. I want to respond."

I looked at Walt, who was motionless, staring into the dining room. I picked up some more dishes to put in the dishwasher. "If he is willing to be available, I'm going. If there is a chance to get to know my father, I want to grab it."

Growing up, the parental catechism was, "Where there's a will, there's a way." I paused, and then wanted Walt to know I was determined. "I'll figure out a way."

Walt looked at me. "Well, I'm not going to pay for it. If you go, the cost is going to be deducted in the divorce settlement. Don't think for a minute that I'm going to pay for you to go to Denver."

The cost of a round trip flight—subtracted from the total value of stocks, dividends, a retirement pension, two cars, two purebred dogs, and an upscale suburban house full of furniture— would disappear in the wash. The cost seemed inconsequential compared to the chance to get to know my father.

I was a kept woman and economically powerless. At that moment, I vowed never again to be financially dependent on a man. I would not put myself in a position of impotence, unable to shape my own life, passively leaving fateful decisions in some man's hands.

My post-divorce plan crystallized quickly. I had to earn money; I had to become a breadwinner. Graduate school was salvation for my intellect and my spirit; now it was my ticket to economic dignity.

As I walked out of the kitchen, my voice was terse, my fury imploding. "Okay. Let it be deducted in the settlement."

We barely talked in the subsequent days. I arranged to go to Denver in July.

CHAPTER 15

....

July 1972

My father loves magic tricks. As a child, I marvel that he can pull a quarter from a child's ear or guess the face card you are holding.

His favorite trick—and mine— is startling people with his magical elevating necktie. Underneath his tie, he installs a wire contraption that has a string threaded down his shirtsleeve. Casually talking to kids at our birthday parties, he pulls the string and the tie rises up, as if by magic.

After pleading with him to tell me how he does it, finally, when I'm eleven, he lets me see him rig it up one evening before a cocktail party. Lurking around the guests, I wait in anticipation for him to pull the string and see his tie rise, startling the onlookers. The sudden laughter washes over me like a balm. I'm on the inside; I'm his coconspirator.

Each tan brick building of my parents' retirement community looked identical—manicured, banal, and sterile. Inside their apartment, I recognized the furniture and decorations, but the place felt small and petty. There was no room to maneuver.

75

Unlike the large house of my childhood, which offered places to hide, to dream, and to capture an unsuspecting beam of light, the cramped rooms dared anyone to have fun.

I suspected my mother didn't know my father wrote me a letter.

The first night, we ate at Luby's cafeteria, with almost nothing to say to each other. The conversation was stilted, formal, anodyne. They asked about the logistics of my divorce, but there was no warmth to make it safe to talk about why.

My mother's judgment seeped through. Her venom silenced me. We all ate too much. Dad, obese, loved ice cream. Mom frowned at him as he ate it. I overate to dull my anxiety.

My mission was to talk to my father, but I knew my mother's anger and jealousy would sabotage me if I tried to do so openly. Her paranoia created demons in her head; she feared she would be excluded. She needed to possess each of us, separate from the other, so she could control and manipulate each marionette who populated her life.

The next morning, I didn't know how I would maneuver to have alone time with my father. I'd have to be cunning. I tried reading the newspaper but couldn't concentrate. I was restless yet enervated to be with people who weren't really there, me included.

My mother was polite. I was polite.

I was ready to explode.

Finally, casually, I said, "I think I'll go to the store for some milk. Anyone want to come?"

I knew I couldn't say, "I'm going to the store. Dad, do you want to come with me?" I definitely couldn't say, "Dad, do you want to get out of here so we can talk?" I knew the subtleties of how to word things around my mother—my invitation had to be veiled, indirect. I knew how to keep my antenna out, engaged at all times. It was exhausting, confining, but useful.

"Brenda, how about you?" my father carefully asked.

"No, I'll finish my crossword puzzle." She turned to me. "You might get some of those little sweet rolls while you're there."

"You sure you don't want to go?" Knowing the rules of the game, I encouraged her. I had to make her feel wanted, so she could turn me down.

"No. I want to finish my crossword puzzle."

"Dad?" Having appeased the tiger, it was now safe to turn toward him. "Do you want to come with me?"

"Sure," he drawled in his laconic way. He couldn't appear too eager. "I'll keep you company."

He said to Mom as he got up, as always, his hip and weight making movement difficult, "Anything else you want?"

"No, thanks." She returned to her coffee.

"How long will you be?" She only *sounded* mild; she was putting her tentacles into our trip. Her need to control leaped unconsciously from her hip pocket.

"Just long enough to go to the store and back. Half hour or so."

We were on notice not to linger. Knowing there was no alternative, I'd fallen for the trap and agreed to minimal time alone with my father.

Having escaped, my heart pounded as my father and I walked out the door. This was my only chance to talk to him privately. I wanted our time to be intimate but never having talked to him about my feelings and my life, I didn't have experience of how to be intimate with him. This was like a first date.

I knew the initiative had to be mine. He had written the letter; I couldn't expect him to open the conversation too. It was not surprising I chose a man who didn't know how to be intimate and with whom I felt awkward when I tried.

Once on the road, with my eyes straight ahead, I said, "Thank you for your letter." I didn't want to waste any of the few minutes allotted to us. When we stopped at the red light, I glanced at him, but I still couldn't look at him directly. "It meant a lot to me."

He doesn't know how to respond in this new emotional territory between us, and I don't know how to let him.

"Is Safeway the best place to go?" I asked, returning to a safe topic.

"Yeah. The one over by Cherry Creek is probably the closest."

I glanced at him, trying to remember if I was on his blind side or his seeing side. He had lost his eye in a hunting accident before my parents were married. He once tried teaching me how to thread a needle while having only monocular vision. I regret that I had been too young and impatient to be interested in learning.

I tried again. "I know that you don't understand why I'm leaving Walt, but it's clear to me that it's the right decision for me."

"No, I don't understand." He paused. "But I have learned that there are a lot of things I don't understand. It seems to me that he supports you well. You have two little boys who need two parents, but as I said in my letter, I haven't walked in your shoes."

"I feel like I'm suffocating. I've tried and tried talking to him about how empty our relationship feels, and he doesn't know what I'm talking about. We've been in couples therapy periodically for two years, and he now admits that he never believed I was serious. He wants another chance."

"Can't you give it to him?"

"It's too late. I've given him everything I've got. He doesn't know how to have a relationship."

I wanted to tell my father about Paul, the man who had taught me what love and sex could offer, but I knew that was unwise. We talked, looking at the road, taking only sidelong glances at each other.

At the store, we both found solace in food. We bought milk, sweet rolls, ice cream, even chocolate bars to eat in the car. Our eating together became another secret. Before driving off, I looked directly at him. "Thank you for your letter and your support. I want you to know that I love you."

He returned my look, was emotional, and said, "I love you, too." We composed ourselves, ate our chocolate, and guiltily went home, silent but full. We became absolutely nonchalant by the time we walked through the door, heartily greeting Mom.

"How did the crossword puzzle go?"

She saw no threat in us being gone only a half hour.

I didn't know it then, but I would be forever grateful I made the trip.

My father would be dead in four months.

CHAPTER 16

....

July 1972

After the evening with my parents, I escaped to spend the night with my college roommate and her husband, who lived outside Boulder. There, I could breathe again; the difference in my body made the comparison stark.

Their friend, Pablo, was also visiting. The next morning, while my friend and her husband worked, Pablo and I set out on a ride— me on their horse Tin Cup, and Pablo on the mule, Strawberry. The sunshine, friendship, and clear air calmed my nerves.

But out on the trail, Tin Cup stumbled. I declined Pablo's offer to ride her back home. When the horse stumbled a fourth time, I was afraid she would fall on me and break my leg, so I tried sliding off her first. Next thing I knew, I was face down on the ground.

Groggy, with my face in the dirt and my hands under my chest, I lifted my head. I saw Pablo's dirt-covered shoes in front of me. I tried using my hands to push myself over, but immediately the pain stopped me. I pushed my feet into the earth to mobilize my hips, creating momentum to roll over.

"I think I broke my wrist."

"Thank goodness you can move," Pablo said, kneeling over me. "You were really knocked out."

Pablo gently helped me sit up. We both stared at the damage. My left wrist was grotesque. My forearm extended to my wrist, then made two ninety-degree angles, like two plumbing elbows on a pipe. My right wrist was swollen, too, but the planes of the bones were recognizably normal. Still in shock, I didn't feel much pain, just curious detachment when observing my mangled wrist.

"Tin Cup must have thrown you." He'd had his back to me and hadn't seen what happened.

"And I must have broken the fall with my wrists." Already trying to be stoic, I looked for the good side. "It's much better than breaking my back."

"Can you stand?"

"I think so." Tin Cup, a few feet away, happily munched the lush July grass, ignorant of how he had just changed my life. Pablo had Strawberry on a lead rope.

"I must have blacked out there for a minute."

Pablo nodded and helped me up. We brushed me off and assessed the situation.

"Can you walk back?"

"I think so, if we go slowly."

I moved gingerly, trying to be smooth as a swan so I wouldn't jostle any joints. It was a long walk back. As the shock abated, the pain began. I hung onto the idea of calling my father for help.

I interrupted Dad's game of gin rummy at the Denver Country Club. "I'm not sure if I should get my wrist set here in Boulder or whether I should come down to Denver."

"Well," he drawled, calm and unruffled, "I think you could drive down to Denver." He paused. "Why don't I meet you at Mercy. Is there someone who can drive you?"

"Yes. Their friend Pablo is here."

"Well," he drawled again, "I would suggest you put a pillow under both wrists to support them while you drive. And maybe take a couple of aspirin if they have any."

On the drive down, I remembered my 4:00 p.m. flight. I'd likely miss it but calculated I could probably get my wrist set and make the one at 8:00 p.m. I did my best to ignore the increasingly throbbing pain.

I asked Pablo, "Do you think you could change my flight for me?"

"I can try. But why don't we wait till we get to the hospital and see what they say first?"

I needed to get home because Walt had to work and didn't have alternative childcare. I felt disoriented but confident I could make the 8:00 p.m. flight.

We arrived at Mercy Hospital, a familiar and comforting sight. I had gotten my first job at age fifteen at Mercy, serving dinner to the nuns. Unlike the other teenagers on the food assembly line, I had access to the cookie room and was charged with sneaking extra cookies for everybody. I tried controlling my own cookie-eating but couldn't; I became a cookie thief.

Dad met us in emergency. After one look, he said, "I think you're going to need surgery." This was not a paternal opinion; this was an expert opinion from an orthopedic surgeon.

"I'll try to find Gene while they take you to X-ray." My father wouldn't operate on me but would get his partner to do the surgery.

The nurse came in to assist me. "We're going to have to X-ray both wrists, and it's going to hurt to position them. I'm going to give you a shot of Demerol, which may make you a bit nauseous, but it will help the pain."

I almost threw up, but within seconds, I also felt ecstatic. I didn't care how nauseous I was. I was high, open, and full of love for the world. Suddenly I understood heroin addiction. Nothing hurt. The excruciating pain subsided, even as the nurse manipulated my wrists.

I was expansive, happy, delirious even. My heart soared when Pablo entered the room. I loved him, as if we'd had had a deep and lifelong friendship. I was spacious. We were connected; the world was benevolent.

Dad was in the background, consulting with his partner about the X-rays. Conclusion: Both wrists were broken, and I needed surgery.

CHAPTER 17

....

July 1972

I asked Dad to call Walt to tell him I'd be home tomorrow. I was rolled into surgery. Someone clamped the ether cup over my nose and mouth. I resisted breathing the awful-smelling anesthetic, but succumbed by the count of three.

I woke up confused. I knew I was in the hospital. But why were both my arms in traction, dangling in the air, immobilized above my head? Why was any arm in traction? I expected a cast on my left wrist but thought it would be lying in my lap, as it was before I went into surgery. And my right wrist was just sprained.

I was woozy, but not too woozy to understand the gravity of my helplessness. I couldn't move and started crying. I couldn't wipe the tears from my eyes. They dripped down my cheeks, into my ears, and puddled in the ear crevices made for tear-lakes. They tickled. I moved to wipe them away, but my suspended arm moved only a fraction of an inch, stubbornly adhered to its metal chain.

I couldn't stanch the flow. Tears flowed down my cheeks, but I wept silently. I couldn't blow my nose. The snot stayed in full flower, having its merry way with my upper lip, covering it like old, yellowed snow.

I looked around the room frantically. How did I get here? How was I going to get out of here? My father stood at the foot of the bed. No longer was he the detached surgeon. With his gray crew cut, and round face red, he looked at me, his eyes filling with tears. I'd never seen him cry.

His tears multiplied my own. If he was crying, I knew whatever was happening to me was serious business. When I was twelve, he was dismissive of my crying when my cat was run over, so whatever had happened to me now was bigger than Stinky's death.

He didn't say anything. He was my best parent. The damage his earlier violence had done to me was buried in my body, lying unconscious, waiting for me to wake up and unspool its torque.

"What happened?" I asked him. "I thought I only broke my left wrist." I was like a turtle on her back, belly open to the world, unable even to flap my appendages in impotent frustration. I tried stifling my sobs. For a second, I pulled myself together.

He reasserted his calm, surgeon's demeanor.

"Well..." his drawl returned. "Looks like you're not going to make the eight o'clock flight tonight."

"I guess not." I smiled through my receding tears.

"I think you'll probably be in the hospital for a few days."

I was too tired to care, too much in shock to process anything.

"Why don't you rest? Soon you'll get moved to a hospital room. We can talk more later."

I closed my eyes and returned to oblivion.

I **woke in the** hospital room, hands still in traction above me, but with the occupational therapist at my side. "When is your next period due?"

Irritated with her irrelevant question, but obedient girl that I was, I thought about the answer. When did I last have a period?

"I think my last one was about two weeks ago. Why?"

"Because you're not going to be able to take care of yourself."

A new reality zinged around my head like a self-propelled billiard ball.

"You're not going to be able to wipe your bottom or change a sanitary napkin."

Shit. Who would ever think of that as the first problem? But there it was.

"If you have your period while you're still in the hospital, we can help take care of you. But it's something for you to think about."

My arms hung in the air for three days of my five-day hospital stay. I was fed, bathed, and toileted like an infant. On the fourth day, I felt better enough that I wanted to comb my hair and put on some perfume. I knew it would cheer me up if I looked better, if I smelled nice. But I couldn't do it myself. *Should I call the nurse?* I suddenly knew how old, infirm people must feel—wanting help but not wanting to be a bother.

I did not call the nurse.

My mother never visited the hospital, but my sister, Laurel, did. "Do you feel helpless?" she asked.

My denial was so thorough, I snippily answered, "No."

No one was ever helpless in our family. Despite my dire circumstances, I couldn't afford to see—or feel—how helpless I truly was. My childhood mantra returned.

I can do anything. It didn't mean I could aspire to any goal like being a doctor or president. It meant I could get through anything, no matter how difficult, and come out mostly alive.

My sisters and I were groomed to perform. We got through by wearing brittle clay masks that ruptured and broke. We reglued the broken shards, hiding our shock and numbness, and licking our wounds in private. Each crack made us more vulnerable, but we were unable to soften our masks, unable to be kinder, especially to ourselves. The fissures became scars, hardened with judgment and certainty. Self-righteousness provided an armor but destroyed our relationships and shaky self-worth.

On day five, my father took me directly from the hospital to the airport. I was mobile but weak. Both arms were in casts from below the elbow to the tops of my knuckles, with a hole on the side for the thumbs. He helped me get my bag checked, and I walked alone toward the plane, my finger hooked into hangers holding my clothes. I was grateful to arrive at the gate and be able to sit quietly alone and gather some strength.

I rested on the plane, willing myself not to cry. Ignorant of the body's recovery needs after a general anesthetic, I assumed I would bounce back and be ready to go. *I can do anything.* I was so tired, I didn't even have the energy to be anxious about Walter and his being inconvenienced by unexpected childcare responsibilities. My brain went in circles about the logistics of the next months. No solution emerged, no matter how hard I thought it through. On the third approach to the same treacherous ledge, I dozed off, my pain meds helping me stay in a fog.

As we stood in the aisle to deplane, a kind gentleman offered to carry my hangers. I nearly cried in gratitude.

"Why are you flying alone in this shape?"

I smiled weakly at him and thanked him. It had not occurred to me that either parent—both retired—could have helped me. I did not ask; they did not offer. Had I asked, my mother's answer would have been, "You made your own bed; now you have to lie in it."

Many years later, after my divorce, Aunt Sally told me, "I called your mother and told her she should go help you. You were getting divorced, out there in California with two babies, and Walt was refusing to give you money. We all need help sometime. Your mother said, 'Kay's an adult. She can take care of herself.' I will never forgive your parents."

At least Aunt Sally had been on my side.

CHAPTER 18

....

September 1972

The following days were a blur. Walt dutifully picked me up at the airport. It was war zone redux. All I wanted was to be with Paul. To be comforted. To be loved.

I couldn't drive. I couldn't see Paul. I needed Walt's help to dress and undress. I needed Walt to take me to my new doctor. I couldn't shower easily. I did not ask for help. Clumsily, I used rubber bands to secure plastic bags over my casts. I didn't attempt to shampoo my hair.

I took care of my own menstrual period. I took care of the children. I asked our sometime babysitter, a new high school graduate, to grocery shop for me.

I grew adept at using my casts to provide strength to lift things. I hired a lawyer. After six weeks, I returned to driving.

I met Paul at a motel in Walnut Creek—more upscale than we were used to. His touch, his kiss, brought me back to life. He shampooed my hair.

I hunted for a place to live, determined to buy a house so no landlord could kick us out at a moment's notice. Walt agreed to loan me $10,000 for a down payment, which I could repay from my half of the proceeds from the sale of our home.

Even though terrified of my new life, I leapt.

The gods were looking out for me. I found a house in Berkeley that was not yet on the market, and I bought it.

Our moving day was September 1, our eighth-year wedding anniversary. It was now public: I was leaving Walter Morgan and the Morgan family. Each of us had made other living arrangements, and we put our house up for sale.

But there was one more blip. Eleanor, the young niece whose mother died in January, was now truly an orphan. After her mother died, being a single parent did not suit her father. Steve didn't know how to comfort Eleanor, how to talk to her, how to make her feel important and loved. He began drinking more, not asking for help.

Steve died on August 28, his death slipping in right before Walt and I separated. Steve was one of three people in a private plane flying in the wilderness in Canada when his plane crashed in a lake. Steve did not survive.

I was sad for Eleanor, but I felt emotionally distanced. Unlike a few months ago, I had no impulse to turn back.

Carol King's "It's Too Late" rang through my head again.

With both arms in casts, I moved.

"This house is so big!" Alan's legs propelled him through the new house at a good clip—he would be six next month. Daniel, just a month into being four, lagged behind, more subdued and dazed by the turn his life has taken.

I was bemused Alan thought the Berkeley house was big. We left a 3,000 square foot house in suburban Lafayette, set on a quarter of an acre with oak trees and a creek, and moved to a 1,400 square foot house on a tiny lot in the heart of Berkeley. Only the width of a driveway separated our house from our neighbors. When the weather was warm and windows opened, we easily overheard their Sunday morning arguments about politics. I gave up square footage but I gained freedom.

I'm glad Alan liked this house. I liked this house, too. It was a charming bungalow on a sweet street. Some previous owner made it into a duplex, giving me flexibility to have a live-in sitter. Even though both my arms were in casts, and the house was filled with unpacked boxes, it provided a foundation of stability and hope. A beautiful pink dogwood tree in the front of the house burst into bloom for three weeks in the spring, bringing grace to the whole neighborhood.

This house was ours. If I earned a living, no landlord would be in charge of my life. But I was scared. I was raised to be a wife and mother, not to be a breadwinner.[1] Even though I had worked summer jobs since I was fourteen, I never expected the responsibility of paying a mortgage. For the first time in my life, I was on my own—and responsible for two other lives besides my own. The idea of earning a living to support myself and my children was terrifying.

My father had disparaged my mother's desire to work. When I was in high school, she found a part-time job working for a local business journal. She loved it. She loved earning money and having a role outside the house.

Privately, my father told me, "She should be at the hospital volunteering, not working."

She quit fairly quickly. I had no model to be a working mother, and no support.

Walt moved to the new Watergate Apartments in nearby Emeryville, the latest magnet for young singles. Immediately, Walter met a new woman.

Twelve days after our separation, Walt wrote to my grandmother:

> I have decided that I can and will find happiness with another woman. Perhaps she and I can be much happier than Kay and I were. I don't know, but I'm sure going to try hard to love and be loved and forget the past. I miss having the boys, but they are close, and I see them often. Kay is good to them, and they are doing well. If Kay can

be as happy as I am, it may be for the better. We both care so much for the boys that we won't let anything wrong come to them.[2]

Walter and I were so different from each other. My wounding made me want to understand and to heal; his wounding made him want to forget, find a new woman and move on.

Nora was an obstetrics nurse who had no children of her own and wanted no children of her own, either. Walt told me Nora felt she dealt with enough children at work.

They moved fast, and within months, they bought a house together. When it was clear she was going to be in my sons' lives, I asked to meet her.

"She isn't comfortable meeting you now. Maybe after we're married."

I didn't push the issue. I also didn't know how big a role she would have in shaping my life.

While my mother was silent during my visit to announce my divorce, she followed with a scathing letter condemning me and my choices, telling me I was selfish, that Walt was a good husband, and how could I ruin the children's lives.

My father enabled her—at my expense. He wrote, "I suspect your mother feels much as I do, but she has not achieved the degree of tolerance to realize how she really feels. I don't know what she wrote to you a few weeks ago, but I suspect that most of what she wrote, you would rightfully reject, and the rest would only make you angry. Please forgive our faults of intolerance and inability to communicate."[3]

First, he patronized my mother by saying she didn't know what she really felt but that *he* knew what she felt.

Then his letter continued, "Please write her to hasten the healing of the breach, which you think now will never be healed."

I needed a good parent desperately—and he was the only candidate. I didn't let myself see how he chose to protect my mother's cruelty rather than protect me. I had neither the energy nor desire to reassure her of anything, yet, dutifully, I wrote a letter of apology.

For what, I knew not.

CHAPTER 19

....

September–November 1972

The external world reflected the chaos of my personal world. The UC campus was tear-gassed to protest Nixon's invasion of Cambodia. Some classes were canceled. I didn't have a clear opinion about the war—another place I felt inadequate, but I didn't have the time or energy to educate myself.

I limped along.

I switched from the master's to the PhD program. If I had to earn a living, I needed credentials. I did not want a ceiling controlling my options.

Still a second year MSW student, I commuted to San Francisco three days a week for my internship at the outpatient clinic at Mt. Zion and had two days a week of academic classes. I didn't care about being a star student; my goal was to survive the year.

With Daniel in pre-school and Alan in kindergarten, I needed childcare. The sometime babysitter from Lafayette became our live-in sitter in Berkeley. I blessed our duplex house.

Two weeks after moving, the doctor removed my casts. My arms were so weak I couldn't lift a half-gallon of milk. I needed more surgery in November, when he would snip off an errant bone from my mangled left wrist, protruding toward my fingers.

It prevented me from lifting my hand at the wrist. This meant another general anesthetic, another four months to recover from the anesthetic, and another rehab.

I was discouraged.

Paul and I spent our two days at school mostly with each other. Depending on his wife and Walt's visitation schedule, I saw him sporadically on the weekends.

The second surgery was November 10. Recovery was slow.

On Thanksgiving morning at 8:00 a.m., the phone rang.

With no preamble, no gentle preparation, my mother announced, "Daddy died this morning. He had an intestinal blockage and died of a heart attack."

My life was in shambles, and now the thin reed of understanding that my father had provided was gone. Thank God I had gone to Denver and had told him I loved him!

Like my wedding, my father's funeral was my mother's creation. It was held in a church he never attended, invoking a god he didn't believe in. To him, original sin wasn't something mystical; it was the impulse toward laziness. My mother was outraged when I wore my red pantsuit, my puny earthly effort to cheer myself up and defy the reality of his death. Besides, it was my only outfit that minimized my hips, which she also found outrageous. She had railed against their size since my puberty ended their androgynous slimness.

I attended the church service, but Uncle Quincy's farm, the farm my father tilled, plowed, hated, and loved, was where he was most alive for me and where I went to say my real goodbye. Uncle Quincy loved me the same way my father loved me—mutely.

I walked past the silo and the pigs, down the dirt road by the dead corn stalks, their juicy kernels of August long withered by a gray December weekend. Soon, I heard the pickup driving behind me. It stopped next to me, dirty with grime that never disappeared from its use on the farm roads.

Uncle Quincy leaned over, calling out the open passenger window. "Wanna get in?"

I really didn't, since I felt awkward around him, never quite knowing what to say. If I got in, I'd have to talk. I was grateful my mother made me develop good social skills as a child, but it was work to pull them out, especially that day.

He peered at me, "Looks like it's going to blizzard."

I climbed into the passenger seat and cranked up the window. We drove for a while in silence. Still recovering from my second surgery, I was too tired, too bleak, to even bother trying to be socially adroit. My father was dead, and he was the only parent who had loved me.

But Uncle Quincy took over, pointing out the fallow field. I was surprised this taciturn man initiated a conversation. "That field will be sugar beets, but we have to let it lie for a while."

Big fat snowflakes began falling. The blizzard had begun, and I was glad to be in the warmth of the truck.

"When do you plant?" I was willing to try communicating.

"Depends on the spring . . . but probably not till March, maybe even April."

I couldn't think of anything to say.

He continued, "Weld County grows more sugar beets than any other county in the state. Our crop next year will be for seed." He was silent again, not demanding much from me.

I watched the snowflakes hitting the dirty windshield. "It looks like you have a new crop of piglets."

"Yeah," he quietly laughed to himself. "That old sow keeps on giving. I don't know how she does it."

"The kids had a great time playing with the piglets last visit."

We drove in silence. He smiled to some inward memory. "Yeah . . . Alan had a hard time milking the cow."

We continued until he said, "Well, we'd better be getting on back," and turned the truck around.

We passed the dead corn stalks, the fallow field. We didn't talk about his brother, my father. Driving together in the blizzard, talking about the farm, the crops, and the pigs, we both knew we're saying goodbye to Frank, in the mute, Harrington way.

After my father's death, my life was in chaos:

To my lawyer, I was a client, an adversary of the father of my children, the man I lived with just four months ago.

To my babysitter, I was an employer organizing her shifts.

To my professors, I was a full-time PhD student, organizing my life around the library hours.

To my clinical supervisors, I was an intern writing process notes and showing up prepared for consultation.

To the waif of a neighbor boy whose mother was an alcoholic, I was a steady grown-up willing to feed him dinner.

For myself and my sons, I was forever a shopper, cook, and provider.

To my sons, I was both a source of solace when they hurt themselves, and I was also the law.

"Pick up your toys. Take a bath. Time for bed."

At bedtime, I read to each boy and had chat time. Exhausted when they're finally in bed at 9:00 p.m., I read assignments and wrote school papers.

And started again the next day.

Neither my psyche nor my schedule had any give. I ping-ponged among roles, reactive to what put itself in front of me.

In addition to this frenzy, a new stress appeared: the oil embargo of 1973. Now I had to use precious time to wait in long lines at the gas station, anxious they might run out of gas before I got to the front of the line. The daily infrastructure of my life crumbled.

A second stress also invaded daily life: inflation. By January 1974, the inflation rate went up over 9 percent, and the following year it went up almost 12 percent. My meager salary supplemented by alimony didn't go as far as it did when it was calculated.

Although our relationship was strained, Walt and I attempted to be friendly. I asked him to help mount shelves in the boys' room. He did.

But the next spring when I asked for help to put up a basketball hoop at the end of the driveway, he said, "I'm not your handyman!"

I never asked for his help again.

CHAPTER 20

....

September 1972

Our lawyers started negotiating. Joint custody was new in 1972. What I wanted was full custody, but ever accommodating, I offered Walt joint custody. He dismissed the idea out of hand, giving me full physical and legal custody. It seemed to me that he did not want the day-to-day responsibility of raising young children.

He picked up the boys for his first visitation weekend. I collapsed into tears after they'd gone.

Like a termite infestation, the disintegration of goodwill between us advanced slowly. Daily interactions weakened the bonds, and then turned the already porous bonds rotten. The first termites used the vehicle of money. I didn't like being a warrior. I wanted to give in. I wanted the conflict to go away, but I knew I needed money in order to finish school and support us. I had grown up in a family where talk of money was taboo, confusing, and dangerous. Walt wanted it that way, and I allowed it to stay that way in our marriage.

I was taken aback when my lawyer's first question was, "What are your financial needs? What is your monthly budget?"

I had no idea. "I don't know. Walt did all the finances in our house."

I didn't know how much he earned—gross, net, by month, by year, by lunar calendar. I was ignorant.

Even though I supported us the first two years of our marriage, I was still dependent. I gave my check to Walt because that was what wives did. I didn't think or act independently. Robot-like, I stepped into my idea of the role of wife and became a Stepford Wife. It never occurred to me I could have separate desires nor actively shape the role of wife . . . or my life.

Once Walt and I were in the legal process, we both had to submit a list of assets and liabilities. I made up a monthly budget, hoping there was some reality to it. Walt had hard facts. It was the first time I'd seen a list of our finances.

I was shocked to learn we were millionaires—$943,249 in assets (house, cars, stocks, and savings)—not counting his salary! The amount of money we had would be worth $6 million in 2024. Walt was also careful to list our liabilities, itemizing a ninety-cent charge for garbage so we could split the debt.

Walt, now my adversary, revealed himself quickly. I was outgunned. He used money—and his cunning and legal knowledge—to get his way. His opening gambit alerted me to his shrewd sophistication. Our legal battles and maneuvering lasted many years with numerous court hearings. (See the Legal History appendix for a chronological listing of all legal events.)

Walt submitted his idea of an estimated monthly budget for each of us, suggesting I should run a household for me and for two children for the same amount of money it would cost him to live alone.

His initial proposal was no child support and alimony for one year only. As a lawyer, he knew that structure would transfer the tax burden to me.

I was unwilling to forgo child support or to accept only one year of alimony. With that as his starting point, we were unable to negotiate a settlement, yet if I disagreed with him, he felt bullied.[1]

Within weeks of separating, I was already facing the likelihood I would need to go to court to protect my children and myself.

This was *not* what I anticipated.

Walt had the boys for Thanksgiving, which passed me by in a fog of surgery and death. Christmas was the first big hurdle I navigated for our fractured family. We did not have an on-site father, but I made sure we had a family.

Even with casts, surgery, my father's death, graduate school, and legal negotiations—I mobilized. I surrounded us with old friends and created traditions I hoped would hold our shaky family together.

I created a scaffolding to get us through the tricky days. Walt scoffed at the idea of me calling us a family on our Christmas cards because we were a mother and two sons—the Harrington-Morgan Family, but I ignored his contempt, sent the cards, and insisted to the boys we *were* a family.

Old family friends joined us to cut a Christmas tree; another helped us decorate it. I spent a week baking the architectural components for multiple gingerbread houses. I bought candy at Sweet Dreams, and we invited two neighbor boys to decorate the gingerbread houses with us. With my wrists weak but functional, I played the flute for our Christmas caroling party to serenade the neighbors.

We made a special Christmas outing to San Francisco with a surrogate grandfather. The boys were too young to shop independently, so he helped them buy presents for me—probably underwriting their purchases. Alan, at six, gave me a small sculpture of a stork feeding her baby. His choice reassured me—true or not—that he felt nurtured. I was trying to minimize the trauma of divorce and keep my boys feeling safe. I didn't know we were all about to go over the cliff.

The new year came, and through our lawyers, Walt and I still wrangled. Walt found more community debts and wanted repayment. He verbally agreed to pay college tuition for the children from the trusts his parents created for our children, but he refused to make the agreement legal.

Walt wrote to me, "I've given in on every significant demand, yet they keep coming. Can't it end? . . . I don't want to go from loving you to hating you in less than a year. I don't ever want to hate you."[2]

After eight months of negotiating, my lawyer told me no agreement was possible.

A court trial was scheduled for May 5.

Morgan v. Morgan, Case 136027, Superior Court of Contra Costa County, May 5, 1973.

A smattering of bored people sat in the courtroom, quietly waiting for their own cases to be heard. Walt's lawyer approached the judge and requested that the courtroom be cleared. The judge granted his request. The bailiff made the rounds of the courtroom, talking to each individual, politely asking them to leave.

One man grudgingly resisted, but the bailiff was firm. As the man walked out, he gave me a dirty look. As a woman walked by, she looked at me with wide eyes, as if she were trying to place Walt or me in her pantheon of known celebrities.

I was confused and disturbed by Walt's power over the judge. My lawyer surmised Walt did not want the public to know about the valuation of the privately held class of Morgan Medical stock.

Each of our lawyers presented oral and documentary evidence. Walt pleaded poverty about the amount of alimony he could afford. My lawyer countered with the observation I had passed on to him: the one time I picked up the boys at Walt's new house, from my vantage point at the front door, I could see a gleaming new TV, a new stereo, and a houseful of new furniture.

His lawyer called me to the stand to cross-examine me. I had butterflies in my stomach, as I knew he would try cornering me.

"Have you looked for a job?"

I thought about the impossibility of having time to even think about it. Instead, I only said, "No."

Later, my lawyer admonished me for not explaining further. I could have said, *"How could I have looked for a job when I was moving homes, was hospitalized twice, had two surgeries, was in casts, was a single parent, a master's student with a clinical placement, and a new PhD student?"*

Walt's lawyer accused me of malingering, using the actual word.

"Why do you need a PhD?"

"Because I want professional options to be open to me."

"Well, you have a master's degree, and you can teach high school Spanish." *Was he inferring I should force verb declensions on unwilling students forever and not be allowed to do something that suits my interests and talents?*

"I don't like teaching high school Spanish."

"You're just malingering, and I think you just enjoy being a professional student. It's ludicrous that you want another degree. It's time for you to take some responsibility, get a job, and support the family."

He ignored that I supported us when Walt pursued an MBA after already having a law degree from Harvard. Even while married, I did not rely on Walt for my education. When I returned to school, I used my small premarital savings from my parents.

He ignored that Walt increased his earning power each year while I stayed home to care for our children. After my education, I would enter the job market fourteen years after Walt. Why should it even be a question why I would increase my professional possibilities and earning power? Women were not seen as the head of a household.

Outcome: We got a temporary support order from the judge on May 16. Walt had to pay me $250 per child per month and alimony for three years ($300 per month the first year, then $250 per month). Attorney's fees would not be considered until the final hearing.

It took nine months, two lawyers, a court hearing, a judge, and thousands of dollars in legal fees to reach an interim, temporary financial settlement. I didn't yet know it would take another four months and another trial to reach a final dissolution order.

Within three months of the court order, Walt wanted to amend our settlement to benefit his tax position. He wanted to keep the total amount the same but reapportion the court award by reducing child support and increasing alimony. He made an argument that this distribution would help each of us lower our tax burden, especially if I had high childcare costs. However, his proposal would also have made me vulnerable to his whim to stop child support, and, at the same time, prevent an increase in child support once alimony stopped because, as he wrote me, "the IRS would then view the whole thing a sham."[3]

This time I was not outmaneuvered. I declined his offer.

Walt was to have visitation every other weekend. His office was just fifteen minutes from our house, so it was easy for him to pick up the boys Friday evenings and deliver them home Monday mornings.

For the first few months, Alan routinely got a fever the night before he was to visit Walt. Routinely, Alan asked to stay home. Routinely, I made him go.

"Your father loves you, he wants to see you, and he can take care of you as well as I can," I said. But inside, I wanted to scoop him up and keep him home, safely inside his mother's bubble.

Rather than a desire not to see his father, I interpreted Alan's fevers as a response to the trauma of the divorce. The fevers subsided over time, even though the transitions from one house to the other remained difficult. I felt guilty. I had brought this on us. The fevers returned years later at the next wrenching separation.

Walt started out consistently, but within weeks, his weekend visitation became sporadic. He often canceled with little notice. He traveled for work. He went duck hunting. He had his new girlfriend. The sudden cancellations upset the boys and increased my logistical and emotional challenges. I tried talking to Walt, but he refused to engage.

I needed to get his attention. After a slew of missed visits, one day when he returned the boys, I insisted on going out to his car to talk, taking a tape recorder with me. I did not want our sons to hear me plead with their father to give them the love and attention they needed from him.

Having had too much experience of Walt misconstruing my words or denying his own, I announced my intention to record our discussion—or rather, my monologue—so there would be a record. In full view, I turned on the recorder and told Walt it was our obligation to be civil with each other and work together for our children's sake. His boys needed him, and they needed him to be reliable and consistent.

Wound tighter than a drum, he stared out the car windshield, totally mute. He neither looked me in the eye nor responded verbally.

My harangue had no impact. He canceled visitation again the following week. When I talked to him by phone, this time without a tape recorder, he told me he wasn't my babysitter.

He totally missed the point.

CHAPTER 21

....

June–July 1973

Nine months after we separated, and after four months of Walter's cancellations of visitations, I tried again to get his attention, this time in writing:

> The boys are being hurt by your continual choices not to see them. A couple of weeks ago, Alan was sitting next to me reading (we were on the Pinel camping trip). All of a sudden, he looked up at me, his face a beautiful radiant sunshine, and he said, "We get to see our dad in three days."
>
> I had to say, "No, you're not going to see him this weekend." His face looked full of pain, then became a mask, and he turned back to his book without saying a word.
>
> That may not bother you, but it sure gets to me. Won't you please set up a regular schedule and stick to it? We can be flexible to exceptions, but let's have not-coming be the exception instead of the rule.[1]

I was a linebacker running interference, so my sons didn't get hurt. The aggression required didn't come easily to me. Mounting the opposition drained the little energy I had, but clarity was on my side. I wanted to protect my sons, not only from their father's abrupt cancellations but also from Walt's new girlfriend, who was willing to be angry at me but not willing to meet me.

Losing myself in passionate lovemaking with Paul became a narcotic to help me escape the struggle of daily life. When the boys were gone with Walt, when lawyers were off duty for the weekend, I pared down my responsibilities to being a student, and allowed myself to enjoy the pleasures of being a lover.

But being Paul's lover was a complicated affair with many limitations. One limitation was my children. I did not want to introduce Paul to my sons, so we had to work around their schedules. A second limitation was Paul's wife. He made up many stories: trips to the library; exercising; or meeting his friend Bill. Mostly, he was in my bed. We talked, we touched, we laughed. We spent time together jogging around the Berkeley Marina—a new activity to me—and I was happy to be losing weight.

Our love grew, our commitment grew . . . yet, he was still married. We avoided crowded public places where his wife might see us. At the same time he was being an adulterer with me, he was being vetted by the bishop of the Episcopal Church to become ordained as a priest. If they found out about our relationship, he would probably lose his professional career. I felt guilty about his wife, and the idea of the consequences to his professional life scared both of us, but we were unable to leave each other alone.

I wanted our relationship to be public. His situation made it impossible. My impatience grew. My anger grew. Multiple times Paul promised to tell Sharon, but inevitably, he chickened out. I had no idea what her understanding was. I assumed she asked questions, and he wiggled out of direct answers—or lied.

One of the sayings he quoted when we argued about this was, "All things come to she who waits."

Betrayed once too often, I drove to San Francisco and waited to intercept him at the Trans-Bay Terminal, where he was on his way to his clinical placement at the Veterans Hospital.

From fifty feet away, I saw him get off the bus. The sight of him triggered an eruption in me. I surprised myself by my own behavior. Without even approaching him, my lungs bursting with venom, I yelled as loudly as I could.

"Fuck you!"

People stared at the crazy lady. My rage was so great, I was not embarrassed. Months of negotiating with Walt, years of being ignored in my family all erupted from my viscera, loosed on the unsuspecting commuters in San Francisco.

"Fuck you!" I yelled again. I indulged in the abandon, the fury that had been building for months. I yelled, turned, and walked away.

I left Paul for good . . . but not for long. He relented first, called me, and I did not hold strong.

I melted; we made love.

We reconciled. More promises, more hope, more touch, more betrayal. The intensity of our sensual life was like nothing either of us had ever experienced—together as one, unafraid to be vulnerable, hungry, passionate, curious. We were as addictive to each other as cocaine was, with a high as dangerous.

Being invisible and second-rate fit me like a well-worn cloak. I told myself once he was safely ordained, he would leave his wife, and we could be together. But history told me it might be a pipe dream. I had no confidence in a happy ending.

Every time I got frustrated at being second, we had the same conversation, yet I was incapable of leaving. I waited impatiently in the shadows.

At Christmas, when Walt had the boys, my cousins in Southern California took me in for the holidays. (Thank goodness for my network of Harrington cousins!) I left their welcoming home to drive two hours in a horrendous rainstorm to wait in an Edward Hopper diner to see Paul for a half an hour. We needed one another like a waning battery needed an electric charge to stay alive. In my depleted world, I pretended crumbs were a full meal.

A year later Paul was still dithering. I was still a side dish.

I got myself into therapy . . . again.

Within four months, my therapist asked me, "Were you ever abused?" She continued, "You have the characteristics of someone who was abused."

I vigorously denied even the possibility. We were an upstanding family. I wasn't able even to consider that my father's "spankings" nor my mother's humiliations were abuse. I dissociated as a child, and I still dissociated as an adult, not able to entertain even a whisper of the truth.

Years later, when I denied abuse to a subsequent therapist, she pointed out, "The footprints of abuse are in the snow." Slowly, I began to tolerate knowing the truth of my upbringing.

After a year of secrecy, Paul got approved for ordination. Even though I was still in the middle of court hearings with Walt, I spent energy helping Paul plan the event. I was thrilled when he asked me to do a reading during the ceremony. A public role at last! I collected rose petals from my neighbor's garden to be tossed as Paul entered Grace Cathedral to his favorite upbeat, non-religious music.

Paul's ordination was beautiful. Being around his wife made me anxious, but I was in total denial about my role as a perpetrator. I somehow excused myself.

His mother was there, too. We all celebrated. Paul and I danced . . . and danced again. Unbelievably, Paul, his wife, his mother, and I lined up for a photo together.

But the next day . . .

"Who is this Kay person?" Paul's wife asked him.

What were we thinking? That I could look adoringly at him while we danced, and his wife wouldn't notice?

He maintained the fiction that I was just a fellow student. He convinced no one. I was relieved the charade was over but anxious about the fallout. *What will happen? What will he do? Who will he choose?*

Weeks after our interim order of financial support, Walt and I continued to disagree about alimony, child support, visitation frequency, and visitation times—in short, all significant issues. Less than three months after our May 5 trial, we needed yet another trial date. We got a date for July 26.

Walt changed the agreed-upon earnings formula for spousal support and also refused to notify me of increases in his income. He would not add anything about using the boys' trusts for college. He insisted I stop school and begin work immediately to support the family. Even though nothing was in any verbal or written record, his lawyer wrote to my lawyer as "fact" what Walt wanted the judge to decide, carefully couching his conclusion in lawyer-like language, leaving himself an out. The judge "indicated in substance" that he agreed the solution to the Morgan family's financial problems would be for Mrs. Morgan to find employment.[2] The lawyer continued, "Mrs. Morgan is intelligent, has three [sic] college degrees and is well qualified for employment." (I had two degrees at this time—Walt also had two.)

My lawyer said we would need interrogatories and depositions. More money. Walt itemized his separate million dollars of property—bank accounts, savings, Morgan Medical stock, partial ownership of a beach house in Santa Cruz, and even listed the down sleeping bag.

My lawyer and I showed up for court July 26, as did Walt and his lawyer, for the final hearing about our financial settlement.

The judgment entered by Judge Abbott on July 30 was the same as the interim order, except this time, Walt had to pay my lawyer's fees.

Even after the judge's order, Walt didn't give up negotiating. Three weeks later, he wanted written into our settlement that he could cancel his visitation at any time.

Finally, thirteen months after our separation, the financial settlement and the dissolution of our marriage was official. Walt then wanted me to do him a favor; he wanted me to sign papers so he could remarry without waiting the six months required by the state. Hoping to create good will, I suppressed my irritation and signed.

We were divorced on October 3. Walt and Nora married on October 9.

Once they'd married, I again asked to meet Nora, since she was now the stepmother to our children.

Walt no longer hid behind, "Wait till we're married." He was direct. "She is not interested."

I was frustrated and angry. She now had authority over my children but wouldn't make any effort to be friendly.

CHAPTER 22

....

August 1973–August 1974

I needed a paying job. I knew I had to adopt a new identity as breadwinner. I got a job at International House on campus as a foreign student adviser, doing academic and visa advising. Only occasionally did I have the opportunity to actually use my counseling skills, but it was a job. I assumed this job was stable and would see me through finishing my PhD.

Wrong. Six months after I started, my boss asked for a copy of my master's courses.

"A man who is on 'preferential rehire' status applied for this job, but we chose you because you're better qualified," he says. "This is just a formality—nothing to worry about."

But then my boss requested descriptions of the course work from all my classes. A few weeks later, he told me that the man on preferential rehire status had appealed and had won. I no longer had a job.

I was frantic. For the first time in my life, I actually had to support a family, and I had lost my job. Walter was no longer a resource for me.

My boss and his supervisor, the Dean of Student Affairs, were so upset by this unfair treatment that they managed to shoehorn me into a temporary job at the counseling center for the summer.

The counseling center had some salary savings and could give me a three-month job through August. It wasn't much, but it gave me time to look for something more secure.

I became the first and only social worker on a staff of seventeen psychologists. I couldn't do career counseling because I hadn't been trained in testing, but I could do crisis counseling and brief therapy.

At the end of the summer, they gave me a lifeline: a permanent job as a counseling psychologist and ongoing training in psychometrics and testing. It was a godsend to have a place where I was treated as an adult during the infantilizing experience of being a graduate student.

What seemed like disaster turned into a blessing. I would learn Walt would try eroding any wisp of my security that he could, but this job provided a foundation for me.

The pieces of my life were falling into place. I'd helped Walt remarry, Paul was ordained, I had a job, the boys were safely with me, and fall semester was starting. There was one exception: Paul hadn't left his wife.

On a fall weekend when the boys were with Walt, I laid in Paul's arms, but the tension of being hidden for months had not dissipated. I was invisible as a child, and I was invisible as a mistress. Now that Paul was ordained, my anger was rising and volatile.

Once out of bed and having coffee, I began, "If you really loved me, you'd leave Sharon. How can you keep living this lie?" I couldn't bear to see who Paul really was to me—a hypocrite, a coward, a selfish man.

"I told you I'd leave Sharon. Just not yet."

"Why not? You've been ordained."

For over a year I'd held onto his promises as my salvation. But he wasn't acting on them.

"Because she's a good person."

"She's a good person! That's the best you can do? What about me?" I flailed on his chest. "I'm a good person, too." I pounded harder.

"What are you doing? Stop it."

I ignored him, crying and wildly hitting him. "You lied. You led me on all year." I hit him anywhere I could find. "You said you'd leave her when you were ordained. You lied."

"I've risked my whole life for you."

"Yeah, while there were no real consequences to you."

He grabbed me, getting angry in return. "I've risked everything for you. My marriage is a mess, yet you act as if I've done nothing."

"I hate you!"

He reeled back, then hit me. We were both so startled, we stopped. We wept. We apologized. We fell into each other's arms. We declared our love. We had passionate, desperate sex.

My eye swelled and blackened. I was ashamed—ashamed of myself and ashamed to be with a man who hit me.

I was also outraged. *How dare Paul hit me!*

I wanted to cancel my next therapy session. I didn't want my therapist to see my black eye. I wanted to protect Paul. I wanted to protect me.

I wanted to hide . . . just like I needed to hide as a little girl.

Lying under the covers of the bed, I could be the sheet. Lying like stillness itself, sinking into nowhere so I won't be found. Instinctively, at four, I know how to be as quiet as a hunted deer—still, unmoving, disappearing into my surroundings. Any slight movement—the flicker of an ear, the twitch of a tail—can be lethal.

I will myself to disappear. I've learned to breathe from the inside out, keeping movement inside my body so no one can discern that I am alive. Miraculously, I have taught my body to make the oxygen-carbon dioxide exchange with pretend air. I inhale one tiny millimeter. No whooshing sound, no sudden intake of breath. Then comes that pause, the pause that is neither breathing in nor breathing out. That pause of nothingness. The same nothingness I want to become, like quivering, shiny mercury, no longer trapped in a body that bruises. I could simply be an element of nature that does nothing more than follow the rules of physics.

Instead, I exhale, a silent, controlled stream of air quietly escaping my body. Using all my powers of concentration, I do the best I can to be inorganic, non-kinetic matter.

Earlier I made the mistake of hiding in plain sight, believing that the kitchen table provided some protection. The legs of the table are chrome and spindly—nothing to offer real security but I imagined the corner placement offered safety. I scrunched down against the far wall, my head next to one cold, rounded, chrome leg. The yellow glossy paint on the wall is unfaded under the table, where the sun is prevented from leaving its mark.

I hide and I hope. Sometimes, if I run away, he won't chase me, his bellowing rage suddenly deflating, having been fed enough by the terror he sees in my little body.

I try not to breathe. But I can't help it. Fear makes me gulp and reach for air, until my will seizes me and prevents any peep from escaping. In spite of myself, while patrolling for sobs, some migrant sounds find their way out.

My whimpering ignites him again. If I can whimper, he hasn't yet shown me who is boss. He grabs me from under the table and drags me out by my arm, a rag doll of tears, shame, and small noises.

He spouts meaningless words into the air. I understand only the cyclone of his fury. His two-hundred-and-fifty-pound quarterback body drags my fresh, spindly, thirty-pound body through the breakfast room and into the living room where he has a chair big enough for him.

He needs to discharge the violence in his body, and he needs an object. As he pulls me onto his lap and flips me over his thighs, he pulls down my pants. He raises his hand high above his head, bringing his open palm down onto my naked bottom with as much force as he can muster. My chest tightens, trying to keep me silent. Fear tightens my belly. I want to run, but I can't escape his grip. In spite of myself, I wail, pain exploding from my lungs.

He raises his hand to pummel me again and again. I gulp for air before another blow lands on my now-tender skin. Only mewls escape my tightly held lips. Some days his handprint is clearly visible hours later. Other days, one handprint morphs into another, leaving a red blob of a welt.

And then he is done, his anger released. I slink away, knowing better than to cry. The final act in this ritual is him saying to my retreating back, "Be quiet or I'll really give you something to cry about."

If I try sitting down, my bottom cries out in pain. If I lie down, with the pressure of my body spread across a greater surface, I can pretend for a few minutes that my bottom is okay . . . but only if I don't move. Moving destroys the illusion.

I know how to be quiet. Stillness itself. I know how to be a sheet.

I do not want to be alive. From a young age, my soul starts to fragment into pieces.

CHAPTER 23

························

August 1974

To my surprise, my therapist did not focus on Paul, whom I wanted to characterize as the out-of-control angry bully; instead, she focused on me. I felt like a victim and had thought I'd get her support by what I thought was true. *Ain't he awful.*

Instead, she made me recount, step-by-step, the antecedents to Paul's blow.

I slowly recognized the part of me that wanted to provoke him, to prove to myself that I was important to him. My father's physical abuse was the only way he paid attention to me when I was little. It took years before I understood that, as an adult, I was reenacting the dynamics of my childhood—something we all do until we heal the original trauma.[1]

A few weeks later, Paul and I approached another physical fight, but I stayed conscious enough to observe myself. I didn't want another black eye, or another round of shame.

I knew I had to leave him.

We separated; we agreed not to talk for two weeks. I was in hell; Paul was in hell. After ten days, he called me. We fell into each other's arms. We inhaled big drafts of each other. In five stolen minutes with him, my nervous system was calmed, my addiction fed. I felt alive again. My desire to die was momentarily dissolved.

I was aware that using Paul as a source of my will to live was a fragile reed. He was conflicted and controlling; I was feisty and resentful, yet submissive.

We continued navigating the tumultuous shoals of a secret affair.

I **had outsourced my** spiritual life to Paul. I attended weekly communion service, always with Paul at the altar. His wife never attended the university community services. I found comfort being in the presence of the sacred ritual, the Gospel teachings, the familiar prayers, my lover—all wrapped up in one. The merged priest-lover fed the numinous need of my psyche. I often wept with relief.

Paul finally told Sharon he wanted to separate. He found an apartment, moved out, and we created some semblance of normalcy. I was hopeful. He met my children. Because of Paul, I returned to the church of my upbringing, and I became uncomfortable with the difference between the boys' religious status. Alan was baptized with Walt's full participation when we were married, but Daniel remained a heathen.

I decided to have Paul baptize Daniel so my children's ability to take communion was undifferentiated, should it ever matter to them. I did not consult Walt because, even though he had agreed earlier, I knew he would object now. I had full physical and legal custody. Our Christmas-family friends became Daniel's godparents.

My toehold on life was tenuous while coping with Walt, lawyers, court preparation, court appearances, children, Paul, work, and school. The seduction of dying whispered in the corners of my mind, and it took energy to hold it at bay. People raved about LSD, the new vogue drug. As much as I wanted to change my perceptions of reality, I knew I was too fragile to risk experimenting.

I stuck with marijuana for relief. I wanted a time out. My sons were the only reason to get up each morning. I wanted to sleep for a couple of years and wake up when this storm had passed. My mother's penchant for threatening suicide paved the way for me to find the idea seductive. Walt's mother and sister succumbed to its siren call, but about one thing I was clear: I would *not* leave my sons motherless.

Walt and I had experimented smoking pot once but did not experience a high. Paul now introduced me to its pleasures. I began smoking with Paul, and separately with a married couple who had become my mainstay friends during this time. Pot helped soften the edges of my harsh reality.

My relationship with Paul was volatile—maybe because the make-up sex was so intense. We fought about time together, time apart, my friendships with others, my professional commitments, our values, our future. We fought about anything.

He thought my tastes were bourgeois, especially my Mustang convertible. I thought he was too controlling. He was upset I had a life before him and was jealous of people I knew before his time. He would have preferred I were an unspoiled virgin with no history. He judged me for having a romantic past yet interrogated me about it. I learned not to tell him stories of old romances because he picked at them again and again, like at a scab he couldn't ignore. Because Paul felt threatened by my male friends from the counseling center, I became fearful of him seeing me have lunch with them. I didn't see yet how dangerous this was.

I stumbled along. My qualifying exams for the PhD loomed in the spring: three days, four hours each day of written exams, followed by a two-hour oral exam with three professors. If I didn't pass, I would have wasted three years of preparation and not been allowed to write a dissertation and complete the PhD.

The logistics of my life were chaotic. Walt continued cancelling visitations at the last minute. The babysitter I hired last summer turned out to be an underage thief. I waited till after my Thanksgiving trip to fire her, but she beat me to it, and in my absence, disappeared with my grandmother's diamond ring. I tried holding our life together for the boys, but I wanted to give up. Instead, I functioned. I put my shoulder to the wheel to find another sitter.

CHAPTER 24

....

April–June 1975

According to our custody agreement, Walt could have the boys for spring vacation and four weeks over the summer. I needed relief and time to study for my qualifying exams, so I wrote Walter, proposing he take the boys for spring break and a week or two early in the summer.

Walt responded quickly. "As the purpose of the visitation is for *me* to see the boys, I want no part of weekday visits when I'm not home from work. For that reason, the idea of my taking them [spring vacation or summer] is just not acceptable."[1]

While I prepared for my exams, I needed certainty in my schedule. I wrote him that if he couldn't promise to follow through on his visitation schedule, I would rather be responsible for them myself.[2] Walt did not argue.

A couple of weeks later, Walt complained about my response to Alan's haircut. "I resented your comments about the haircut for Alan more in the manner of delivery than in the substance of the message. Your comment came across to me in an angry tone of voice with a lot of criticism. As it was, I got mad, and Nora got even madder. It was just another incident for her to salt away in her mental little black book on Kay."[3]

I needed a new babysitter immediately. With little choice, I found Joan, a thirty-something woman who had been a nanny before and seemed competent, even if not particularly appealing. Within weeks, she acted petulant and was irritating. When I would leave notes about the schedule, the boys' homework, or shopping, she would leave notes for me with the tone of a jealous lover, saying I hadn't been paying enough attention to her. With exams looming, I couldn't afford to fire her.

Since Walter would not take the boys for spring vacation week, I paid Joan to take them to Santa Cruz while I did my final preparation. Once she returned from the vacation week, I learned she had called Walter and told him I was an irresponsible mother because I kept knives in a kitchen drawer accessible to the boys. I fired her.

On short notice—again—I scoured for another babysitter. The only one I found was a young woman who was pregnant and needed a place to live. Not ideal, but I hired her.

I took and passed both my written exams and my orals.

In June 1975, I was advanced to candidacy for the PhD. I was elated! A major hurdle was behind me, but I still had to work, feed, and care for the boys, deal with Walt, and write a dissertation.

Paul now had a new demand.

"Give up your kids, car, and career."

He hated my Mustang convertible for being too bourgeois— but he didn't mind driving it. I didn't want to give up my car and especially not my kids or career. Even thinking about giving up my kids was foolish.

But think about it, I did. Totally separate from Paul's edict, the idea of letting Walter have the boys for a bit was appealing. I longed for relief, for fewer responsibilities with just time enough to finish school and get back on my feet. I felt caught in a vice.

Every time I passed the local hospital, I was filled with envy of the patients; I wanted someone to feed *me* and to take care of *me*.

Sensitive boy that he was, Alan dreamed he was alone in the desert.

I ached for him; I ached for me.

Choice One: Give up Paul and the healing balm of being wanted.

Choice Two: Give up my children.

I smoked marijuana to help me survive, but it was contributing to my depression. I continued struggling with wanting to die. My therapist helped me do a tai chi move: I called Paul's bluff and told him I would give up my children temporarily. I didn't want to, but it was the only way I could see out of the dilemma I was in.

I talked to Walt. I asked him if he would take custody of the children for a few months or a year while I sorted out my life.

Walt said no. No surprise.

At last, I had clarity. My responsibilities, my children, and my life were mine. The only big decision facing me was how to leave Paul. I'd made another mistake in the choice of a man, and I vowed to stay in therapy long enough so I would never repeat the same pattern again. Paul and I agreed to have no contact.

I became a dead woman walking. I felt like I'd lost a limb. A zombie. I functioned. I got dinner on the table. I went to work. For the first time in my life, I was unable to listen to music. If I did not turn off the car radio, I dissolved in tears.

To stay sane, I walked. I walked the seven miles to Paul's house, turned around, and walked home. I was not able to sit still; I had to stay in motion to discharge anxiety. Paul called me, saying he had coughed up a piece of his esophagus because he was so upset. I did not understand why two people who were so powerfully connected couldn't be together. But I knew we couldn't.

I wavered. I held strong. I wavered.

I dreamed I was at the bottom of a steep hill and needed to get to the top. I started hiking up the switchbacks but, when I looked up, I realized what a long, difficult path it was. Then, to the left, I saw an escalator going in the same destination. All I had to do was get on the escalator, skip the switchbacks, and ride effortlessly to the top.

Every waking hour, I focused on my dream and the escalator. Actively, minute-by-minute, I chose the escalator. I chose not to return to Paul. I had no idea what life would be like as a single woman, but I was determined to stay that way till I could choose more wisely.

CHAPTER 25

·······················

November 1975–March 1976

Soon, I would become a published author, with a chapter in a book. I did not want to carry Walter's name into my newly crafted professional identity, so legally, I reclaimed my maiden name and left his surname in the history bin.[1]

When I told Daniel, age seven, that I was changing my last name, he immediately asked, "Will you still be my mom?"

He was scared. Scared of being abandoned. Scared that his parents were fighting. Scared he might not have a dad, and now he might not have a mom. I hugged him and reassured him.

"No matter what my name is, I will always be your mom."

The Berkeley Unified Teachers' strike in fall of 1975 changed my life. The disruption provided Walter an opening for the camel to get his nose into our tent, and he used it to try to destroy the life I had created with the boys.

The facts seemed simple: school wouldn't start in the fall. The rhythm of life ground to a halt, as if the gears were stuck. No harvest of the crops, no Back-to-School night, no clean folders to get dirty. Eighty-five percent of parents kept their children home. It became a polarizing political issue, neighbors shaming neighbors. At a core level, the strike disoriented the whole community.

I was taut, like a guitar string about to snap. My life had no place to absorb the full-time care of two young children while I worked and went to school. Day by day, I put a patchwork quilt of caregivers together. I skipped my own classes; I took vacation days from work; my neighbor helped as she could. The anxiety of finding coverage was mitigated by knowing the strike would only last a day or two. Maybe a week, two at the most. But days passed with no settlement. Week Three. Week Four. Week Five. The strike dragged on nine weeks, almost into November.

Everyone was on edge. Working mothers were having nervous breakdowns; kids were bored and getting into trouble. Family therapists' schedules were full. I ran out of childcare options, and I was behind in my doctoral work.

One evening, Daniel went over the edge, and I wanted to join him there in crazy-land, not responsible for my actions. I don't remember what precipitated his freakout—probably I asked him to pick up his toys. He started shaking, and his eyes rolled up into his skull till only the whites were visible, almost as if he were having a seizure. I held him, I talked to him, I reassured him, but I couldn't get the pupils of his eyes to reappear. I was scared.

Life was out of control, and I could do nothing to stabilize our careening family. After what felt like forever, Daniel's eyes finally returned to normal, and he stopped shaking. I needed help. I needed relief, but there was none.

I fed them dinner. I got both of them to bed. It was up to me to keep our family on track, contained, and moving forward.

Once they were in bed, though, I collapsed into tears and let myself feel the terror I had held at bay for two hours. I called my doctor cousin—sort of a paterfamilias—to get medical counsel and comfort. I described Daniel's physical symptoms, and he reassured me it was probably no more than a panic attack. I couldn't afford to have panic attacks; Daniel had them for me.

Discretionary time was nonexistent. However, I made time to visit several classes at Malcolm X, where Alan was slated to be bused the following year. I was appalled at the level of teaching— English teachers misspelled words and used poor grammar. I was also worried about bullies holding up fourth graders for their lunch money. Alan hadn't had to develop street smarts; he would come out on the losing end.

I was willing to be shamed and labeled a traitor for not supporting public schools. I started investigating private schools. I tried including Walt, asking if he would like to be involved in the school research and decision.

He preferred I did the work, although he helped with the final choice. We selected The Academy, a small, academically-oriented school near home. I relaxed some, knowing that next fall they'd be eight blocks from our house, safely in a good school.

In March, Walt verbally agreed to pay tuition at The Academy for both boys for one year, starting fall of 1976. Walt had never had the boys for more than one week at a time, but he suggested the possibility of them coming to live with him and Nora.

I was startled Walt had suggested the idea. I didn't want them to move, but I needed help to maneuver this difficult terrain, so I turned to my therapist for counsel. Luckily, she was a family therapist in addition to doing work with individuals. She already knew our circumstances, so I didn't have to pay for sessions to fill her in. I scheduled a few family therapy sessions with the boys, and I invited Walt to join us. He declined.

My therapist used the modality of Sandplay, which allows clients to express themselves nonverbally by making scenes with miniature people and objects in a tray of sand. Justine showed the boys the sand tray and demonstrated how to make "water" by brushing aside the sand to expose the blue bottom of the tray. After showing them the array of miniatures, she invited them to play by themselves while she and I talked.

At the end of the session, Justine and I looked at their sand tray. Because it was nonverbal, a sand tray often revealed knowledge unconscious to the person doing the tray. With Alan and Daniel, there were no surprises and no subtleties. They made a river down the length of the tray, placing competing armies on either side of the river. The bridge across the river was toppled over—no bridge over troubled waters.

I stared at it, wanting to cry.

I paid for the sessions, but I asked Walt to submit the claims for our family therapy to the insurance company.

He answered, "I am frank to say I am strongly opposed to therapy. Money has nothing to do with it. I feel it would do more harm than good and am opposed to the boys participating in it."[2]

Walt and Nora bought a new house in Marin County. I wanted to provide a thread of safety from one house to the other. Before their first visit to Walt's new house, I asked Daniel, "Would you like to take something from here to have in your new room at your dad's house?"

"I don't know." Daniel was evasive.

I knew about "object constancy," and I knew Daniel. When he would be at his dad's new house in Belvedere, he would find comfort in having something to tether him to the daily home he knew. I suggested a toy, or maybe a found treasure, a gift from a friend or from his adopted grandfather. He could choose anything he wanted.

He seemed hesitant.

"What about Rabbit?" I knew Rabbit was his favorite stuffed animal.

"It's okay. I don't . . ." He looked away from me. "Maybe not . . ." his voice trailed away.

"Maybe the ceramic lion you made in school?"

Again, he turned away, but this time he didn't answer.

I looked around the room to find another object, maybe something dropped from the sky that I hadn't seen before. As I scanned the room, suddenly I understood. "Are you afraid that your dad and Nora would be mad if you brought something from here to their house?"

He dared to peek at me from the corner of his eye. His voice wasn't strong, but it was honest. I heard his quiet assent, "Yeah."[3]

I gave up the quest. There was no object that could bring him comfort while dancing cheek-to-jowl with fear.

CHAPTER 26

....

April 1976

Four years after Walt and I separated, Alan came home from a weekend at Walt's and announced, "Dad says we can live with him if we want."

Daniel, as usual, was silent, but when he looked at me, his eyes confirmed the truth of what Alan had said.

I was stunned. What did this mean? It was a legal decision, not something for Alan to deliver as if it were, "We need dress-up clothes next weekend." They were not old enough to choose where they lived. They were in second and third grades.

I crouched and looked Alan directly in the eyes.

"You are too young to make that kind of decision." I called on all my strength to be clear and matter-of-fact, to ignore the sudden fear and molten putty inside.

"Your father and I make that decision. We've already decided that you live here with me."

Daniel observed the whole scene. I looked at him and repeated the facts.

The moment passed, but the tension stuck in my brain. The return from Walt's house was never easy, but today they seemed particularly feisty.

"Would you please set the table?" I asked Daniel.

"I don't want to."

"It doesn't matter whether you want to or not. It's your turn."

He ignored me.

"Daniel, I asked you to set the table."

"Dad doesn't make me set the table."

"It doesn't matter what your dad makes you do. When you're here, you and Alan set the table, and tonight is your turn."

"I wish I lived at Dad's."

His words were like a knife in my heart.

"I know sometimes you wish you lived there, but you don't. You live here. And here you set the table. So . . . do it."

I started getting testy. I wanted to swat the kid. I wanted to swat Walt. *How can I get Daniel to set the table—or do anything– when Walt tells them I have no authority in my own household?* I was shaken, but I acted like I was in charge and put on a good front.

By Monday morning we were back to normal. I got up at 6 a.m., showered, got ready for work, and woke them up at 7 a.m. Daniel had a harder time waking up than Alan did, and finally I had to get firm and nearly pull Daniel out of bed. They dressed in their sturdy jeans and striped T-shirts and stumbled in to eat breakfast. They got their own cereal and milk, and I made the toast.

I didn't require much in the morning—no formal table setting, no conversation expected. Their one job was to help make their lunches. If we could all get dressed, fed, teeth brushed, and out the door on time, I was grateful.

"Do you have your assignment about birds?" I asked Alan. His last report card made comments about what I already knew: "Alan has made satisfactory progress in all academic areas. However, he needs to be neater, and more careful with his written work— very forgetful."

He looked startled, clearly having forgotten about it. He went to his bedroom.

"I think I saw it on your desk," I called out.

He returned, paper in hand, relief written on his face.

On the small table in the kitchen, next to their little metal suitcase lunch boxes, I put out all the ingredients for lunch. "Come make your lunches."

They brought in their breakfast dishes; I rinsed and stacked them. With no dishwasher, we waited to wash our breakfast dishes with dinner dishes. I went into my bedroom, brushed my teeth, and then scrambled through the papers on my desk.

"Five more minutes. Finish up lunches, and don't forget to brush your teeth." I tried to manage them from a distance while I figured out what I needed to take to work and school today. I stuffed more than I needed into my briefcase—quick insurance for whatever I might have forgotten.

I cleaned up the kitchen mess, put away lunch material, and wiped the counters. Not yet enrolled at the Academy till the coming fall, they walked the three blocks to John Muir Elementary School. I hugged them as they grabbed their jackets and ran out the door.

"Don't forget, Dave will be here this afternoon, and I won't be home till dinner." The boys loved Dave. He took them to the park or Bott's to get ice cream and played games with them. He had been with us almost a year but wanted to go to culinary school. I dreaded the interview process to find another good sitter.

The days flew by—almost fourteen of them—till Walt picked up the children for his weekend with them. I would be free from parenting and have two days to do dissertation research.

Walt delivered the boys Monday morning before work. He rang the doorbell, and they came in—quiet, subdued, uncommunicative—as they always were at transition times. Walt said Daniel had the sniffles and might be getting a cold. As usual, we passed only logistic information, never information about what they did, or the texture of their weekend. Walt talked to me as little as possible. My gestures of friendliness had gone nowhere, so I, too, had become withdrawn at transition times.

I closed the door and breathed a sigh of relief that we three were safely inside, securely a family again. My eyes devoured my sons, gorgeous and precious. Beautiful, sturdy-torsoed boys with rangy limbs. Although nearly two years apart in age, they were almost the same height—a source of great distress and competition between them. Daniel, eight-and-a-half pounds at birth, was born with big, wonderful paws of hands and feet, and was growing into them quickly; Alan, four-and-a-half pounds at birth, was leaner and lankier. They had their father's blue eyes, and my fair coloring. Their towhead hair was beginning to darken—Alan with straight, fine hair, while Daniel's curls had tamed to waves. Daniel had a round, open, cherubic face—one that old ladies loved caressing. Alan's face was longer, narrower, but not yet angular. Alan had grown into his permanent teeth; Daniel's new teeth still looked large for his head. Their healthy beauty made my heart catch. Like all parents, I could stare at them forever.

They carried their small suitcases into their bedroom. I followed.

"How was your weekend?" I was cheery in the face of their disinterest.

"Dad says we can live there if we want."

"Yeah, Dad says we can live with him." The fact Daniel was also verbal this time told me Walt pushed harder this weekend.

"We've talked about that before. Nothing has changed. It is still a decision he and I make. And we've made it. If we change it, it's between your dad and me. You're both too young to make that kind of decision."

"If we live there, he said he'll get a sailboat."

I felt like I'd been stabbed. Walt and Nora lived in Belvedere, one of the three most expensive areas in California—right up there with Beverly Hills and Atherton. Not only did they live in Belvedere, they lived on the *water* in Belvedere, and had a dock on the San Francisco Bay. Walt's money could buy worlds that young boys wanted. Walt offered a sailboat; I offered Monopoly and Clue.

"I don't know if he's going to get a sailboat, but that has nothing to do with where you live. We've made the decision, and you're living here." I wanted to run to my bed, crawl in, and pull the covers over my head and cry. I felt so impotent, envious of Walt's money and ease of life. I was so tired of struggling to be a good parent by myself, trying to be frugal, trying to be a good student, forcing myself to leave Paul, trying to be a good employee.

Be steady. Save the tears for later.

"What did you do this weekend?" I asked, hoping to change the subject.

"We went sailing." Daniel, younger and not yet able to repress his enthusiasm, was willing to be more forthcoming than Alan.

A lead balloon landed in the room. We're back to the sailboat. No free pass, no passing Go.

"And if we live there, we'll get a sailboat, too." Daniel continued with full enthusiasm, unaware of any meaning beyond the excitement of sailing and the anticipation of having their own sailboat.

I considered saying my mantra once again, but thought better of it. There was no point. If Daniel was willing to talk to me, I grabbed the opportunity, no matter what the subject. Alan had his back to me, unwilling to utter a syllable.

"Who did you go sailing with?"

I tried keeping the conversation going with the only willing participant. Maybe we could build a tenuous bridge between their Berkeley lives and their Belvedere lives. Maybe Daniel would let a tiny light shine from one to the other. Maybe . . . maybe . . . maybe even Alan would join us.

Daniel answered with names I didn't know, describing a life where I didn't exist. I was swimming through heavy mucus toward my children, trying to find them in an unknown space, unable to reach them. But at least Daniel was talking. The gulf felt large and growing, their secretiveness increasing. I wanted to cry. I wanted money. I wanted a sailboat. *I* wanted a dock on the bay.

For the next weeks and months, I rallied myself to be competent in all my roles. I went through the paces, always aware of the threatening drumbeat in the wings, a drumbeat that wouldn't go away.

CHAPTER 27

....

April–July 1976

Every time my sons came home from their father and stepmother's house, the pattern repeated itself. Both Alan and Daniel would go directly into the bedroom they shared, and I would become an actress, going into their room with a smile on my face. At least an hour or two would pass before they returned to the boys I knew.

Their choice now was to please their father or to lose him. So, they pleased their father, which meant all of us were in purgatory for a while when they came home. With their return from each visit, that "while" elongated.

I knew if we could get through the first hour, the first day, the first evening, they would start talking, and life would slowly return to normal. They would let me be their mom again. The wounds of that first hour—or day—were always hard for me. I wanted to rage and scream.

Self-control was the only way out. They did not need a hysterical mother yelling, "How can he do that? You can't live with him. He doesn't love you enough to put you first. He doesn't love you enough, and I do!"

I wanted to be the kind of mom they would never *ever* consider leaving, yet every two weeks they told me they did not want to live with me. I knew it had nothing to do with me being a good or bad mom, but I only knew that intellectually.

The soil eroding from under my feet made my heart break. I was *not* always a good mom. I was juggling too many balls to be as attentive as needed on any given day. I escaped through marijuana. Sometimes, I wished I didn't have the responsibility of children.

I struggled.

Why did Walter want the boys now? Why now?

The tension between Walter and me mounted. The boys felt it. Daniel told me he felt caught in the middle, like Olive Oyl in a tug-of-war between Popeye and Pluto; Alan described us as a family at war.

I couldn't afford ongoing family therapy, so I continued my individual work. Having a witness provided me a place of sanity for this ongoing war that sadly, only got worse.

During visitation weekends with their dad, my sons were not allowed to speak to me nor speak of me. From pickup to return, we had no contact, not even a quick phone call. I was filled with apprehension, wondering what was happening to them.

I was the child of a narcissist, hoping—if I did it just right, if I worked harder—I could create understanding and connection. Still captivated by the delusion that peace was a possibility, I was like a child, believing if I just crossed my fingers and closed my eyes real tight, if I explained it just right, he would understand.

Without meaning to, or even knowing I was doing so, I capitulated. Half doormat, half high ground, I continued to believe going more than halfway would engender harmony. Even though I thought the boys were too young to move, I still hoped that if I agreed they could move to live with him in a year, maybe he would put down the sword and cooperate. Maybe he would refrain from challenging them every time he saw them, tearing them apart and turning our lives into a tug-of-war between Popeye and Olive Oyl. Maybe we could have a sane year.

Through an attempt to find a compromise—and pure naïveté on my part—I sealed our fates. In spite of all evidence to the contrary, I made a proposal based on the premise that Walt would be able to control himself for the sake of his sons.

I wrote the fateful letter. "I would hope we can spend our energy not in a standoff over the boys but in cooperation about their future. In order to avoid creating more struggle between us, I am willing to give them their choice of where to live as soon as a year from now if I can have them with your support and blessing for this coming year. I feel that my willingness to agree to a year more and then a choice is a great bending on my part, but I am willing to do that if it will help avoid increasing the conflict in them. Will you help, too?"[1]

Walter responded as if I had promised the boys would move to live with him the fall of 1977, without him having to change any of his behavior. "We will plan on having the boys with us after the '76-77 school year. If our concern for them is at least as great as it is now, I will go to court if necessary."[2]

My fatal flaw was overlooking the reality that Walter was not capable of my conditions of "an uninterrupted year without competition." I wanted to clarify his misunderstanding, but my lawyer suggested to clarify would risk his suing for custody immediately. She knew me well.

"It is, I'm sure, foreign to you to permit him to continue with a mistaken understanding . . ."[3]

I left him with his misunderstanding. At least I would have the boys for the summer and one more school year, even if the year was filled with ugliness from Walt and Nora.

By spring of 1976, I was on the home stretch for a PhD—on track to finish in five years what many people take seven or eight years to do. I'd passed my qualifying exams, collected the data for my dissertation, and completed my classes. All I had to do was analyze the data and write the damn thing. I was still working 80 percent of the time, being a single parent 100 percent of the time, and a litigator and strategist 50 percent of the time, but the worst of the academic grind was behind me.

I had made plans to take some time for myself and meet my sister and her family in Spain. I was exhausted and looking forward to two weeks singing and drinking Rioja wine with our friends in Totana, leaving behind parenting, work, and school responsibilities. Walt had made plans for the boys to be at an expensive new summer camp while he was in Germany.

But then a friend asked why I wasn't taking the boys with me to Spain.

The question stayed with me. I began wondering, *Why not?* I could introduce them to a new world, to a group of people who thought I was terrific. They could see me as a light-hearted person—no school, no work. We could just be together, outside the pressure cooker of our lives. They could be with their young cousins. We could have fun. If I didn't take them, I wouldn't see them for six weeks.

So, I posed the question to the boys. No point in creating unnecessary upset with Walt if neither of them wanted to go.

Daniel rejected it immediately. We had just made a Christmas trip to Mexico for a disastrous visit with my mother.

"I had enough trouble understanding Spanish in Mexico."

But Alan wanted to go. And I wanted him to, even though this would also complicate camp plans. Daniel no longer wanted to go to a new camp alone without Alan; he preferred to return to the familiar AdventurePlus, the camp he went to last year.

In June, 1976, I wrote Walt about my unexpected decision to take Alan to Spain, explaining my rationale, my choices, and

Daniel's decision to return to the camp he knew. I gave him a month's warning and offered to be fair in working out any non-refundable deposit for his Sequoia Camp.

"On June 13, I will be delivering only one boy to you instead of two. They have both made their decisions with the hope and expectation that they can go to Sequoia Camp next summer."[4]

Walt was going to pay the whole cost of Sequoia Camp; I suggested we split the cost of Daniel's camp at AdventurePlus, as we had in the past.

And then I tweaked him, just for the perverse pleasure it brought me.

Because Alan's trip to Spain will be educational, I suggested Walt might want to help subsidize Alan's trip, either by cashing in a CD or selling some Morgan Medical stock.

Walt responded that I could not take Alan without Walt's consent or an order from the court, and he would oppose me if I tried getting a court order.

"[This change in plans] is the most deceitful trick you've pulled since we split up. As far as I'm concerned, plans for the summer remain the same. Kay, I've let you walk all over me in regard to the boys for too long. There will be no more baptisms without my prior knowledge and consent." He refused to pay half of Dan's camp, and also opined that if I used any of the boys' money for which I'm custodian (money my parents gave to them) to pay for camp, he would consider it illegal under California law.[5]

I'm surprised he threw in the baptism of two years ago. When Walt gave me legal and physical custody, I believe, in his mind, he expected me to remain as subservient as I had been in the marriage. He did not envision me truly having agency to make independent decisions.

Walt filed a complaint in court, known as an Order to Show Cause (OSC), to prevent me from taking Alan to Spain and from sending Dan to his familiar camp.[6] I responded, asking the court's permission. This July 6th court date was our third time in court, the first since the financial settlement of the divorce. The judge asked why I needed to go now; I explained my sister's travel dates, which were determined by her relocation in the Foreign Service, and I offered to make the children available to Walt any other time in the summer.

The judge ruled in my favor on all counts. I could take Alan to Spain, I could send Daniel to the camp he wanted to attend, and Walter must pay my legal fees.[7]

Alan and I went to Spain, and we loved it. Alan draped himself over the men in the group, he ate watermelon with his cousins in the hot sun, and he had a big smile when we sang. He saw his mother happy; he saw his mother loved.

Daniel went to AdventurePlus; I paid my half. Not surprisingly, the camp wanted the other half, which Walter paid under duress while I was gone, but then deducted that amount from my next child support check. Doing so was illegal; he was in contempt of court, but I didn't sue over the $225 he owed me.

CHAPTER 28

....

September 1976

Back in 1963, when we were courting, and before Walt would marry me, I had to pass the Backpackers Test—a two-week backpacking trip in the Sierra. When Alan and I returned from Spain, the Backpackers invited us to go camping over Labor Day weekend.

The Backpackers were a group of twenty families originally led by Walt's Uncle Harry. In the 1940s, they split off from the Sierra Club so they could enjoy a cocktail in the high Sierra without withering disapproval. Walt had backpacked with them every summer since he was a teenager. Once I passed muster and we married, we continued backpacking with them, introducing Alan and Daniel to the rigors of carrying a sleeping bag at ages five and three. The Backpackers became our extended family.

Now that I was a ship without a rudder, their continued inclusion had been a balm for me. I had been camping with them for almost ten years, two or three times a year. They had seen the boys grow up, they cared for their safety, and I trusted them implicitly.

In 1976, Walt had learned that the Backpackers continued to invite me to outings, and my involvement with them was radioactive to Walt. Jack, the unofficial leader, invited me for Labor Day, but for the first time, he articulated conditions.

"Kay, I can only invite you if Walt is not coming, but we wanted to include you." He then explained when Walt and Nora had hosted the Backpackers the previous Christmas, Walt had pulled him to the kitchen to inform him not to invite me anymore. He pulled everyone in the club into the kitchen, one by one with the same demand. Walt never addressed the group as a whole.

I said, "I'm sorry, but not surprised." I controlled my voice even as my heart sank. I didn't know what more to say. Newly out of court for our third time, I wanted to keep the peace. I was furious at Walt's manipulations to get others to shun me. I didn't know he would be so blatant.

"Since we don't want to offend Walt . . ."

I wanted to yell and scream *Why not?* but it was Walt who put Jack in this untenable situation; Jack was simply doing his best to be a decent person.

". . . Our solution is to invite him first and, if he's not coming, we'll invite you."

If you're so offended, why do you take his side? I was frustrated, but I didn't want to unleash my fury at Walt onto Jack's innocent head.

"Jack, I really appreciate your efforts to continue including me. But you know how that's going to work." I paused, hoping he would speak, acknowledging the inadequacy of their solution. "He will deliberately not give you a response until it's too late for me to be able to come."

"I worried about that, too. But this seems like the best solution."

"Thank you. Let me check with the boys, but I'm sure we would love to join you on Labor Day."

"That's great. Everyone is eager to see all of you. We'll meet on Friday at six." He gave me the logistical details and directions.

I felt grateful to Jack and the Backpackers for not shunning me completely, but at the same time, I was angry they were willing to put me second. At least Walt had not completely gotten his way.

When Walt and I camped together in the past, he did all the organizing of gear. I didn't like that chore, nor was I good at it, but the boys wanted to camp, so I tried to make it happen. The camping equipment was in disarray, most of it having migrated to Walt's house. Desultorily, I tried organizing it. I couldn't find enough Sierra Club cups. My boots didn't really work. We didn't have enough rain gear. We had only one backpack and needed three. At least they would be providing the cooking gear.

I began losing my enthusiasm for the trip. I couldn't even imagine what Walt would do, but I knew he would find some way to get back at me. I didn't have the energy needed to collect gear, nor to drive on a holiday weekend, and then deal with whatever repercussions would follow.

We had just been in court three months ago over the trip to Spain, and I didn't want to stir things up. I wrote Walt, saying I hoped we could turn over a new leaf and "work together for the best for Alan and Daniel." As a demonstration of good faith, I told him that two days before our trip with the Backpackers, I canceled our plans "in the face of the likelihood that it would bother you."

Then I proceeded to make a foolish confession. "I was also able to recognize my vindictiveness of wanting to go somewhat in order to make you mad. Once I recognized that in myself, I really did not want to act on it."[1]

Ever hopeful . . . and misguided . . . that was me. Maybe if I talked about taming my own vindictive impulses, he would have enough insight to control his own. My abusive childhood lurked in my every interaction with Walt. I believed if I just tried harder, he would be appeased. Dumbly, compulsively, I didn't give up trying to create cooperation.

The school year started, and the boys attended the new private school. Since Walt and Nora continued to say they wanted to be full-time parents, I was willing to give them a chance to be involved. I wanted to be able to take the boys to school their first day, but work conflicts made it impossible. I wrote to Walt, suggesting he take them; he worked nearby, so the logistics would have been easy for him.

Our next contact was by telephone.

"You have custody now, and I am not going to be your babysitter. It's your job to take them to school."

I mumbled something about his saying he wanted to be involved, but he continued. "While I have you on the phone, I'm damn tired of you intruding on my life."

"How did I intrude on your life?"

"You keep trying to come to my house, but you can forget it. The one time you saw my house after we separated, you misused it."

The TV again. I'd heard this before.

"You had your lawyer take cheap shots at me in court when he said I had a new TV and stereo."

"But you did." When Walt pled poverty while negotiating alimony, I'd told my lawyer Walt had furnished a whole new house. I didn't know those facts would live as weapons for decades to come.

"And another thing. Even though I'm paying child support, Daniel got blisters on his feet, and Alan has athlete's foot because you're not taking good care of them."[2]

I was irritated that he blamed me for the daily bumps of life, as if I could prevent blisters and athlete's foot. I was angry at his arrogance but gave up trying to defend myself. I confirmed I would get the boys to school and hung up.

I generally avoided calling Walt; it was always unpleasant, and I risked having to talk to Nora. I had to call a few days later to make pickup arrangements, and Nora answered. I hadn't talked to her in weeks, but she immediately started on a tirade as I tried confirming logistics.[3]

Ignoring what I had said, she responded with, "One of our grievances is arrangements for school on Monday."

I was taken aback at her aggression. I tried to diffuse it with reason. "I just thought you and Walt ... might want to be involved."

"What you have done is horrible."

"I don't understand why it's horrible. I wish I could take them to school, but I can't. I simply asked Walt if he wanted to take them instead."

Nora continued, "They're *living* with you. It's your *job*. If the boys were with us, believe me, a parent would be taking them to school."

"I agree with you, and that is why I'm offering a parent a chance to do just that." It was hard for me to include Nora in the category of "parent," so I pretended to myself I was just making the offer to Walt.

"You shirk all your responsibilities."

"I don't agree. But clearly, we have different values, and I'm not sure there is any point in discussing this further."

I hung up.[3]

When the first day at The Academy arrived, Walt was MIA, I had to work, and it was left to the babysitter to take our sons to their new school.

CHAPTER 29

....

September 1976

I had forestalled Walt's suing for custody in the summer by promising custody in a year *if Walt and Nora were cooperative*. My offer was conditional, hoping for a year of peace and keeping the boys at least one more year. He acted as if I had promised.

The week before school started, Walt made a major change in his agreement to pay the school tuition. He made it conditional on my promise to give him permanent custody of the boys at the end of the school year.

"My commitment to pay tuition for The Academy depends on knowing what lies in store the following year. Nora and I are not going to make the emotional commitment and the substantial change in the way we live that would be necessitated by having the boys here on a full-time basis for just one year."[1]

The truth was my sons were too young to be forced to move, especially to a home where the stepmother refused to meet me and the father wouldn't talk to me.

I wrote to Walt. "I expect you to honor your commitment to pay for The Academy this year."

But I was also like the enabling wife of an alcoholic, not wanting to share our dirty linen with the school. I covered for Walt by explaining to the headmaster that Walt was in Germany all summer. "I'm not sure what arrangements he's made for tuition, but if you have questions, you may call him at work." I paid the $60 milk fee . . . and hoped Walt would come through with the tuition.

Because Walt often changed his promises, I needed a record of history. I told him I would not talk to him about the big issues without either a tape recorder, a lawyer, or a therapist present.

Nine months later, in a court filing, he mischaracterized my tactic of trying to hold him accountable as evidence of my insecurity.[2]

Our lawyers talked about custody, tuition, his illegal with-holding of child support payment, and his unwillingness to submit therapy claims to insurance. His lawyer stated that Walt wanted custody "as soon as possible," and was, "unwilling to pay tuition without the promise of custody."[3] He reiterated his belief that I was not capable of rearing the children and threatened to litigate if I didn't voluntarily give him custody. "Mr. Morgan believes that Mrs. Morgan is not capable of providing the children with the environment they need to grow and mature. He believes it is in the children's best interest to have the issue of custody reviewed at this time."

Because he thought I had acted in bad faith, he wanted the court not only make me pay his attorney fees, but also "any other sanctions felt by the court to be appropriate."[4]

I was exasperated . . . infuriated, and tired of being told I was an unfit mother. I was tired of Walt using money, yet again, to try bending me to his will. I was no longer interested in being cooperative; I was ready to fight back. If Walt could play hard ball, so could I.

Only four months after we were last in court, I took the reins. I filed a complaint with the court, an OSC, to make him pay tuition, as he had promised, without tying it to me giving him custody. I got a court date for Oct. 20, 1976. I boldly said I thought the boys were better off in my custody . . . and I did not plan to transfer custody in the fall.

Our lawyers took over.

After school had started, Walt paid the tuition.

Walt responded to my OSC by asserting that "he is better able at this juncture to provide the love, discipline, and the type of home environment that his sons need to grow and mature."[5]

It was war.

In spite of Walter's views about therapy, we needed a neutral place where he and I could make plans for our children and help the boys maneuver through this minefield. I did not want to end up in court again in a few months for a fifth time. Hoping Walter would feel we were in a neutral field, I found a referral of a highly-reputable male therapist I'd never met. I invited Walt to see Dr. Friedman with me and the boys, and I asked him to submit the claims through his insurance.[6]

By getting a court date, I had maneuvered Walter into meeting with a third party. To my surprise, Walt did make an appointment with Dr. Friedman but made it clear it was not for any help for himself but "to discuss his sons' visits to Dr. Friedman and Dr. Friedman's impression concerning his sons."

Ignoring that I was no longer "Mrs. Morgan," his lawyer responded that Walt would not submit the claims. "Mr. Morgan is not against therapy . . . he is against Mrs. Morgan dragging Alan, age nine, to a psychiatrist because he allegedly loses things occasionally."[7]

I had to get a court date to demonstrate my strength. Just having the date got us through this particular Gordian knot without going to court. He paid tuition, was threatening a custody investigation because I hadn't promised a transfer of custody, we were each paying our own attorney's fees, and Walt had made an appointment with Dr. Friedman. I hoped maybe we had some breathing room. Maybe . . . maybe . . . we had a chance, with help, to talk about custody and communication issues. I released the court date.

Dealing with the boys, I had to have the delicacy of a butterfly to explain my choices without disparaging their father. Dealing with Walter, I had to have the strength of a Mack truck.

I paid yet another bill for my lawyer. I kept notes about the boys' behavior. They were not sleeping well. I desperately wanted to protect them from this maelstrom, but it permeated the air they breathed, wiggling its way into their unconscious, interrupting the regulation of their autonomic nervous systems.

By the end of October, 1976, we had all seen Dr. Friedman individually. Dr. Friedman did his assessment and came to a conclusion, obvious to me. The children were developing normally, and the problems were between the parents. He suggested seeing Walter and me together. (Eureka!)

I wrote Walt, asking him to join me at the subsequent evaluation appointment. "I would certainly like to start a process of constructively talking about living, schooling, and summer arrangements to find a resolution to the problems now—with time—rather than wait till next spring or summer and reach a decision through the courts."[8]

On November 3, Walter agreed he would see Dr. Friedman with me. It had cost me a lot of time, oodles of dollars, and even more anguish to get my children's father to talk to me directly about parenting decisions.

Amen.

But Walt felt no urgency. He traveled for work, he canceled his visitations with the boys (including his entire Christmas week), and we didn't manage to schedule a joint meeting till the new year.[9]

While Walt and I argued about tuition and where the boys should live, Daniel didn't want to go to his father and stepmother's house on his weekend visitation. I knew Daniel didn't want to mix his worlds together, but I asked anyway.

"Why? What's going on?" I didn't expect much of an answer.

"Nothing. I just don't want to go."

"Tell me. What do you do when you're there? What's bothering you?"

"It's nothing."

I could tell it was *not* nothing. After a bit more back and forth, he finally confessed the truth—and I nearly burst out in tears.

"Nora weighs me when I arrive. If I weigh too much, they won't let me have any dessert."

I was appalled. "They weigh you?" Daniel was a little overweight, and, given my propensities, I worried a little, too. But I would never publicly *weigh* him. Like me, he stress ate, and God knew, we had enough to be stressed about. He was not fat, and I believed his impending growth spurt would release any chubbiness.

"Yeah." He hung his head and looked at the floor.

I wanted to pierce their guts with a sword. How could they do that to this precious boy who just wanted to be loved? I felt impotent to help him.

"They keep track, and if I weigh too much . . ." His voice trailed off.

"How long has this been going on?"

"I don't know. A long time."

I put my arms around him. "I'm so sorry, punkin'. I'm *sooo* sorry." I held him, not knowing what more to say. "I wish they wouldn't do that to you."

He sniffled a little. I sniffled a little.

"I'm *so* sorry."

And there we sat, impotent, hugging each other.

I wanted to help him without shaming him, but when life was too much, which was often, he saw me surrender into a bag of cookies. I didn't have much high ground to stand on. Once Daniel had accidentally told me the truth, he wouldn't talk about it again. He had to keep his universes separate. How much energy that must have taken!

I couldn't stop Nora, and I could do nothing to protect Daniel. All I could do was love him and be furious at my own helplessness.

Soon after, I discovered a marijuana roach in Alan's toy, newly returned from Walt's house, on top of the C batteries. It was still a semi-triangle shape, one end charred, the whole thing squished. The brown stains on the paper were irregular in color. Uncomprehendingly, I stared at it. How did it get there? Who put it there, and when? Most critically, *why* was it there?

The bright blue walls of the boys' room started swimming; nothing seemed stable. The children's bunk beds were behind me, their desks to the left as I faced the windows. Painting the walls bright blue when we moved in was my attempt to make the room cheery for latency-age boys. I made their curtains of bed sheets—white with block letters in primary colors, showing the names of professional football teams—Oakland Raiders and Los Angeles Rams.

But suddenly I was chilled. The only way the end of a marijuana joint could have ended up in this toy was if Alan had put it there. Walter was getting ready to sue me for custody, and the radioactive knowledge popped into my brain. *Alan planted the roach in the toy to help Walt's case.* Alan had become a spy. My body went cold.

Occasionally, I smoked for relief from the constant stress of a fifteen-hour-a-day schedule. I didn't smoke in front of the boys, but I didn't lie to them, either.

I reviewed the whereabouts of the toy—when it was home and when Alan took it to Walt's. I struggled to piece together the shards, as if remembering accurately would help me make sense of the story. As if the story *could* make sense.

I mistrusted my reality. I reviewed every detail with a close friend who knew our comings and goings well. She concurred: There was no way for that roach to have traveled to Walt's house and back without Alan deliberately and consciously inserting it into the toy, making the toy a secret compartment to transport evidence against me. He probably intended to show it to Walter, but I doubt Walt would have allowed the evidence to return home, so maybe Alan changed his mind or chickened out.

I knew I was going to lose Alan—and ultimately Daniel, too. I could barely cope with life: consulting lawyers, making life-altering decisions, fighting about money, trying to parent, paying bills, working and finishing a Ph.D. So, I self-medicated. I smoked too often. I would stop but later succumb when I couldn't help myself. Marijuana was my friend and savior, my Achilles heel, and Alan was being programmed to exploit it.

I felt betrayed.

I worked to remind myself Alan was too young to be fully responsible for his behavior. I knew how intense Walt's pressure could be; it was much easier to succumb than to oppose him. I despaired. I would not be able to fight what I knew was coming.

CHAPTER 30

·····················

January 1977

Even though tuition was paid, and the boys were successfully enrolled at The Academy, Walt and I still fought about where the boys would live in June. In January, Walt had finally made the time to meet with Dr. Friedman and me to discuss custody arrangements. Even though Walt and Nora had been married for four years, I still had never met her. I insisted Nora be present when we met with Dr. Friedman. Walt and Nora had to accede to reality: No judge would give them custody if she refused to meet me.

I had pushed for this meeting, known it was necessary and right but I didn't want to be present. My nervous system was strained beyond its capacity, and I had to go alone into the lion's den. Two against one. If only I could send a doppelgänger. I didn't want to have to defend my right to be a mother; I knew they would double-team to assault me and malign my character.

My good friend, Vicki, agreed to wait for me in the car and help hold together whatever shards of me returned. I was grateful. Already knowing how Nora's tongue lashed out, I anticipated needing triage care immediately.

I walked to the door of the office, mustered all my courage, painted myself *Resilient* (the latest Sherwin-Williams color), and opened the door to the waiting room. *Resilient* had deep-hued, bold tones. *Resilient* had depth and courage.

Seeing the empty chairs, the veneer of *Resilient* evaporated from my body . . . but only momentarily. Anticipating Walt and Nora's arrival, I quickly applied another coat.

Luckily, there was no awkward togetherness in the waiting room. As soon as Walt and Nora arrived, Dr. Friedman opened the inner door and ushered the three of us into his office. Walt and Nora sat together on the couch, and I took a small chair. Dr. Friedman settled into his large leather chair.

"What can I do for you today? Tell me what is on your mind."

I wanted to cry out, *Save us!*

Since I was the one who called this meeting, I felt responsible to start. To avoid an awkward silence, I began immediately. "As you know from seeing us individually, Walt and I disagree about where the boys should live and who should have custody. I'm hoping you can help us communicate better about these issues. We certainly haven't been able to do so on our own."

I waited for Walt to offer his views. Silence.

Nora's dirty-blond hair was pulled back into a bun, emphasizing her long, narrow face. Walt had the same dark hair as when I met him, the same blue eyes. He oozed superiority as his customary smirk danced across his face. He struck a pose of confidence but revealed his discomfort by not looking at me. I sat back in my chair, but my body was vigilant, already anticipating their paranoid, twisted accusations about my motivations. I looked directly at Nora and then at Walt, and then turned back to Dr. Friedman.

"With a few sessions and your help, I hope we can work out a plan together and not end up in court again." There, I've made my opening gambit.

Walt responded. "I don't really see any need to be here. We've made our position clear, but Kay seems overly emotional and unable to understand."[1]

The assault had already begun. The rest of the meeting was a blur, a continual thrust and parry. Very little stuck in my memory.

Nora brought up my negligent parenting, using the example of me not taking the boys to school on their first day at The Academy.

I parried. "You say you want to be full-time parents. My offer was a way to help you be involved in their lives."

Nora snapped. "I have better ways to spend twenty dollars."

I was befuddled by what she meant. I tried to make sense of her snark and assumed she must be referring to the cost of gas and the bridge toll. I tried to get back in balance.

I pleaded that we must be positive about each other in front of the boys. Nora disagreed.

"I'll tell the boys that you're a bad mother, a liar, untrustworthy, and mean because I tell the truth to children. I only tell them the truth so that they know they can trust me."

I was shocked but tried carrying on. "We need to communicate about logistical arrangements, summer vacations . . ."

Walt said, "We want as little communication with you as possible."

"But we have to talk about plans and be able to talk if there are unexpected changes."

"No. I want you to think twice, and hopefully you will decide that you don't need to communicate." He was definitive and firm.

That shut me down. *Where do I go from here?*

Where was Dr. Friedman? Why wasn't he helping me? He occasionally asked them to clarify a statement, but they both mostly ignored him and continued on their harangue. He seemed to be as impotent as I felt.[2]

Throughout the appointment, I was stunned by Nora's venom and Walt's passivity. I said that no matter where the boys lived, the three of us would need to communicate.

Nora responded, "I want to get rid of you."

I knew that to be true, but I was surprised she was so blatant.

The final outcome of the meeting: they wanted no communication with me.

When they refused a second appointment, Dr. Friedman invited them to reconsider and call him if they changed their minds. In hindsight, I realized his skill as an individual child psychiatrist did not give him the training in couples therapy that we needed.

I walked out, trying to appear normal. *I cannot cry.*

Totally disassociated and still in shock, the vacant shell of my body crossed the street. Once I was safe in the car, I burst into tears. I tried describing the conversation to Vicki but only bits and pieces remained. My body had a new visceral knowledge about how much they disliked me, and how intransigent they were in their views.

My shock did not abate.

I was shaken but clear about what I wanted. No matter what compromise I offered in the previous April's letter, I did not want my children to live with Nora's vitriol, Walt's collusion, nor with adults who refused to communicate with me. I wanted the boys to live with me and to continue at The Academy.

If I didn't capitulate, Walt was prepared to litigate, eager to testify that I was an unfit mother.

My attitude had changed. Let the battle begin.

CHAPTER 31

....

April–May 1977

I was tired of going to court, but if it was the only way to protect my children and get them a good education, to court I would go

I took the offensive again a month later. I aimed for a long-term settlement, not just one year of tuition. I filed another Order to Show Cause, asking Walter to pay tuition, increase child support, and reveal information about the boys' trusts. Since Walt had refused to meet together with a private therapist, I also wanted us to be required to go a joint meeting in conciliation court. I got a court date for May 26, 1977.

Walt refused to pay for private school, and he refused to reveal information about the children's trusts. He painted the problems as mine alone. He would not go to conciliation court to address "any problems that Ms. Harrington may have."[1]

Two months later, Dan, age ten, approached me late on a Thursday night, saying he didn't want to go to Walt's the next day. Nora had told him he would be fined $2.50 if she found a "sticky spot," a dab of jelly he failed to wipe up. I was furious that my little boy had become anxious, made to be fearful of punishment for being a child.

I spent all of April and May preparing for court, an enormous expenditure of energy and time while concurrently working, parenting, and writing my dissertation. I needed to offer evidence that the children were succeeding in school, the local public school would not offer a good education, and Walter had enough money to pay private school tuition.

Each lawyer deposed the opposing party, and we each had to produce—under oath—all our financial data, check stubs, W-2s, invoices, etc. for the previous two years.

I went into overdrive to prepare.[2]

I got a letter from my original divorce lawyer stating I had offered Walter custody, and he did not want it.

I researched statistics on the cost of living increase during this highly inflationary period to justify an increase in child support. I showed that $500 in 1973 now was the equivalent of $640 four years later in 1977.

I gathered their school records to counter Walt's argument that they weren't performing well. They both had the highest marks possible in all behavior categories; in academics, they had the highest possible in everything but spelling and French. Both were above grade level on the Stanford Achievement Test.

Neither one had ever been tardy! I felt vindicated—a negligent mother was not able to pull off zero tardiness. In the nine-month period available, Daniel was absent twice, Alan four times.

Their teachers wrote very positive reports about their academics and behavior. They were well-liked by the other children.

I obtained data from the public school district, showing that the testing outcomes were low.

I solicited a letter from Dr. Friedman. He confirmed the boys had split loyalties, but that the work we did was focused entirely on the boys, not any therapy for me.

Once Walter was finally forced to reveal his financial life, the differences in our circumstances were stark: Walt earned $3,459 per month; I earned $844 per month. Walt was the beneficiary of six separate trusts and received $1,100 per month from the trusts alone; I was the income beneficiary of no trusts. And Walt's house in Belvedere was valued at $260,000; my house in Berkeley was valued at $37,000.

Walt had a power boat and a 27-foot sailboat valued at $20,000; I had no power boat nor a sailboat.

Walt had $233,000 in savings, stocks, and investments; I had $198 in savings and $200 in stock.

Walt spent $1,371 a month on housing for two; I spent $290 a month on housing for four, which included the sitter.

Walt spent $200 a month on clothes for two adults; I spent $75 a month for myself and two children.

Walt spent $602 a month on his gun club, yacht clubs, health clubs; I spent $70 a month on entertainment for myself and the boys.

Walt spent $0 on psychotherapy to gain self-insight; I spent $150 a month on psychotherapy for self-insight and support in parenting.

In 1976, Walt's canceled checks revealed the following:

Securities for $16,171
New car for $15,957
Duck hunting expenses of $6,473

Those were only the top three major expenses out of nine. He spent $1,387 for the boys' private school and $165 for their medical costs. However, each child's trust paid $3,000-$4,000 a year in dividends, twice the amount needed to cover school tuition of $1,500 per child.

Walt responded to my filing. He refused to increase child support, pay school tuition, or pay my attorney fees.[3]

Even though I had given Walt copies of all my canceled checks and signed my financial declaration "under penalty of perjury that the foregoing is true and correct," he questioned my integrity.

"I very frankly question that the five hundred dollars per month that I am presently paying for child support is actually being spent for the benefit of my children."

I had no idea what he found suspect.

Walt's defenses against my requests were:

1. It would be a financial hardship on him to pay for private schools . . . "burdensome, punitive, and violative of my rights."

2. He and Nora have been fully able to communicate with me. "If a problem exists, it is of [Kay's] mental making."

3. The distrust between us results from my adultery and their disapproval of how I care for the boys.

4. "[Kay] manifests her insecurity by saying she will talk to me only in the presence of a tape recorder, lawyer, or therapist."

5. "My wife and I can clearly communicate. [Kay] may be incapable of understanding what is said."

6. He denies there is any disharmony between the parents which affects the children.

7. He believes, "[Kay] wanting us to go to conciliation court shows her dependence on psychological counseling . . . and by taking the boys to therapy, [Kay] is trying to use the medical insurance I carry for the boys to help solve her own emotional problems."

8. He questions whether the child support is actually being spent for the benefit of his children.

9. "I am at a loss to understand why she feels compelled to spend 13 percent of her net monthly income on therapy . . . when she could get it for free at the university." (His facts were wrong. Long-term therapy was not available through the university, and I was the staff person providing the short-term therapy that *was* available.) I was willing to spend 13 percent of my net monthly income

on psychotherapy because I was determined to protect my children. In order to be able to do so, I needed help to heal my own childhood trauma.[4]

The court date on May 26 loomed. On May 23, three days before the court date, Walter's lawyer offered me a "compromise." Walt would pay tuition for a second year (1977-78) if I promised permanent custody of both sons at the end of the school year and agreed to no increase in child support. If I agreed, he would withdraw the threat of custody court proceedings.

To me, this was no compromise. He thought I would be so cowed by his threat of a custody investigation that I would surrender and give him custody.

Wrong. I was ready for him to bring on an investigation. Yes, I smoked marijuana for comfort. Yes, I ate too many cookies. Yes, I had trouble controlling my weight. That was about the worst they were going to find. I got the kids to school every day, on time. They were healthy and succeeding in school.

I told my lawyer to decline Walter's offer. After I declined, Walt continued to push for full custody. He had never had the boys more than two weeks at a stretch, so I suggested an interim measure as an experiment: the boys live with him for the summer.

Our lawyers hammered out an agreement for the boys to live with Walter and Nora for two months.[5] I would have visitation, and we would adjust child support accordingly. Walt made my visitation schedule conditional: I would be allowed to see the boys *if* the boys were available, and Walter and Nora would decide the "*if.*"

A single little word slipped in to disenfranchise me. It made me angry, but there was no way to protest without bringing the whole negotiation to a halt.

For this June and July experiment in full-time parenting, they decided to send the boys to camp for all of July.

Right before the boys left, it became clear that our lawyers created a $200 misunderstanding about what Walt owed me in child support during this experiment. He went apoplectic.

"This is exactly the kind of hassle I told you I would not tolerate. This is why I feel compelled to issue the April 20 deadline [for you to sign papers about summer arrangements]."[6]

For $200, he was willing to give up the chance to have his sons live with him.

We were in court last year over summer plans.

We currently had a court case pending over tuition, mediation, and child support.

I refused to open yet a new court case over $200.

I let it go.

On May 26, 1977, we appeared in Contra Costa Superior Court for three issues only: school tuition, increase in child support, and mandated conciliation court meetings. Custody overhung everything but wasn't being litigated.

On June 6, the judge ruled the following: Walt's child support was increased by $75 per child per month. My request for private school tuition was denied. Walt must pay $1,000 for my attorney's fees. The court was silent about a referral to conciliation court.

The increase covered about two-thirds of the school tuition. The $1,000 attorney's fees covered about two-thirds of my lawyer's fees. No luck getting Walt into a room for mediation with a third party.

It was not a total win, but it leaned in my favor—and was enough for me to keep the boys, pay for private school, and run our household.

The resolution of custody still loomed.

CHAPTER 32

························

June 1977

In order for me to see the boys during the summer experiment at Walt's place, I had to drive in traffic an hour each way.

As I crossed the bridge at the inlet, I looked for their house, one-third of the way up the hill. The skyline of San Francisco was visible, as were two piers of the Bay Bridge. The sailboat masts of the Yacht Club swayed to-and-fro, their gentle clanking audible through my open window. I turned left and started up the hill, almost exactly a mile to their house.

As I drove, stone retaining walls cradled the road on the right, the bay on the left. I passed fences, garages, and shrubbery; all the houses were hidden and private. I wound up the narrow road, careful in the spots only one car could pass. The mansions were mostly hidden from view with elaborate fences, stone walls, or landscaping. Walt's house was on the downward slope from the road, with curving steps descending in switchback fashion.

Prior to my first pickup, Walter told me, "Just use the back door. We use it more frequently, and you're welcome to use it."

I saw it as an invitation to familiarity, thinking maybe this was new territory for an amicable handover of the children my first time at their new home. Maybe the punishment about me having seen his new TV and stereo five years ago was over.

When I arrived, the front porch light shone brightly, and I was a little confused where the back door even was. Guessing it was to the right, I carefully picked my way across the brick patio and found a door. There was no light; there was no doorbell. There was no socially acceptable way to make my presence known.

I could bellow, "Stella!"

I smiled at the idea as I turned away from the door, careful of my step in the enveloping darkness.

I went to the elegant, well-lit front door and rang the bell. As I waited, Alan and Daniel spilled from the darkness at the side of the house. I was amused that Nora didn't open the front door and let them join me where I was. The boys and I hugged, and we started walking up the steps to the car, talking as we went.

Suddenly, I heard a shrieking. "Kay!"

Halfway to the car, I saw Nora coming from the back door. "The back door is *here!* Walt told you to use this door."

I was trapped again in his half-truths, his twisting of reality. No way did he have the courage to actually tell me I was a second-class citizen. Instead, he hid behind nice words as if he were offering me a friendly invitation, when, in fact, he was giving instructions to a subordinate.

Afterward, I told the boys that I refused to go to the back door. I would honk, and they could come up to the car.

After this greeting for my first "noncustodial visit" with the boys, I took them for dinner in Tiburon.[1] They were glum, silent, and a little edgy.

Alan mumbled, and when I asked him to repeat, he said, "Oh, never mind."

Toward the end of dinner, Alan said, "I might want to live with my dad next year."

Daniel piped up and added to the assault. "I might want to, too."

I felt stabbed. I was in court fighting for them and their education, but we seemed to be on different sides.

I asked Daniel why such a change from a month ago, and he said, "Well, after being here all this time, I'm used to it and it's not so bad. I think Nora is changing."

Alan said, "Nora probably isn't changing, we're just getting used to it."

They initiated the subject of why I was banned from the front door. "It's because of the thing in court about the TV and the stereo."

Why did they even know of such things? And it was five years ago.

Alan offered reasons why living there was positive. "Learning good manners could really help us at camp because the person with the neatest footlocker gets a prize."

Maybe I could think of the Walt Side as a finishing school for manners.

Daniel then switched to the subject of court. "There have been too many courts this year."

I agreed.

"They said that you brought them both."

I didn't want to belabor this discussion. "Eight and ten is too young to be caught in a spot like this."

Alan said, "When we get old enough, we'll probably have to read the court record to really know what happened."

I was reassured Alan was so discerning but sad he thought about such things. He managed to come to an adult-like conclusion.

Walt now had total control of the boys and of my access to the boys. A few days later, he declared that I must forfeit custody by June 30 (in ten days) or he would sue.

My lawyer called to give me the most shocking news yet. During this summer "experiment," Walt had taken ten-year-old Alan to a lawyer's office to have him deposed to prepare him to testify against me in court.[2]

"You mean *officially* deposed? In a lawyer's office?"

My voice squeaked, high and tight. I inhaled deeply, hoping my voice would return to a normal pitch.

"Yes. In a lawyer's office."

"He wasn't just talking to someone casually, telling him what he wanted?"

"I'm sorry. No. It was not casual."

Alan was in fourth grade! He didn't even know how to write cursive. How could he be forced to choose between his parents? Knowing there was no way to be safe in a deposition, I couldn't imagine him being grilled by a lawyer. Lawyers could kill with contempt, distortion, and words. When I was deposed, the opposing lawyer twisted my words, and then used them against me. He dissembled and jabbed until I felt bruised, as if I were hanging on the ropes, recovering from a boxing match. I could not believe Walt would put Alan through that.

I was dazed as I put down the phone. I stared at a list of phone numbers on the bulletin board, but no meaning penetrated. The neighbors, the pediatrician, the babysitter. For all my brain comprehended, it could have been a list of the minerals found on Mars.

Next to the phone, my eyes landed on the receipt from the Roto-Rooter guy who unplugged the drain last week. One hundred and five dollars, a lot of money for me as a graduate student. My 80 percent civil service salary wasn't enough to pull me from the mindset of being poor.

In slow motion, I picked up the receipt and started filing it. *Walt had Alan deposed.*

I later learned from my professor, Judith Wallerstein, world-renowned expert on children of divorce, that in all her years of practice, consulting for hundreds of cases, she had never heard of a father having his own child deposed.[3]

Before my body made the six steps to my desk to file the receipt, I remembered my grocery bags, abandoned when I grabbed for the phone. I put down the receipt. I brought in the groceries. I couldn't focus. I was mechanical as I unloaded groceries, my mind far away and nowhere all at once.

Walt had Alan deposed.

I was irritable with the groceries. There was never enough room in the vegetable bin, and I knew half would spoil before we ate them. Angrily, I shoved the celery in, as if that would hold Walt at bay.

Walt had Alan deposed.

I saw the broom. My brain sent commands to my body.

Keep moving. Sweep the front porch.

I picked up the broom.

Why didn't Alan tell me?

I put the broom down.

Alan said he does not want to live with me.

My world had irrevocably changed. Walter crossed a divide I never even imagined was there. I was numb, wanting to hold the knowledge out of my awareness, yet unable to think about anything else. The thought was like a sore in my mouth that I felt compelled to explore again and again to see if it still hurt.

I repeated the words to myself, as if that would help me understand.

Walt had Alan deposed.

My breathing was shallow, as if taking in too much air would crack me open. I was in too much shock to cry. The constrictions in my throat, the fear in my gut—my body already knew we were in danger.

I released summertime as an "experiment" so Walt could experience extended parenting. Instead, he cunningly used it as an opening to make a legal maneuver and "win."

I had no protection against Walt. He was their father.

I was in shock. *Who can I lean on?*

CHAPTER 33

························

June 1977

My mother never liked me, and my father was dead. I made an SOS call to my adopted parents, Arthur and Rosie, the only elders I knew who were on my side. We made plans for me to visit them over the weekend in Cayucos, at the ocean.

I had met Arthur when he was a dean at Berkeley. When I lost my first post-divorce job to the preferential rehire system, he helped finagle the summer job for me at the counseling center. Beloved, he was the only administrator trusted by both sides of the Free Speech Movement. At his retirement party, the Cal Band played, the Cal mascot Oski danced, and over twenty student body presidents showed up or sent a bottle of wine, vintage of the year each was president. This was the man who would take me in and help me think through the unthinkable.

Arthur and I found each other a few months after Walt and I separated, four years ago. We each had a hole the other filled. My father had died suddenly about the same time Arthur's daughter began withdrawing. Both Arthur and Rosie introduced me as their adopted daughter. I was grateful they made me feel like I belonged.

I bought sweet rolls and cookies to prepare for my trip. On Friday night, between spasms of tears, I alternated treats as I drove the four hours to Cayucos.

After breakfast Saturday morning, Arthur and I bundled up against the wind, clambered down the wooden steps carved into the stone cliffs, and headed down to the sandy beach. There was only one other person on the beach, far down at water's edge, angling for fish. I linked my mittened hand through Arthur's arm. The physical touch helped me.

Creating a mutual rhythm with our steps without speaking, we automatically turned toward the pier. Silently, we watched the terns scamper along the edge of the incoming wave, scurrying to avoid it, yet staying close enough to find a meal. A couple of brown pelicans glided by, perusing the ocean for fish. I watched, hoping one would swoop down and dive-bomb unsuspecting prey. But no luck. Just a gentle meandering above the water, which was a pleasure to watch. A grayness painted the sky, monotonous in its unchanging color.

More of the cliff had eroded away.

"Was that from the big storm a couple of months ago?"

"Yeah, over there, too." He pointed farther north. "It's becoming a problem."

The pier was over a mile away and still looked small in the distance. As we walked, Arthur waited for me to speak. Arthur knew I needed to reinforce the leaky walls of our castle after every one of my sons' visits with their father. He knew the ever-rumbling argument about custody had been gaining steam.

We continued on in silence.

I matched his gait, enjoying holding onto his arm. I remembered a few weeks ago when we were all here and he taught Alan and Daniel how to fish in the surf. He had a bucket of bait, set each boy up with a pole, and patiently showed them how to hold it, where to put their thumb, ways to control the reel, and how to cast. It was a moment of rightness in our lives. Arthur, a former athletic coach, was like my own father in many ways, laconic and calm.

The sand crunched under our feet. I was so weary of this ongoing battle with Walt that I just wanted to curl up and die.

Finally, I took a deep breath and plunged in. "Walt took Alan to be deposed. Alan testified that he does not want to live with me." The sentence nearly got swallowed as my mouth quivered, and I started to cry.

Arthur stopped. He looked directly at me, as he waited to hear more.

"I don't know when Walt took him. My lawyer called me this week." I pulled out my Kleenex.

We resumed our matching gaits, me sniffling, both of us watching the waves crash and recede. The tide was going out, leaving exposed, newly firm sand. We stayed in the crunchy area, avoiding the softer sink-where-you-are sand.

"Has Alan said anything to you?"

"Not a word. But I've only seen him for one dinner."

We walked on. "Did he take Daniel, too?"

"Apparently not." My guess was that Alan was totally alone, unable to talk even to his brother.

"What does your lawyer say?"

"Not much. We have an appointment this week. But the inference is that if I don't let Alan live with Walter, he'll go to trial and have Alan testify against me in court."

Silence. We both understood the enormity of what that meant. More crunchy steps.

"What will you do?" Like my father, Arthur was a man of few words.

"I don't know." *Do I fight this?*

The pier grew closer. Our habit was to walk there, turn around, then walk back.

We arced around and headed back toward the house. It was still gray and cold; the fog was not lifting. "If I fight it, Alan will have to go to court and testify in front of me that he doesn't want to live with me. I have no idea what reasons he'll give."

We walked farther. "I'm sure Walt has coached him in what to say, and whatever that is, Alan will say it. He's a smart enough kid to do his father's bidding." I looked at the gray sky. Arthur waited for me. "If he doesn't say he wants to live there, Alan knows he will lose his father. I think he knows that I'll love him no matter what. Besides, I'm sure part of Alan *does* want to live with Walt. Walt takes him on fancy skiing vacations, he's promised him a sailboat . . . what ten-year-old boy would turn that down?"

"You're right," Arthur said. "Testifying against you would be devastating." It was not clear if he meant it would be devastating for Alan or for me.

"When do you have to make a decision?" Like my father, he was also practical.

"Not immediately. I'll find out more this week."

"Why don't you talk to Rosie? She'll have a different take on this. And come back and see us when you know more."

We continued walking in silence. Every now and then he looked at me, his face full of sadness, slowly shaking his head in disbelief. Our silence provided a communion greater than words. Slowly, we climbed the steps, bodies burdened by our heavy hearts.

After lunch, Rosie and I walked in the other direction. This time, she put her hand through my arm, as if I were the caretaker. Having already described the horror to Arthur, it was easier for me to begin this second telling. Her hand tightened on my arm.

"Oh, sweetie. I'm so sorry." She knew what it meant to be a mother denounced by your own child. She knew there was no way to stop loving your child, no matter what the child did to you. "I'm so very sorry." Her hand squeezed my arm again.

As we walked, we shared the intolerable truth in silence, the silence itself acknowledging the depths of the dilemma I faced. If I fought, we all would lose. If I didn't fight, we all would lose.

Still numb, I drove the four hours home on Sunday. I imagined the scenario of putting up a fight. I saw little sixty-three-pound Alan on the stand in the courtroom, mumbling answers, afraid to look in my direction. I saw Walt at the other table, smirking triumphantly.

I saw myself being brave, holding back tears, caught in the impossible web of explaining to the judge how stability and playing Monopoly with my sons was better than abruptly wresting Alan from my breast and giving him ski vacations and a twenty-thousand-dollar sailboat.

My mind froze. I couldn't tolerate the scene. I grabbed for some cookies.

CHAPTER 34

....

July 1977

I wanted to take the boys and run away, disappear into the great unknown—to Texas, maybe, where I spent vacations as a child. I was able to speak with a Texas twang.

Walt's attempt at control would meet my cunning—the boys and I, on the lam, the open plains, swirling dust hiding his sons' very existence from his controlling grasp.

I could earn a living in Texas. I could become whoever I wanted—a retail clerk, a stripper, or an exotic bird disinherited by her wealthy parents. Unwilling to puncture my fantasy of escape, I savored the idea until I bumped into the reality that I would need childcare while I worked. But the more I envisioned a life without lawyers, without bickering about pickup time or clothes, the more I was drawn to the open road. Let McDonald's do our cooking.

I consulted with my lawyer. "What are my options?"

"You can do nothing and see what happens."

"I've been doing nothing for over a year, and things are only getting worse. Walt's willingness to depose Alan tells me they're not going to get better."

"Right. Walt will probably demand that Alan come live with him this fall, arguing that Alan wants to."

"Let's assume that happens. Then what?"

"Then you either let Alan move . . . or you fight it."

"What does fighting entail?"

"If we go to court, which is what we're talking about, it would be a minimum of five thousand dollars. It could be as much as ten thousand, depending how they play it."

I stared at her. There's nothing to say. I didn't have a spare five thousand dollars, much less ten. My alimony of $600 a month was stopping next year, and my child support was just $250 per child. She was neither avaricious nor hard-hearted, just practical, realistic, and being as kind to me as possible under the circumstances.

"What are our chances of winning?"

"It's hard to say. It depends on which judge we get. I wish you were in Alameda County because the judges are better. They have a good family court system."

I looked at the most recent OSC, holding back my tears of frustration. She went on. "If we were in Alameda County, maybe we could get your case evaluated by Elizabeth Crocker. She would understand this case and recommend that Alan not move."

This was not the first time I had yearned for the magic of Elizabeth Crocker. I was like a kid in a candy store, the sugar tantalizingly visible. But I couldn't have it. Instead, I was in a different county, at the mercy of an archaic court system where male judges had the power to rule—judges who were ignorant about child development and about the manipulations of a narcissistic parent.

"What are our chances here?"

She recited a list of judges' names from memory, annotated with a sentence about each. None sounded good. They were all male, conservative, old-school, disapproving of working mothers. They'd certainly lean toward a two-parent home with a woman who didn't work, a home like Walt and Nora's. What was not visible on Nora's resume was that she didn't want children—her own or others. She wanted her house to be orderly and clean. I was in cold fear of the damage she could do to young sprouts trying to grow in toxic soil. I wanted to keep her away from my boys.

"The real question is, do you want to put Alan through having to testify against you?"

"How seriously will they take his testimony?"

"Hard to say about age ten. At fourteen, the court lets the child decide; at thirteen they'd probably listen some, but ultimately decide for the child."

"Can't they see Walt has coached Alan? Even his language is adult. His words are not words of a ten-year-old."

She looked directly at me with compassion in her eyes. "There's no guarantee a judge will see that," she said gently.

"So, the risks are that I put Alan through the horror of having to testify in a courtroom against his mother, I might lose, and have him go live with Walt anyway, and I spend five or ten thousand dollars to do it."

"Exactly."

"The alternative is to let Alan move before he's even started fifth grade."

"Yes. Not a good set of choices, I know."

A "choice" is choosing between cake or pie for dessert. To fight for the salvation of my sons hardly felt like a "choice." Every choice was bad, especially when Nora had said she would tell the boys that I was a bad mother.

Days passed, but the *only* thing I thought about was this "choice." *Fight? Don't fight?* The sword of Damocles hung heavy over my head.

Alan was definitive; he wanted to move.

Daniel was ambivalent; he changed his mind daily.

The next weekend with the boys, I retreated again to Cayucos for counsel. While Alan and Daniel played at a distance, Arthur, Rosie, and I walked the beach, a trio trying to figure out what

I should do. We were bundled up against the wind. Mercifully, no rain.

We walked to the pier.

We walked back toward the house.

We turned around and walked some more.

We talked.

And walked.

We walked till we could no longer stare at the problem. No one had words for what was making itself clear. There was only one answer: I had to let him go. I had to make a Solomonic decision. I could not put him through testifying in court. Alan had spoken; the courts would probably agree. I must allow Alan to live with his father and a stepmother who hated me.

Maybe I could hold onto Daniel one more year.

On our drive home from Cayucos, I diverted us to Cambria and The Soldier Factory—a magical store overflowing with miniature objects made of pewter, such as animals, mythological figures, and military figures. As a treat, I let each boy pick one miniature. Each boy looked, each was uncertain, but eventually, each one was definitive. Alan chose a dragon, tension coiled throughout its body—a formidable beast ready to spit fire. Daniel picked a mother whale swimming with her baby beside her.

I interpreted that Alan was ready to take on the dragon. I interpreted that Daniel needed a mother close at hand. My interpretations brought me some comfort, suggesting maybe I had made the right decision. At least, I chose to believe that.

Three days ahead of Walt's June 30 ultimatum, I bent to the reality he had created.[1] On June 27, 1977, I made a legal proposal about custody arrangements. My goal was to protect both Alan and Daniel, while also maintaining some flexibility.

I would allow Alan to move September 1.

I would not give up custody.

I wanted an evaluation procedure in place for the spring.

I wanted until September to decide for Daniel.

Walt's response sounded good—politically correct, but empty. He said he wanted to be as generous with visitation as I had been.[2] He hoped I would give him "a free hand without interference. To put it another way, I won't press the question of legal custody at this time," but he implied the threat.

"Your desire that we agree now upon a method to decide how to evaluate the experience leads me to believe that you view this as an experiment or trial. I, on the other hand, look upon it as a simple change in place of abode."[3]

His ability to minimize trauma astounded me—this was *not* simply a "change in place of abode."

Then he said, "I could force a resolution of the question immediately by starting a custody proceeding. I'm not willing to commit now to some sort of procedure."[4]

He was adamant. I took solace in retaining legal custody, and I gave up on getting an evaluation procedure.

Both boys were gone for the summer, and my heart was breaking. I would get both of them for a week vacation in August, and then . . . that was it for Alan. I would have to relinquish Alan to the Walt Side on September 1; I had until then to decide about Daniel, but I knew, inevitably, the best I could do would be to keep him another year.

I couldn't afford to feel the impending loss, so I worked. The subject of my dissertation was Intimacy and Autonomy, clearly an academic inquiry into my own life struggle: self and other. *Who am I? Do I have agency?* I completed the interviewing and testing of my research subjects a year ago. The past year, I did the statistical analyses of the data and started writing. In order to graduate in May next year, I had to submit a complete draft of my dissertation to my committee by November, only four short months away.

I doubled down. For the whole summer, I did nothing but work or write. I was determined to complete writing a book by November. *I can do anything.*

On August 12, I met my own deadline and submitted a draft of my first three chapters.

On August 13, I took the boys and their cousins on vacation to Santa Cruz. We knew that in seven days, there would be a "before" and "after" in our lives, an earthquake of life-changing proportions. At the end of the week, I was losing Alan permanently, and I would have to declare where Daniel would live in the coming year. We needed the young Colorado cousins, Bonnie and Nate, with us to make this final vacation tolerable. Alone, our vacation would have been a disaster.

Alan, an old hand in Santa Cruz, showed his cousins the thrill of crossing the estuary on the old railroad bridge.

"Look. From here you can see all the way down to the water."

The vertical drop was far enough down to create vertigo. The horizontal slats were far enough apart to imagine slipping through the gap. The frisson of fear was just right for their gang—enough to cavort, brag, and show off, drawn like magnets to the rickety bridge as a moth is to flame, but without any real danger.

The daily crossing became a game as we made the trek to the boardwalk.

"Who wants a corn dog?" All dietary restrictions were suspended.

"I do."

"I do." A chorus of voices took us along our well-trodden path to the corn dog stand.

Sitting in the sunshine, eating the first of many delights that would make us sick by the end of the day, we jostled to plan what was next. The bumper cars usually won. Everyone was tall enough to have their own car. The buzzer sounded. I spied Daniel within range. I rounded the corner and made a beeline for him as he was on his way to cream Bonnie. Alan and Nate were in another part of the oblong track. I T-boned Daniel, sending him off course, and now I lined up for Bonnie. We spent four minutes ramming each other, laughing, and forgetting that Alan was going to be wrenched from our family in a few short days.

We moved onto the Giant Dipper, built in 1924. Alan and Daniel were behind me as the wagon went through the tunnel and cranked up to the tippy-top. Then *whoosh*! Stomachs dropped as we sped down to the next dip. We were serial riders, debating in between rides which car was more exciting—the first car or the last—and then someone tried to snag that car on the next ride.

A short stop for cotton candy, then onto the arcade. All the kids tried their hand at throwing darts at balloons but quickly gave up. The calliope of the carousel called us, giving us a face-saving way to rest while still being on a ride. Every day, we came home dirty, tired, and sick from our carnival eating.

In the evenings, once we were safe at home playing Monopoly or Sorry, I went to the bedroom, closed the door, and smoked some pot to help me forget I was losing my son.

Even if the weed relaxed me, I was never off duty. My antennae were always on. When I heard Bonnie ask Daniel, "Are you gonna move, too?" My body went rigid as I waited for the answer.

Silence.

I strained to hear what Daniel would say.

More silence.

Nate came to the rescue. "Whose turn is it? Do you have a 'Get Out of Jail Free' card?"

Alan's body kept the score, revealing what he could not talk about. The move to leave me and live with his father was not "a simple change in place of abode," as Walter had characterized it. Alan's body disclosed the strain infiltrating his cells.

The week before the move, Alan regressed to four years old— the last time he had wet the bed. Not only did he wet the bed twice the week before his move, he also spiked a fever of 102 degrees, reminiscent of his fevers when we first divorced. Daniel, losing his brother, tagged along with a fever of 101.

The last day of vacation, we all fell apart. Nate slammed the car door on his finger, maybe breaking it. I twisted my ankle as I ran to help him. We all went to the emergency room, got Nate's finger treated, and I assumed my ankle would improve with time.

We drove to the SFO airport, put Nate and Bonnie on the plane, and morosely went home to face what awaited us: losing Alan.

CHAPTER 35

....

August–September 1977

Once home from Santa Cruz, I returned to work during the few days before Alan moved. My ankle did not heal. The doctor diagnosed a torn ligament and put me on crutches for six weeks—a significant problem for daily walking across campus. I was teaching a ten-day gig for resident hall assistants: how to identify mental health problems in the dorms, do crisis intervention, and make referrals to the counseling center. I was depressed about Alan, and I was scared. I had never done a teaching gig this large or for this long; I was afraid I was going to bomb. I walked across campus painfully, bruised armpit by bruised armpit.

I carried on. There was no choice. *I can do anything.*

Opening day came, and I jumped in. Once I got going, I lost my stage fright and actually enjoyed myself. Each day I grew more confident. I was a success! At the end of ten days, all sixty RAs gave me a standing ovation!

That didn't make up for Alan leaving, but even if only temporarily, it cheered me up.

Daniel made up his mind about where to live, then changed it. Then changed it again.

"I feel like I'm missing somebody, but I don't know who."

The idea to split them up was agonizing. No one would win. I thought it would be harmful to Daniel to live with Walt and Nora. He was two years younger and more vulnerable to their rigid rules. Our hearts would break to have Daniel stay or to have him leave. I reassured him I would tell his father it was my decision, not his, to provide him some measure of protection.

I strongly encouraged Daniel to stay with me. Once the deadline was upon us, I wrote Walter that Daniel, with my help, had decided to live with me the coming year. He wanted only two things from Walt: "To be included on your mid-winter ski vacation and to be part of the hunter-safety course."[1]

Walt declined both these requests. "The hunter-safety course is a father-son thing."

I tried again, reminding Walt that Daniel *was* his son. I said nothing to Daniel. My negotiations with Walter to secure Daniel's requests required multiple letters throughout September.

Walt still declined. "The logistics are too difficult."

I wrote him a third time; I offered to do all the driving so that Daniel wouldn't be left out. "I'll be glad to take care of logistics."

Walt agreed to enroll Daniel in the hunter-safety course if I did the driving, but he continued to refuse to include Daniel in the mid-winter vacation. When I pushed again for Dan to be included, Walter wrote, "For reasons I don't understand, the Reed school mid-winter vacation is something you won't let go of."[2]

On Friday, September 2, the actual day of Alan's move, Alan, Daniel, and I spent most of the day crying. A friend who was like the boys' godmother came for dinner to provide reinforcements. We were exhausted by the time Walt arrived to move Alan out.

After Alan was gone, we "left-behinds" ate, talked, coped, and cried. When I put Daniel to bed and had chat time, he cried and cried. "It just doesn't feel right without Alan here."

"I agree. We both already miss him."

"One thing I learned today is never to leave your brother if you don't have to."

"I wish neither one of you had to leave the other . . . or me."

"Sometimes I'm mad at Alan, but today I found out how much I love him."

Nothing could paper over the hole in our hearts. This was the third time Alan had been taken from me before he was ready—and I had been unable to prevent any of them.

At birth, he was in an incubator, and I couldn't hold him. At two and a half years old, a nurse peeled him from my body to take him to surgery for enlarged adenoids, refusing to let me be with him till he was under anesthetic. And now, this third time, ripped from my bosom and taken to a place where they wished I didn't exist.

I was grieving his loss, my loss, and my deep-seated fears for him. *What repercussions will there be in his development because of this premature move? How will his living under their scrutiny shape the relationship he and I will be able to have? Will they cut him off from me?*

After Alan left, I focused on Daniel, who was young, healthy, and energetic. I was depressed, I was tired, and our September weather was hot, hot, hot. I put the dissertation aside, and we went swimming. Dan's calls from the diving board were incessant. The towhead curls on his gorgeous, chubby, eight-year-old body twitched with impatience.

"Look at me."

I looked, smiled, and waved at him from the side of the pool. My attention satisfied him no longer than an empty snack keeps hunger at bay. He jumped from the board, popped up from the water, and immediately swiveled in my direction to confirm with his own senses that I was looking.

"Did you see me jump?"

I put on a big, encouraging, mother's smile and waved. Over the space between us, wordlessly I let him know his jump from the board was terrific. Absolutely terrific.

It was. I was grateful for his exuberance and confidence, touched by his poignant neediness for my attention. But even though he deserved my attention, even though he was trying to earn it with repetitive jumps from the scary board, my well was empty.

He *was* admirable. He *was* beautiful. He was life, daring to jump into the deep, not knowing where he would land, how he would surface, risking being a jack-in-the-box pop-up. He knew how to pivot to find mother, an instinct even under water. He needed more from me than I was able to give.

Three jumps. Six. I hoped it would end by ten.

It wasn't his fault. He was just eight. He had lost his brother. I had lost my son. I smiled beyond my capabilities, waved more times than I was able. I was an actor-mother, trying to give him his feed, like the daily ration of grain needed to maintain good equine nutrition. I depleted every nerve ending in order to create a bright smile, sending a wave-beam of love toward him on the diving board, my corpuscles shrinking as the energy traveled the fifteen yards from the chaise lounge over the water to the tip of the bouncing board, curved downward with the weight of his eight-year-old glorious body and soul.

"Look at me!"

I existed but was inert, so I pretended. "Good jump!" I called out. "Good jump!" I was physically with Daniel, trying to be present, but I was preoccupied about how bereft Alan must be feeling, alone and without either of us.

Fall quarter started in September. My dissertation was due in November, in nine weeks, but only fifteen days were available to work on it. All the other days were committed either to work or to children. I was fearful I couldn't actually finish the dissertation in such a short time. *I can do anything.*

Our situation was intolerable, but I tried constructing a silver lining. Maybe now that Walt had won, maybe now he would be more cooperative, but I was soon disabused of that notion.

Walt and I quarreled over everything. Alan's first year there was a nightmare of tension and disappointment.

Roles morphed. Walt and Nora insisted Alan call me Kay, not Mom. I was horrified.

Alan called me Kay only once. I grabbed him by the metaphorical short hairs he hadn't yet grown and made it clear to him. "I am 'Mom.'"

Walt made it difficult to see Alan, even on my weekends. He knew I had an hour's drive to get there, but, unilaterally, he changed the pickup time from 7 p.m. to 5:30 p.m. on Fridays.

"I can't get there that early."

"Well then, I'll just take him with me on my weekend plans."

"Why can't he stay home alone for an hour?"

"We're not negligent. Besides, we don't want him setting the alarm. If you can't get here by 5:30, you'll just have to skip the weekend."

Walt canceled his weekends with Daniel. "I'm going to Germany, so I can't have Daniel on my regular weekend."

"Why discriminate against Daniel? If Nora was eager to be a stepparent, Daniel could still have his weekend with Alan."

"For Nora to take care of Daniel would be babysitting for you, and she doesn't want to do you any favors."[3]

Walt demanded pristine clothes, clothes that were nonexistent in a ten-year-old boy's wardrobe. "We would like you to take responsibility for Alan's cleanliness and dress when he's with you. You've said that the responsibility is his, but we feel that you should be sure that he is clean and neatly dressed for school (when I pick him up)."[4]

"I will wash his clothes and have him bathed, but at ten years old, I expect Alan to dress himself in the morning."

Walt does not trust me with Alan's clothes. "I will not provide Alan with clothes to take to your house as long as I believe that they might be returned in an unsanitary condition."[5]

I asked to be notified about school open house. "I assume it's all right with you if I attend such events."[6]

"I will tell you of teacher conferences and open houses at Alan's new school, which we don't plan on attending. We do not want to participate in these types of things with you due to the obvious friction between us."

I answered, "Although I would like to attend, I will not go to the Reed open house this Thursday. This is a difficult time of transition for all of us, and I do not want to aggravate matters. However, I want it clear that, as the transition difficulties subside, I hope there will be little enough friction so it will not be difficult for you to participate jointly in events such as open house. The sooner we can be neutral and civil to each other, the better for the boys."

I invited him to Daniel's open house in November. He didn't come.

I had the boys on September 24-25. When Walt asked to change dates because he'd been invited on a Backpackers trip, I said I had plans, but I didn't tell him that we, too, had been invited on the Backpackers trip. The host somehow had inadvertently invited both of us. I checked with our host, and she reconfirmed our invitation.

Once I learned Walt was going, I changed my plans. I couldn't imagine spending the weekend with him and Nora.

First, I missed the open house, then the Backpackers trip. Delusional that it could be possible, I wanted some credit for my selfless actions. I wrote Walter, "Deference to yours and Nora's feelings is the reason I bowed out of the Backpackers trip this past weekend. I was invited and accepted based on information that you wouldn't be there."[7]

"Your deference to my feelings is pure balderdash. If you hadn't decided not to go to the Backpackers, you'd have been uninvited, and you know it."

Walt changed my visitation weekends with regularity. "Your weekend falls on cleanup from duck season, and the boys have enjoyed helping in the past and want to go."

"I will trade if there is another weekend that I can have them."

"You can have Jan. 21-22."

I agreed. Then . . .

"Your weekend of January 21-22 is the same as ski weekend."

I changed weekends again.

"Your weekend is the same as a Boy Scout event, and Alan really wants to go."

I didn't have a weekend with Alan for two months. I was angry at their success in excluding me, and I was filled with uneasiness at the void. What stories were they feeding Alan about me? Were they telling him that I didn't care? That I didn't want to see him? Alan and I needed time together to keep our relationship alive and healthy, but I couldn't seem to make that happen.

CHAPTER 36

....

September 1977–January 1978

The Friday night pickup time was a constant source of tension. By coincidence, Nadine, a teacher in Alan's middle school, was the older sister of an intern I was supervising at the counseling center, and Nadine lived in Berkeley. We had met, and we liked each other. She offered to drive Alan from Belvedere to Berkeley on Friday nights to help me out. Such help would be a godsend for me. Not wanting to impose, I demurred till December, when I had a conflict I couldn't solve. She agreed to bring Alan that Friday, and I called him to let him know.

A day later, she called me. "I really would like to help you out, but I got a call from Nora exploding at me. If it were up to me, I would ignore her . . ." Her voice trailed off, then continued. "I hope you can understand. I'm a semipublic figure in the community. If I were to bring Alan to Berkeley, Nora would make a stink, and it would become really ugly. I'm a representative of the school system."

Neither of us knew what Nora would do, but we both knew she would create trouble.

Arrrgh! They'd done it again. First the Backpackers, and now Nadine. I compartmentalized my fury so I could speak graciously to her.

"I understand. I'll figure out some other way to handle it. I don't want to put you in a hard spot." I canceled an important meeting and drove two hours to pick up Alan and return to Berkeley.

Mid-winter vacation was coming. I made another plea to Walt to take Daniel, pointing out that Daniel's good test scores should allow him to miss a week of third grade.

"His test scores may look great to you, but Nora said Daniel's spelling and penmanship were not up to snuff."[1]

Then, Walt acted as if he were an administrator in charge of attendance-based funding, quoting statistics of state school subsidies that would be lost if Daniel missed a week of school. The next justification was nonsensical accounting.

"Also, remember that the February vacation was Alan's special week off. He viewed it that way. Daniel had his [vacation] the four days after Labor Day when Alan was in school."

I wrote, "I find it appalling that I am in the position of asking you to take your own son on your vacation. He wanted to be with you enough to have made it one of two requests for the year. For a son to feel loved and included by his father is of far more lasting importance than any improvement in spelling or penmanship that might be made that week. I hope you will reconsider and invite Daniel."

"I will not act in such a way as to instill in him the idea that I think school days can be traded for four days in the snow. If he had the time off from The Academy as Alan does from Reed, Daniel would be invited if you approved. He does not, and I will not invite him."

I had to let it go.

Alan, Daniel, and I savored being reunited as a family in Berkeley for Christmas week. We cooked, laughed, and played, but sadness was ever-present in my psyche. I knew Walt would be angry when he learned that Daniel brought home head lice from school, and now both boys had lice. I had been shampooing them with Kwell the entire vacation. Always fraught, I knew Walt's pickup at my house would be tense, but the lengths to which Walt would go to use the head lice against me was, as yet, beyond my imagination.

At turnover at the door, I said, "Here's the Kwell. I've shampooed both boys daily since we discovered the issue."

Walt just stared at me. I empathized. "I know it's a drag. There's an epidemic of lice at John Muir right now. It was even reported in the Berkeley newspaper."

Walt said nothing as he reached for Alan's suitcase.

"I've washed all their clothes. We're on the downward slope now, but to be safe, you should probably use the Kwell for another day or two."

He ostentatiously ignored me, took Daniel's suitcase, and then gestured with a nod of his head. "Come on, guys. Let's go."

I hugged each of them as they left. "Have a good time."

They trooped out to his car silently.

I closed the door, then turned around and looked at the Christmas mess. Just me and leftover clutter. The tree lights were still on. Christmas Eve dinner was cleaned up, but just barely. Furniture was still askew; dishes waited to be tucked away.

Memories of our morning filled me with pleasure—the boys up early to find stockings filled with candy, trinkets, and nuts, all of us opening presents, cooking breakfast together, just hanging out.

"Look, Mom." Daniel had demonstrated a magic trick he had taught himself, using the magician's table I'd given him just hours before. Instead of a voluptuous magician's assistant, he had Alan, still in pajamas, holding a handkerchief over an empty glass, awaiting further instructions.

With their absence, I felt as empty as the house. I turned off the Christmas lights so they could cool. Dismantling Christmas was nearly as much work as assembling it. The sooner I got it done, the sooner I could get back to work on my dissertation.

The new year brought a letter from Walter, unilaterally announcing his "new rules" for 1978. He wanted to put a protective shield between himself and me, to make himself immune from head lice and my irresponsible ways. Therefore, he announced, there would be no more suitcases or transfer of clothes between houses.

He was angry and blamed me for the head lice. Until now, he had paid the out-of-pocket medical expenses for Daniel, but he was going to stop because having done so "does not seem to have improved Daniel's lot."[2] He believed that, "Lice reflect[s] improper personal hygiene," and he "proved" my personal negligence by confirming with the county health department there was no lice epidemic. (Untrue.)

Walt unilaterally changed my Friday pickup time from 7 p.m. to 5 p.m., maybe because he wanted his Friday evenings unencumbered, and he did not want to make accommodations for my work and driving schedule.[3]

I responded, "I'm tired of fighting about what time I pick Alan up on Friday night. Hereafter, I'll pick him up on Saturday morning at 10 a.m." I was willing to forgo a night with Alan to stop the ongoing bickering.

In order to survive at Walter's house, Alan had to demonstrate a dislike of me. Over the last seven months, Daniel watched the abnormal transformation in Alan and told me he was terrified of being "brainwashed" like his brother.[4]

Because Walter had proven himself untrustworthy with Alan's move, I would allow Daniel to live there *only* on a temporary and conditional basis. No way would I allow Daniel to move without an iron-clad legal agreement. And I wanted Nora contained.

Instead of being laser-focused on my April deadline to submit my final dissertation for May graduation, I diverted myself in January, February, and March to deal with legal arrangements for Daniel's move. Guardian ad litem, where the court assigns a case worker to supervise a highly contentious divorce, had not yet been invented in 1978.

If Daniel was going to move, we needed a claw from the sky to pull us from this morass. How in the world could I get us from here to there? We needed a trained professional to mediate, but Walter refused private mediation.

We didn't have a pending court date, so conciliation court was off limits. Ignoring the rules, in January, 1978, I made a plea to the court that we needed to use their services to forge a legal agreement before I allowed Daniel to move. I succeeded in getting an appointment with a social worker, then invited Walt to join us.

Walter saw no reason to meet. "To be frank, I view that as another effort on your part to get me involved in your psycho-therapy. You've been projecting your need for therapy on me and even on Alan and Daniel, and I just don't buy it."[5]

I ignored Walter and marched forward, writing a letter to both the social worker and to Walter, outlining what I wanted in a legal agreement before I would allow Daniel to move. My demands were rather standard visitation practices, but because of the difficulties with Walter the previous five months, I also included nonstandard conditions, such as immediate access to the kids by phone with no conditions imposed by Nora, leeway in pickup time, and reevaluation in a year. I wanted both Walter and Nora to promise not to denigrate me in front of the boys. I wrote Mrs. Daltry, the social worker, with copies to Walt and Nora. "In the past you have told them that I'm mean, I'm a bad mother, I lie, and recently you have been overheard saying that I'm crazy."[6]

I met with Mrs. Daltry in February, 1978.

In spite of his objections, Walter met with her in March.

Daniel observed me spending hours at my typewriter, writing my dissertation. When I was not at my desk, Daniel liked to mimic me, typing on my trusty Smith-Corona. He knew Walter and I were working out arrangements for him to live with Walter next year.

One day he gave me the following typed note:

Dear Kay

You are very nice even if Walter (dad) hates you.

I am sad I am going to live with WALT (or my dad),

but I like Alan TO [sic]

Love,

Daniel Morgan[7]

I nearly cried when I read it. It warmed my heart that he was sad to be leaving me but broke my heart that he knew his father hated me and that he missed his brother. He was so open, heartfelt, and innocent; I wanted to scoop him up and hold him forever in my arms.

On April 6, 1978, Walter and I met with the conciliation court social worker.[8] My goal was to create some kind of legal, stable structure for us, and I knew this was my only chance to get help.

We hammered out agreements about visitation, pickup, clothes, and interference with my phone calls. Walter agreed keeping Nora and me apart was the best for all concerned, and Nora would give me immediate access to the boys when I called. I wanted it in writing.

I insisted on retaining custody of Daniel just as I had custody of Alan. I wanted Walter and Nora to make it easy for the boys to talk to me and see me. Throughout the session, I gave examples of the many ways Walter and Nora had disrupted my visitation schedule and discouraged Alan from seeing me. In addition to not denigrating me in front of the boys, I wanted no moral lectures, no snide remarks, and no letters to "teach" me.

Mrs. Daltry asked many questions, probing each of us separately. She knew better than to try to make Walter respond to me directly.

At the end of the session, Walter refused further mediation. We were back to square one.

CHAPTER 37

·······················

March–May 1978

I can do anything. My childhood mantra helped me.

With dread in my stomach, my Sunday morning breakfast churning, I crossed the bridge and drove the hour to Richardson Bay to Alan's soccer game. If I wanted to be part of Alan's life, I had to shoehorn myself into places where I knew no one, and where I knew, for sure, that I was not welcome.

Just beyond the expansive green soccer field, sun sparkled on the water. The well-groomed parents clustered at the edge of the field, chatting with each other. I envied their wealth and comfort. My brain knew they were not deliberately excluding me, but my body tightened. I played it safe and stood alone. I didn't approach anyone nor try to be part of any group. They probably had been told I was mentally unstable.

I cheered for Alan when he scored. Other parents looked at me with curiosity but maintained their distance. I made myself stay for the whole game, determined to say goodbye to Alan rather than just fade away. I found him and congratulated him on his goal. He shyly accepted my praise and allowed me to hug him, even while he turned his head away and only limply hugged back.

I didn't linger, I didn't make him talk to me or introduce me to his friends. Instead, I strode back to my car, head held high.

Once out of sight, I collapsed in tears. My dignity was intact; my confidence had grown. Wanted or not, I could show up for my son.

I can do anything.

The social worker's final report outlined our negotiated structure of visitation and access. Walter and Nora agreed they would not speak of me in derogatory terms nor interfere with phone access. I insisted on maintaining legal custody and wanted to reevaluate the living arrangement at the end of the year. Walter described my need to retain custody as my "psychological hang-up." Walter continued refusing mediation. The rudimentary (and unenforceable) structure we worked on was a mere drop in the bucket compared to the help we actually needed.

Because we did not have a court hearing scheduled, Mrs. Daltry withdrew from further mediation. If we needed more help, we would have to resort to paying private lawyers to negotiate—an expensive and unproductive step.

But we had a basic structure. I felt some relief.

Walter took only two weeks to undo our agreements. Walt instructed his lawyer to prepare a legal document for me to sign. Unilaterally and without consulting me, Walt changed the pickup time back to Friday evening instead of the Saturday mornings we had agreed to in conciliation court. I did not sign it; I left the pickup time on Saturdays, but in practical terms, I knew it wouldn't make any difference.[1]

Trying to find new ways to see Alan, I invited him to see Carol Channing in *Hello, Dolly*. Walter had loved *Hello, Dolly* since high school and introduced me to it early in our marriage. Walter considered *Hello, Dolly* to be his. Alan declined to go with me.

Months later, Victor Borge was in San Franciso. Since my verbal invitation for *Hello Dolly* had been unsuccessful, I invited

Alan by letter to see Victor Borge. I said I would like to take him, but I would understand if he already had plans to go with his father.

Alan wrote back:

> *Kay, I would like you to stop sending me letters because most of them are about plays or musicals that you have most likely found out that we are going to. Since Hello Dolly you have gone to or wanted to take me to most of the plays that we have gone to. I would like to know why you didn't take me to plays or musicals when I was living with you? I would also like you to talk to Dad about plans that will involve Dad's time schdeule [sic] or in any other plan that in any way involves Dad.*
>
> *I don't want to go to Victor Borge with you. Alan*[2]

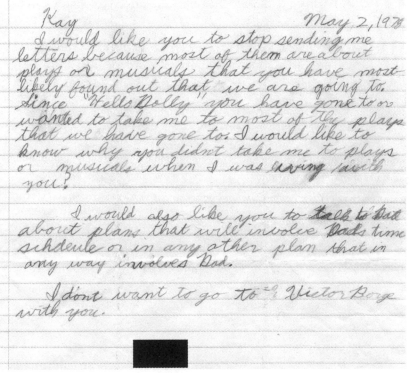

Alan's letter regarding Victor Borge's letter

I wanted to fold up my tent and disappear. *Bury me, please.*

I knew they were making Alan call me *Kay* instead of *Mom*, but it still stung to see it in writing. Walter might as well have dictated that letter—maybe he did? I knew it was not the voice of my son, a boy who just a few short months ago bought me a sculpture of a mama stork feeding her baby. The letter made clear that Alan was fully in their clutches, and I feared he might stay inaccessible to me forever. I wished I could magically get him back to live with me.

Like Walt, Nora distorted the truth. "We never asked Alan to live with us, but rather, it was his choice. If you had taken care of him properly in the first place, he would never have asked to leave you." [3]

It made me furious to hear her false narrative. What bullshit!

Sometimes I had to show up even when Alan asked me not to. *I can do anything.*

When I skipped Alan's open house in the fall, I announced I would go in the spring. Not wanting to surprise Alan, I wrote him a note to tell him I was coming. I offered to see his work before, after, or with Walter and Nora, however he preferred.

When I answered the phone the day before the open house, I was surprised to hear Walter's voice.

"I'm calling because Alan wants to talk to you."

My stomach churned. Alan had never called me from Walter's house; it was verboten. Why was Walter intervening in this call? My eyes grabbed for safety—the bulletin board, the artwork in the hallway—anything familiar, any crumb to steady myself as I sat down on the kitchen stool.

Alan came to the phone.

"Hi, punkin'. What's up?" I tried being casual and intimate at the same time.

Long pause. I knew Walter was at Alan's elbow, listening to every word. I let the pause extend until it got too uncomfortable. I threw Alan a lifeline.

"Your dad said you wanted to talk to me."

Another pause, but shorter this time. Short enough I could tolerate it. Then suddenly, "I don't want you to come to open house." He hurled the words out, trying to reduce his job to one sentence. His voice was tight. I inhaled, taken aback.

"I know. It's difficult for you; that's why I didn't come last fall."

Silence.

I continued. "But last fall I said that I would come in the spring, and I'm coming."

He started crying. I wanted to scoop him up and comfort him (and kneecap Walter and Nora).

"Sweetie, I'm really sorry it's so hard for you, but I've always gone to your open house. I love you, and I'm coming."

"If you're coming then I'm not going."

"That doesn't make sense. You don't have to spend much time with me. Just say hello and show me your work. Then I'll leave."

"I don't want you there."

"I'm sorry you feel that way, but I'm coming, and I hope you come, too."

Silence.

I was not sure how to end the call.

"I'm sorry it's so hard, but I hope I'll see you there."

We both hung up.

The next month, to prove what good mothering Nora was providing Alan, Walter wrote me, "It was to Nora as well as me that Alan took his tears and upset caused by your insisting that you would go to the Reed Open House."[4]

It was crazy-making. Walt manufactured a problem for Alan, blamed me for the problem, then used Alan's reaction to the invented problem as evidence of Nora's superior mothering, proving they were more caring parents than I. *Aaarrrgh!*

CHAPTER 38

· ·

April 1978

Soon after our conciliation court meeting, I received a phone call.

"May I speak to Kay Harrington? This is Greg Fortner, Chairman of the Sociology Department at the University of North Carolina, Wilmington. We received your application and are very interested."

Application? I hadn't applied for a job. But here he was, offering a pathway to something new. I suddenly remembered. In January, I'd given the department permission to release my name to schools looking for entry-level professors. Three had responded. One day when I was bored with my dissertation, I had applied to all three, and then I had forgotten about them entirely.

What I wanted right now was a year of rest which, to me, meant working full-time and being a parent. I wanted to finish my degree, be out of survival mode, and have time with my boys.

"Are you still interested in us?" he asked.

I was so startled, I answered honestly. "I don't know. Where is Wilmington?" As soon as I blurted out the words, I wanted to take them back. What a clumsy way to start a job interview! I didn't even know where I had made an application? Lame.

"On the coast in southeastern North Carolina," he answered, seemingly unflustered. "Next to the ocean."

Ocean? "Well, yes. I'm interested." The ocean had an allure. I wanted to be comforted by waves and sea air.

He invited me to visit the school so I could meet the faculty and give a "job talk." Now I had a moral dilemma. I knew I was not going to move; I needed a year with no major changes, so it seemed dishonest to let them pay for me to visit. I consulted my friends. They all said I should go.

"You never really know."

I continued being honest when I called the chairman back. "I'm interested, but I need to tell you that the chances of me moving are very small. If, under those circumstances, you still want me to visit, I'd like to."

He agreed.

I flew to Wilmington in early May and had a grueling day of interviews. I gave my job talk, based on my dissertation, then flew back home the following day. They offered me the job the next week—and then my real dilemma began.

I wanted out of Dodge. I was physically, emotionally, and spiritually spent. I wanted to be with my children without continual harassment from Walt and Nora. I considered Alan on loan to Walt. I believed having full legal custody gave me some power over Alan's fate, even though I knew I would have to convince him to come. I had firm control of Daniel's custody because he was too young for a court to fight me.

I wanted, with all my heart, for the three of us to have a year together with no courts. They could grow in peace, and I could let down my guard. I could have a year's extended leave from my job at the counseling cente and still have the job upon my return.

I asked Walt to extend our visitation Memorial Day weekend and told him I was considering a job offer as assistant professor at UNCW. I wanted to take them with me for a scouting trip. I wanted them to see the beach and consider living with me the following year. Walter was upset, but he gave permission to take the boys out of state.

Should I move? Should I not? It was like asking the daisy, "He loves me, he loves me not."

One day I was clear I should move and felt the strength to do it—rent my house, pack everything up, close my private practice, and start a new life. The next day I would feel overwhelmed at the thought of moving and decide it was too much.

I made lists of advantages and disadvantages, giving weights to each variable, hoping it would reveal an answer. The lists made no difference, and the analytical exercise ended nearly as soon as it began. I had to make a decision. Stay? Move? The conundrum never fully left my mind.

I got Daniel his breakfast, sent him off to school, went to work, fixed dinner, supervised his homework, checked the chores chart, made him brush his teeth. We had chat time, I read him a bedtime story and said, "Sweet dreams."

I grocery shopped, got gas, paid bills—and yet—I was always assessing.

At Safeway, checking off items on the grocery list, I looked for catsup. As I reached for the smaller jar, I heard myself think, *We won't need the larger bottle before we move.*

Eureka! I'd made a decision. We were moving to North Carolina!

I talked to the boys about my desire to have all of us move to North Carolina together. Alan balked; Daniel was enthusiastic.

Daniel was in a pirate phase of life. He liked to write secret pirate messages on a paper whose edges he had charred, making it look like parchment. I prayed he wouldn't burn the house down. One night I came home from work to find a charred note on my bed.

I hope we can get Alan to go to NC: If you go, count on one boy at least. Love, Dan[1]

Dan's Pirate note regarding North Carolina

Later, Alan wrote me a note.

I will do anythink to live at dad's!! I can't stand it.[2]

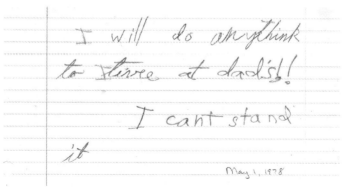

Alan's note regarding staying with his father

If I moved, it would likely be without Alan.

On May 19, 1978, the University of California, Berkeley conferred a doctoral degree to my exhausted, depleted body. The five years of doing my PhD were a blur. I was always a "someone to a someone else"—a parent, an ex-wife, a litigant, a respondent, an employee, a client, a therapist, a student, a friend. I never had time for my own needs. The compacted, over-scheduled minutes of each day became like an overripe melon, ready to explode.

It would take years for me to savor the triumph of my achievement—of my mere survival—and find my way back to health.

CHAPTER 39

May–July 1978

I made reservations for the three of us to fly to North Carolina on Memorial Day weekend, crossing my fingers we could have a peaceful year together. I expected North Carolina to be an interim life. I didn't see it as a long-term solution since I knew Walt would keep the boys in California one way or another . . . but if I could persuade Alan to come with us, it would be a no-brainer. I wanted a year to live at the ocean with my boys, leaving Walt and Nora three thousand miles away, unable to create weekly discord. A year together without interference would provide a solid foundation for the inevitable antagonism to come. They would each be a year older, less vulnerable to being damaged, and we would have had a year to solidify our bonds before the onslaught from the Walt Side.

I acted as if Alan were coming with us. I looked at three-bedroom apartments, making sure he would have his own bedroom. I rented an apartment directly on the beach, a hundred yards from the fishing pier. I hoped the setting would seduce him.

When I told Walt I had accepted the position and that Daniel and I would be living there the following year, I said I would love for Alan to join us. Alan liked North Carolina, but no way could he buck his father.

"I will not let you remove either boy from California," he wrote. "I have no choice but to begin a custody proceeding."

I expected him to refuse permission to take the boys, but I was surprised he moved so quickly to legal action for full custody.

He filed for custody on June 12, 1978. "I very frankly do not feel that Daniel is being provided with the type of home environment that he needs to grow and mature."

I filed, asking to modify our decree so I could take the boys out of state. The court scheduled us for a hearing on June 28.

I was angry at his characterizations of me in the court documents, but I burst out laughing at his descriptions of my bad parenting. "Kay has exposed him to everything from psychiatrists to head lice to smoking marijuana."[1]

Driving to my lawyer's office, once again, I passed the riotous bougainvillea on a nearby corner. Its petals spread up, down, and around. The fence supporting its structure was no longer visible, swamped by the capacious beauty that conquered every object within its reach. The scarlet-pink color, draped in the intense morning sun, called out to me as I passed, highlighting, by comparison, my own dullness. I reached for the vitality of that scarlet-pink celestial color, imploring its wavelengths to enter and feed my despondent body.

I responded to Walter's filing, paying my lawyer another retainer fee. Dealing with Walter sucked the life out of me. Always waiting for his next blow, I spent my energy defending, gathering evidence, and mobilizing others to testify on my behalf.

In late June, Walt wrote me again about Alan's clothes. "We're not willing to entrust his gray slacks to your care because of the condition in which you returned them the last time."[2]

I had no idea what he was referring to.

Since Walt had brought up the lice infestation as evidence that I was negligent, I received a note from our pediatrician, attesting that head lice last winter was "in epidemic proportions, usually associated with close contact at school."[3]

Walter asserted that Daniel's school performance had deteriorated due to my negligence. In fact, Daniel's school performance was good. I got teachers to write letters attesting to Daniel's achievements.

I got a letter from the psychiatrist we saw together stating that Daniel's development was normal; any problems Daniel might have were due to the discord between his parents.

The lawyers' schedules forced the custody hearing to be rescheduled for a month later, from June 28 to July 24. Easy for them to delay, but hard on me. *Aarrgh!* I'd done nothing but prepare. I didn't want to wait another month, yet again accommodating the needs of others.

While I was getting ready for court, I helped Daniel prepare to go to Sequoia Camp in August—the rich kids' camp Walt had sent him to last summer. I didn't particularly enjoy the camp prep tasks such as organizing name tags, buying clothes, or getting his flashlight ready, but I loved being part of any aspect of Daniel's life, so I did it happily. He loved the camp and had been looking forward to it for weeks.

Final payment for camp was due July 1.

On June 28, Walt canceled Daniel's enrollment, writing me, "Since the extension of time you sought makes it impossible to know whether Daniel will be with us or with you, I am turning over to you responsibility for Sequoia Camp. The fee of $895 is due July 1."[4]

Because I hadn't promised him custody, he transferred Daniel's deposit to pay Alan's fee and left Daniel with no guaranteed space. Walt knew I couldn't afford such a camp, but I was not going to have Daniel broken-hearted because suddenly his father wanted to pull a power play. I was custodian for about $3,000 that my parents gave Daniel at birth. Without hesitation, I used a third of that money to send Dan to Sequoia Camp. I seethed inside that Walt would do such a thing. Part of me wanted to tell Daniel, so he would know about his father's dirty tricks. The more mature part of me wanted Daniel never to know what his father had just done.

I said nothing.

On July 14, ten days before our court date, Walt's lawyer sent a proposal for change of custody. Because I managed to get us into conciliation court, we had already hammered out most of the details. Child support would be further reduced and terminated in a year, and I, of course, was to do all the driving when it was my time with the boys. Walt conceded that I was allowed to call him at work.

Walt also sent a proposal outlining his rules if I wanted to take Daniel with me to North Carolina. Walt would maintain "care, custody, and control" of both boys but would allow Daniel to live with me one year in North Carolina if I promised Daniel would live with Walter thereafter "because Daniel has expressed a desire to move there."

Walt's proposal primarily used what we agreed to in conciliation court, with an additional nod to me, because it included a clause I wanted: Neither of us would speak of each other in derogatory terms within earshot of Alan or Daniel.

My lawyer advised me, "Please think on this in your usual, clear, creative way, while keeping in touch with what are the meaningful and less meaningful provisions of this lengthy proposal."

The bottom line was this: To keep Daniel one more year and take him to North Carolina with me, I had to relinquish custody of both boys and promise delivery of Daniel at the end of the school year. I knew Walt eventually would get custody of Daniel. I just hadn't been sure exactly how it would play out. Now I knew. I had tried creating a peaceful year for the three of us, but I couldn't pull it off. I had known for years that the end game was coming, but that didn't stop me from being grief-stricken. The only comfort was that I would get Daniel for one more year.

I wanted two more items in the legal agreements:

1. The boys must have their own phone.
2. Nora must be included, legally, in the pledge to agree to good behavior and friendly cooperation.

I added a memorandum of agreement to be signed by Walter, Nora, and me. It confirmed that Alan and Daniel needed my love and guidance, Walt and Nora must encourage visitation with me, and they would accomplish transfers without conflict, unpleasantness, or embarrassment. Even though I knew it was unenforceable, it felt satisfying to get Nora to legally agree not to speak ill of me in front of the boys.

I signed the memorandum, and my lawyer sent it to Walt and Nora for their signatures. They signed, but not before gutting it. They added, "This agreement has no legal force or effect . . . and shall not be admissible in evidence or used for any purpose in this or any other proceeding. [Observance of the agreement] shall depend solely on the honor and integrity of the undersigned."

My lawyer gave me some much-needed validation. She donated two hours of her time "as a comment on the good sense and high level of parenting you have shown during this demanding process. It's a pleasure to work with you."[5]

I didn't get both boys, but I got a year with Daniel in North Carolina without Walter and Nora, and right now that sounded like heaven.

In September, it was time to celebrate finishing my PhD. A friend, whose two sons were longtime friends of Alan and Daniel, offered her spacious property with horses and a pasture as a venue for my party.

Alan and Dan knew about their father and clothing, and we agreed they would change out of their good clothes as soon as they were done eating. My rules for their clothes were iron-clad and repeated ad infinitum. At the party, I was watchful toward Alan and Daniel as we ate, mingled, and talked. As soon as I saw them head for the pasture, I yelled for them to go change. Thanks to my vigilance, we finished the day with their dress-up clothes in pristine condition—and secondarily, me with a PhD.

CHAPTER 40

....

September 1978–September 1979

Daniel and I lived at Wrightsville Beach, a few miles and a drawbridge away from Wilmington. Our new apartment faced the ocean, one hundred feet from the fishing pier, and three thousand miles from the legal system that had absorbed the previous months. For the first time in three years, there was no weekly pugilistic ambush from Walter or Nora. Daniel and I had an empty room announcing Alan's absence, but we lived in peace. We heard the ocean from our open windows.

An older fisherman befriended Daniel. He taught him how and when to fish, instructing him about the benefits of a good catch when a storm arrived. I insisted Dan gut and clean the fish outside before he brought them in for me to cook. He glowed with pride as we ate a dinner he provided. He was growing. He was happy. I was happy.

He attended Tileston School, fifth grade, with Miss Billie Jean Glover as his teacher. On his third day of school, as he was leaving the house, I said, "Bye."

He replied, with a strong Southern drawl, "*Baihhh . . .*" I smiled. He was adapting quickly.

His fourth day of school, he told me that Miss Glover asked him a question, and he answered, "Yes."

She said, "Yes what?"

Confused, Dan said, "Yes, that's right?"

She said, "Yes, ma'am."

He had no idea he had to add "ma'am" to every response. He was learning about Southern rituals and manners, and I was happy he was expanding his experience of other cultures.

After the intensity of life in Berkeley, I found Wilmington's pace unnaturally slow. People in line were patient while the clerk visited with the paying customer. After two weeks, I began joining the Southern pace with gratitude instead of frustration. I found the community more friendly than Berkeley. After our trip back from California to see Alan at Christmas, the clerk at the post office exclaimed, "Miss Kay! You've been gone. Welcome back."

Teaching was demanding. I had four course preparations, each of them new to me. May Sarton, the poet, likened teaching to raising an elephant anew each day. It took me at least a day to read, condense, and prepare a lecture, and once delivered, it was over in an hour with barely enough time to prepare another one for tomorrow. I was always behind.

I shopped at Kroger's. The biscuits at Hardee's drive-through were irresistible. My new bank in Wilmington was being used as a pilot for a new-fangled machine—an ATM, which I used for the first time. Daniel found a friend, Terry, who taught Daniel to crack his knuckles.

When Alan came out for spring vacation, we went to Williamsburg with my sister and her girls. Every time Alan and Dan found a postage-size piece of green space, they were immediately on the ground, wrestling with each other. We ran a 5K race together. Watching them, I deeply wished the three of us could have had the year of peace together to solidify my bond with them, to give each of them another year to mature before being snatched away from their mother.

Daniel must be turned over at the end of the school year like booty, the spoils being handed over to the victor. To Walter,

Daniel was a prize won; to me, Daniel was more complex. He was a little boy who missed his brother, who loved his father, and who didn't want to have to choose. He was a little boy with a face of sunshine who loved me. I knew I would soon be persona non grata, but I still had no inkling how bad it would be. I thought the last year was bad; I'm glad I didn't yet know it was going to get much worse.

In April, the days grew bittersweet as June approached with relentless regularity. Each day became one day closer to giving up custody of Dan, now ten years old. I savored our time, knowing the clock ticked down each day. I focused on today's pleasure; I couldn't afford to contemplate the grief awaiting me.

I hadn't had much contact with Walt, but now that the transfer was approaching, the wrangling about child support and travel costs started up again.

Then my life shifted. I met and developed a romance with a visiting speaker. After a few weeks of correspondence and a visit, he invited me to spend June traveling with him. He was giving workshops in Greece, Yugoslavia, and Germany, and we would ride on his motorcycle from place to place. I answered with a resounding, "Yes!" After years of courtroom battles, financial struggle, bickering about clean clothes and pickup times, there was no question in my mind. I was going. The chance to be carefree with a man who thought I was the cat's meow? Yes!

More importantly, it was just the adventure I needed to distract myself from the loss of both children. I could leave, go somewhere exciting, have company, and avoid raw grief for a few weeks.

Yes, it meant Daniel would miss the last two weeks of fifth grade.

Yes, it was selfish.

Yes, it meant, I could stick it to Walter. As the visiting parent instead of the custodial parent, I could work the schedule around my convenience instead of Walter's. Having custody meant he would have to make whatever arrangements he had to make. I was finally out of his clutches.

At last, I could be without obligations for three weeks. Walt couldn't do anything more to me.

I informed Walter that Dan would be returning May 25 or 26.[1]

Walter responded, "Kay, for once you must put your interests aside and do what is best for Daniel. I, as his custodial parent, demand it. Live up to your responsibilities."[2]

But I did not capitulate. I returned Daniel early. I wrote Walt, "If the 'demands' of the custodial parent didn't work when I had custody, there is no reason they should suddenly start to work now."[3]

My new beau, Myron, and I had an adventure during the summer and into the fall. He was in charge, I followed—a relief for me. Over time, I realized I scarcely knew him; I'd read his books, he was famous in his circles, and I admired his stated values. We traveled well together.

After the trip, I visited him in Connecticut with his family; he as much as announced I was "it," intimating marriage. He was absorbed in his world, attentive but disconnected from me, and assumed his reactions were my reactions. I started having second thoughts about being with him. He visited me in Berkeley, and it became clear to me I did not want to hook my star to his, or rather, I did not want my star to be his satellite.

I needed to end the relationship, but when and how? Myron had invited me to join him in November in Florida. I longed for a nice vacation in a warm place, but I didn't long for Myron. As appealing as it was, I knew I had to say no.

I didn't want to break up over the phone—we had been too important to each other. I decided to wait till I would see him in two weeks and quipped to my sister, "By waiting to tell him in person, at least I'll get a free dinner."

My mother overheard me and made no effort to hide her judgment. "You're no better than a prostitute!"

CHAPTER 41

······················

September 1979–March 1980

Walt had both boys, and now paid me neither alimony nor child support. With these new conditions, I had hoped we could be civil, but instead, my life became Kafkaesque again.

Legally, Walt was required to have a phone solely for my use with the boys. I called and called, but no one answered. Weeks later, I found out the phone was installed in the basement, where no one could hear it ring.

On my weekends, Walt offered the boys fancy activities—a river trip on the Delta, skiing in Sun Valley, and then said, innocence personified, "If they don't want to see you, I'm not going to *make* them."

If I had to delay pickup time by an hour because of work, he would tell me I could not see them at all. Wearily, I called my lawyer. She would call his lawyer. His lawyer would tell him he could not withhold visitation if I had to change the pickup time. We averted going to court, but we each spent hundreds of dollars on this aggravating ritual. I wanted to wash my hands of the whole business, but I couldn't; I didn't want to wash my hands of my sons.

The foundation with my sons eroded, like sand under my feet as the wave washes back to sea, the rhythm powerful and inevitable. I orchestrated our precious visitation weekends—the only time I could directly talk to the boys, now in sixth and seventh grades. If I needed to say something important, Friday night was too early. We hadn't yet been able to reknit ourselves into a lumpy, bumpy, family unit. Sunday was too late. No time left to pick up the pieces from a fraught topic.

In March 1980, I chose the intimacy of our tiny kitchen, our bodies within a foot of each other as we improvised the choreography of clearing, washing, and drying the dishes. I inhaled, paused—and then plunged in. My voice was tight, but outwardly I maintained a careful nonchalance. "I plan to go to your school open house in a couple of weeks." My attendance should have been assumed, part of the normal course of parenting. Instead, it revealed the fault lines, deep and unfathomable, growing daily between my sons and me.

Neither son spoke. Wires of tension suddenly materialized with electricity zapping back and forth on every wire.

The discussion about whether I was "allowed" to go to their school open houses had intensified the last few weeks like a sudden summer storm. When I had talked to Alan about it, he was vague about the date, so I called the school and got the date.

Tonight, in the kitchen, Alan expanded his chest, pulled out the big guns, and tested his testosterone on me, his mother. "You think it's because of Dad and Nora that I don't want you to come. But it's not. *I* don't want you to come to open house."

Alan liked showing me he had joined the enemy camp, proving to me there was nothing I could do about it. If I went to open house, it would prove to him that Walter and Nora were right—that I didn't pay attention to his needs and only cared about myself. If I didn't go, it was another step in disappearing from his life.

Daniel cast a sidelong glance at his brother and slightly nodded his head in agreement, trying to support Alan without alienating me. Daniel neither looked at me nor spoke; his open house wasn't for another few weeks.

Alan, in his third year living with his dad, played the "Get Mom" game with vigor. Daniel had been there only eight months; the tender chord to me was still moist with the love and salt air of our previous year together at the beach. It was not as easy for him to betray me, but Daniel's gestation period in his new, arid environment had tamed his juicy exuberance. Daniel had grown cautious. Like a baby who changed dramatically each month, Daniel's posture in the world had contracted visibly between each visitation. He still called me "Mom," but he knew he was supposed to call me "Kay." He often went blind and mute, trying not to see or feel the terrible fissures asked of him.

"Except for last fall, I've always gone to your open houses. Why would this year be any different?"

"Because we don't live here anymore."

"But that's even more reason for me to go."

Alan chewed on that for a minute, and then said, "Because it's embarrassing."

I bristled inside, but calmly said, "Why? I don't understand."

"Dad and Nora don't want to have to see you. They don't want anything to do with you."

"Well, we can go at different times." Silence as I stacked the dishes for the boys to dry. I continued. "I didn't want my coming to be a surprise. I just want you to spend fifteen minutes with me."

"I don't want you to come."

Alan's rejection hurt. He was not usually so blatant, but I didn't let myself respond to his defiant attitude. Alan's words revealed Walter's self-righteous encouragement to "just say no." Still, knowing I couldn't afford to feel at that moment, I focused on arrangements for open house.

"I'm coming. I don't think fifteen minutes is too much to ask." Silence.

"I'll call your father and see if we can arrange to be there at different times, so he and Nora won't be uncomfortable."

More silence.

"Okay. We'll talk about it next time you're here."

We were done drying by now. Sullenly, they hung up the towels and as a unit, moved to the living room and zombie-like, started the Atari game. A pall descended over the house.

I gave up. I was out of juice. Feeling defeated, I retreated to my bedroom. As the sole adult in this mix, I didn't have it in me to try to stir up any cheer for our fracturing family unit.

When I am six years old, if I reach up stretching from my tippy-toes, I can grab onto the clothes rail in my closet, swing my legs up as if I am on a jungle gym, get my feet onto the lower closet shelf, then launch and slither my whole body onto the upper shelf. The naked light bulb hangs down from the ceiling. I then grab a pillow, put it on the shelf, lie back, and disappear into a book.

During the summer, the bookmobile comes once a week, parking at the corner of Cherry Street and Fifth, a half block from our house. It's hard to sleep Tuesday nights, savoring the anticipation of picking out new books. As if it were a clandestine act, I take my new books to my safe spot in the closet, toss them up on the shelf, and pull myself up.

My favorite story is The Little Lame Prince. *The prince can't walk and is very lonely. His nursemaid, the only person who loves him, gives him a magic carpet. He can fly anywhere he wants, see anything he likes, and forget that he is lame and lonely.*

The upper shelf swaddles me in safety. If I make myself invisible. No one hits me, and nobody can pierce me with hateful resentment, reaffirming what I already know to be true—I shouldn't be alive, that life would be easier without me.

So, I make myself as scarce as I can till I can't.

When I can no longer sustain my disguise as a ghost child, I have tantrums. I scratch my older sisters. I bite. I wet the bed. I make my presence known in the only ways I know how.

I then retreat to my closet shelf, back to safety and to my pretend nonexistence.

Knowing it wouldn't end well, I dreaded calling Walter about open house; yet, to protect Alan, I felt compelled to try. The rock in my stomach made me procrastinate till Friday, when I finally mustered the courage to pick up the phone. I chose a time to call when I could collapse afterward, when nothing professional would be asked of me.

CHAPTER 42

....

March 1980

Walt was unhappy I called him at work, so I spoke quickly before he could hang up. "I wanted to check with you about open house, so we could arrange so Alan would be comfortable."

"It would be best if you did not come at all."

"I'm not calling about that. I've always gone to their school open houses, and I just thought it might be easier on you and on Alan if we went at different times."

"Well, you don't need to be there. Nora has replaced you in that function."

"What do you mean, she's 'replaced' me? I'm their mother." I was aghast.

"As I said, she's replaced you in that function. To come to anything in Belvedere is simply intruding where you're not wanted."

I started to respond, but he continued. I'm jelly with fear—and rage.

"The boys are embarrassed to be from a divorced family, and Nora and I are acting as their parents."

I thought of Daniel's class in Berkeley. Of twenty-three students, only four lived with both their parents. Alan and Daniel had lots of experience with divorce; I'd never tried to hide the facts, and they were never embarrassed.

I shook from frustration. I was caught up in my own compulsion of trying to make him understand, caught in the illusion that if I just tried harder, if I found the right words, he would see the light. "Walter, they've never been embarrassed before about being from a divorced family, and if they are now, you and Nora are helping to create that."

"They are embarrassed, and when you appear, it forces the fact on them that they have a mother living elsewhere."

My brain had trouble receiving oxygen. "But I am their mother, and I do live elsewhere."

"Nora and I have talked about it, and we both agree 'out of sight, out of mind' is best for them. We want to keep it that way."

My heart raced. It was hard to stay calm and to think.

"There's no place for you in Alan and Daniel's lives except for planned visitation on weekends and vacations."

"What do you mean there's no place for me? I'm their mother! Open house is a public event, and I have a right to be there."

"Nora and I are married and providing them a home. I see no purpose for you to come to open houses, or to their graduations, or weddings either. Your presence is intrusive and unnecessary. You know you're doing this for some ego need of your own. It doesn't have anything to do with what's best for Alan and Daniel."

I tried staying rational. "I will always be their mother, and I expect to be included at major events in their lives. Our job as parents is to work out a way to be amicable at these events, not to avoid them. We can start with the open houses."

"I can't be bothered."

"But Walt, we have to be bother—"

The line went dead.

I sat on the stool. A long time. Numb. Staring into space.

Why be so militant about open house?

Slowly reality pierced my denial: they were actually pretending Nora *was* the boys' biological mother, and they didn't want me to blow their cover.

They actually believed they could make me not exist.

Nora wrote to me. "I will further remind you that I take care of your child for you, with no thanks or monetary compensation. I deserve nothing but thanks from you, which I have never received. It was not my choice to raise your children."[1]

I had one more weekend with the boys before open house. When I drove them home, I used my last chance to talk to Alan.

"I can come early or late. I can see your classes with you alone, or with your dad and Nora. We can work it out however is easiest for you, but I'm coming, and I expect you to spend some time with me."

We went around and around about. I had only one demand: Alan needed to see me and speak to me at some point during open house.

We continued arguing as I delivered them home. I said I'm coming; Alan said he wouldn't talk to me. We're outside the car when I finally I lost my temper and raised my voice. "All I want is fifteen fucking minutes of your time!"

That shut both of us up. I was as startled at myself as he was. Unwittingly, without thinking, after years of prohibiting curse words in our home, the word "fucking" left my mouth in the presence of my sons; I'd just given Walt and Nora ammunition. What I didn't yet know was that my single "fucking" would live in infamy for years to come, showing up in court documents to deny visitation and prove I was an unfit mother.

CHAPTER 43

....

April 1980

The following Friday, I honked as I passed their house, giving the boys time to come up the stairs to the street while I went fifty feet beyond to turn around. The light was on at the gate, but there was no sign of my sons.

I waited a few minutes, decided they didn't hear my honk, and lightly tapped the horn again twice, trying to make the sound loud enough to be heard, but soft enough to be courteous, an impossible volume to achieve. I resisted my impulse to lay on the horn.

Nothing. Twilight darkened into night. No signs of life. I got out of the car, leaving the door open with the inside light on so I would be as fully visible as possible. I peered through the gate. I could see nothing but the light above the front door, the ivy-covered hillside, and the switchback pathway leading from the gate down to the front door.

Suddenly, from the darkness on the right side of the house, Nora emerged and strode up the steps toward me. My heart started pounding. The boys were nowhere to be seen. I quickly assessed my options. I did not want to retreat to the car, trapped inside with her looking down at me. I decided to stand my ground; I waited for her at the gate.

In eight years, I had met her only once, at the consultation with the child psychiatrist. She was slender, slightly taller than I, with shoulder length hair. She was dressed in slacks, blouse, and a sweater. Her face was tight, pinched, and angry. My adrenaline had me on high alert, but I tried to appear calm, as if standing at their gate with her charging toward me were an ordinary event.

She opened the gate, stood two feet from me, and assaulted me with her voice.

"What are you doing?"

"Waiting for my sons." I sounded defiant, taking a confrontational tone in return.

"You didn't honk."

"Yes. I did. I honked twice."

I answered calmly, staring at her with cold, steely eyes. If we were going to have a fight, my raw will was staking out my physical territory, bending to no one.

"You're lying. You didn't honk."

"I honked twice. You didn't hear."

"You didn't honk. You're lying."

I switched gears. "I thought you didn't want anything to do with me."

"I don't. I want nothing to do with you."

"Then why did you come up here?"

"To see what you were doing. You want your sons? Well . . . I'll go get your sons. You lost them long ago. You don't want them."[1]

The energy in her body became so volcanic that she was unable to contain it. She started to erupt in fury, Kali personified. "You don't want them. I never asked for them, and I don't want them, either." She spit words at me, her foul resentment surging up and spilling out her mouth.

"Then I will be glad to have them." I wanted to get away from her but did not want to wait passively in the car, giving her the power to fetch or not to fetch my sons.

"I never wanted to raise your sons, but you don't want them to live with you. Let me hear you ask them to live with you."

I worked at not responding. I simply stared at her, trying not to show the rage I felt.

She lapsed into a taunting, singsong rhythm, hoping to provoke a fight. "You won't because you never wanted them. Let me hear you. Just let me hear you."

She worked herself up, ever higher, twisting into a tornado.

My rage was about to erupt. She wanted to fight? Well, then, we'd fight. My impotence, my efforts to be deliberate and measured in order to protect Alan and Daniel—rational impulses were nowhere that dusky evening on the streets of posh Belvedere. She was the cause of unspeakable heartbreak and pain in my life, and now she had the gall to taunt me?

We were in a visceral standoff, a down-and-dirty cat fight, hating each other with every cell, pore, wisp of hair. Inside my head, a four-star general suddenly took over. I commanded myself, with a very authoritative, brook-no-discussion kind of voice, *Kay, you cannot hit her.* I told myself to behave. I left no room for uncertainty.

She continued her taunting. "Let me hear you ask them to live with you. I never wanted to raise your children." Her eyes had such hatred in them, my overwhelming urge was to scratch them out.

Kay, you cannot hit her. I yield to the authority of the inaudible voice. This voice controlled my nervous system, instructing my muscles to stay still, not to give in to the impulse to raise my fingernails to her deliciously close face.

"I came to pick up my sons." I became an automaton, both inside and out. I appeared to be a flesh-and-blood person, but I was a bombed-out carapace.

"I came for my boys."

I knew I had to get away from her or I would hit her. I lifted my right hand, put it on the top of the gate, and moved to push it open. She grabbed my arm, scratching my right cheek, and held onto my wrist, restraining me from opening the gate. We shared a hard, fixed stare, each of us daring the other. I was glad not to be in high heels and professional clothes, which would have made me feel constricted right now. I was comfortable in my standard casual clothes of a turtleneck and pants.

My inner voice became audible, menacing. "Don't you dare hit me," I threatened her. My provocation threw gasoline on the fire.

She raised her right hand and with all the force of her body, she slapped my left cheek. The instant sting made my eyes water, and I could tell welts were on their way. The boil was lanced, the danger passed. I had won. I knew that I would not hit her now.

She stared in satisfaction and hatred for a split second, swiveled, opened the gate, and marched down the steps, snorting and swinging her arms. I sagged, relieved that I didn't have to hear her taunts. I provoked her, but I did not hit her. I did nothing she could use against me.

I looked down at the house. The front light was on, but all was quiet. I could not make myself go down and ring the front doorbell. I knew I might have to, but I needed to collect myself before attempting Round Two. They might refuse to let me have the boys, and I didn't know what I would do then. I couldn't think of any option but to be angry, protest, and then slink away.

I was shaken and shaking as I stood on the street, thoughts racing through my head. I forced myself to consider the next scenarios and potential options. I felt drained, close to despair. I looked at both the illuminated front door and the darkened right side of the house. Who knew where the boys would come from or if they would come at all.

Within a minute, Dan, duffel bag in hand, emerged from the dark at the right of the house and started up the steps. I was grateful and relieved to see his flesh-and-blood body, his presence revealing that this standoff was over. I yelled down to him to provide a thread of sound to help him climb toward me to safety. "Hi, kiddo."

He called back, "Hello" as he walked toward me. I was relieved he had a voice. I was still shaking as I hugged him. I pretended it was just another Friday evening pickup, business as usual. Luckily, Daniel had no idea what had just transpired between his stepmother and me. Gently, I stroked my hand on my scratched cheek, as if one touch could caress my whole traumatized psyche.

I opened the car door for him, and he climbed into the back seat of the station wagon. At eleven, he was still a boy with no hint of adolescence about him. He was a few inches shorter than I, with a cherubic, rounded countenance framed with blond curls.

After helping Daniel in the car, I turned back to look down at the house. All was quiet. Were they going to hold Alan hostage? Would I have to risk approaching their front door in order to retrieve him? I waited another few minutes, hoping he would appear. I didn't want to leave Daniel alone in the car by going to the door, nor risk another shouting match. I prayed Alan would soon appear.

To keep Daniel occupied, I made inane conversation. "I'm glad you brought your jacket. It's already getting cold." No response. "I was thinking we might go to the movies tomorrow. How does that sound?"

I waited some more. I heard noise below and Alan appeared from the dark side of the house. He was not alone.

Nora became visible in the light cast from the fixture above the front door, still yelling. "You don't want your children to live with you. Let me hear you ask them. I never wanted to raise your children."

Alan at thirteen was slender, also blond, and my height but still a boy. His body was changing, but he was not yet in the full flower of adolescence. He had his brown winter jacket with the fleece-lined hood slung loosely over his head. Both his hands were holding either side of the hood over his head to cover his ears, leaving the body of the jacket to flop out behind his shoulders.

Alan did not run but was deliberate and fast in coming up the steps. I watched this scene in horror, unable to do anything but pray. I wanted to get out of there as fast as we could. *Please, Alan, just keep coming. Please, Alan, don't trip. I'm sorry. I'm so, so sorry. I don't want you to have to hear this, I don't want you to have to live this way. You're close. Don't stumble. Keep that jacket over your head. Don't listen. Protect yourself as best you can. Keep coming. I'm here. I'm here. I promise you we'll get out of here. Please, God help. Please.*

Alan made it to the top of the stairs, beyond the gate, and into my keeping. "Hi Punkin." I hugged him quickly and hustled him into the car. "Let's get out of here." Nora had never stopped taunting, "Let me hear you invite them to live with you."

He climbed into the back seat but didn't stop there. He hoisted his leg over the back of the seat and crawled into the way-back, and Daniel immediately followed suit. I got into the car and started the engine. I had my children safely with me. I wanted out of there.

"Put on your seat belts." Wearing seat belts was a routine family rule. We never drove without them. My admonition was habitual, part of the unconscious sequence of putting the key in the ignition and starting the car. I looked in the rearview mirror; they were nowhere near their seat belts. I decided not to make an issue of it till we got to the bottom of the hill. Getting out of there was more important than seat belts.

I pulled away from the house, still shaken, and slowly crept down Seaside Road. It was dark by now, easier to discern the headlights of oncoming cars around a bend in the narrow road. I was always more comfortable driving this nearly single-lane road at night than in daytime, when a car could come barreling around a curve with alarming speed and nearly cause a head-on crash.

Alan and Daniel immediately started wrestling with each other. Spontaneously, they created a game.

Alan said, "Put on the brakes."

Dan responded, "I can't."

They wrestled some more, then changed roles.

Daniel said, "Put on the brakes," with Alan responding, "I can't."

They never stopped wrestling with each other, staying in close body contact, alternating lines.

I gave up the idea of seat belts. Playing their repetitious game—perseverating, trying to master the recent scene—was more important than seat belts. I sent up a silent prayer and hoped the odds of a car accident were low tonight. Still shaking, I gripped the steering wheel and forced myself to focus on the movement of other cars as I heard the boys playing their game during the long, hour-drive home to safety.

When we're ten and eleven, my father captures my sister's arm in his hand while his other hand grabs my arm and roughly pulls me toward him. He lines my sister and me up, facing each other.

Once he has us positioned, he pauses. He is a photographer. We hold still, staring at each other while he takes a picture of us. Each of us curls the edges of our lips upward, smirking away the pain we know is coming.

He puts down his camera and returns to the business at hand. His large hand calmly cups the back of my skull as his other hand simultaneously cups the back of my sister's head.

With his superior strength, he headbutts our foreheads against each other.

We are experienced enough to know not to cry.

We stay silent until he is gone.

He does this to teach us to stop bickering with each other.

The bump on my forehead swells. It hurts if I touch it.

I memorialized the events of Nora's rant and physical assault in a letter to Walter, with copies to both lawyers.

My lawyer wrote me, "I think this situation is very unhealthy with no obvious solution. One wonders if lawyers and judges are even relevant."[2]

I had no illusions of trying to be friendly anymore.

Unwanted, I went to Alan's open house.

Alan was absent. I did not see Walter or Nora.

CHAPTER 44

· ·

April 1980–September 1981

After the winter rains, spring burst forth. The sun was out, a cool breeze teased the senses, and vivid green leaves pushed their way out of barren branches. A good day to be alive.

I was to pick up the boys Saturday afternoon at 1 p.m. Like Goldilocks's porridge, my arrival time had to be *juuust* right—not too early, not too late. Because traffic and crossing the bridge was unpredictable, I always left early; I wanted to deny Walter and Nora a chance to find one more reason to berate me. I arrived early. To wait for the magic minute, I parked in the pullout on the road above their house, from which their house was not fully visible.

The day sparkled. The water and sailboats looked like a tourist's postcard of life on San Francisco Bay. I got out of the car, breathed in the fresh air, and just stood there, enjoying the beauty.

At 1 p.m., I did the three-point turn, pulled into their pullout, and honked. The boys came up; we left. Uneventful pickup.

I repeated the same procedure the next time I saw them. Alan got in the car. He announced, clearly charged to deliver a new decree, "When we come home, you have to let us off down at the market."

Not only was I banished from their front door, but I was also now banished from Seaside Road. The shopping mall was a mile down the hill from their house, and they were now to walk home from there. "Why? I don't understand."

"Because Nora saw you spying on us last time you came."

I was astonished. "What do you mean, 'spying?' I was parked on Bella Vista waiting for pickup time."

"She thinks you were spying."

"I can't even see your house from where I was. How could I be spying?"

"You have to let us off at the bottom of the hill. You can't bring us to the gate anymore."

"That's crazy. I won't do it."

"Please. We'll get in trouble if you drop us off at the house."

We go around in circles. They agreed it was a crazy request but begged me to let them off at the bottom of the hill. "If you don't…"

They didn't have to say. Nora or Walter would make their lives miserable. They would get in trouble. If I loved them, the best way to protect them was to go along with the craziness.

So, I did.

I'd entered *Alice in Wonderland* where there was no logic. For more than a decade, I let them out at the market, pained every time I saw them trudging up the road, knowing they had a mile to walk for no reason except Nora's ability to create threatening stories in her head, stories in which I was the villain. Even after they graduated from high school, I was to let them off at the market. The walk up the hill never stopped.

The next big issue was when Walter told me I couldn't come to Alan's eighth grade graduation from Del Mar Middle School. I maintained it was a public event, and I would be there. Knowing I needed support to enter enemy territory, and hoping to lessen the awkwardness, I invited Roy to go with me. Roy was no stranger to Walt; as young married couples, we had a monthly dinner party together. Alan also knew Roy, as part of our Christmas-tree-cutting friends.

When I told Alan that Roy was coming, I also told Alan he had to acknowledge me, talk to us for a few minutes, and pose for some pictures. Alan was silent, avoiding agreeing or disagreeing.

Except for my feeling numb and anticipating an assault, it was a sunny, joyful occasion. The girls were dressed up beyond their years, and the boys were dressed up beyond their comfort. The boys, in sport coats and ties—awkward and gangly—roughhoused with each other, denying the garb and the occasion. The girls were floating pieces of beauty, suddenly young women, with hair coiffed, makeup cautiously applied, looking more like nineteen than thirteen.

As I idly surveyed the scene, I suddenly caught a glimpse of one girl standing with the sun behind her, turning her dress into a gauzy mystery, outlining a slender, developing body. My first thought was how much older she was than my son, and of course, thought how he wouldn't be interested in such a mature girl. Quickly, I burst the bubble of my own illusion: they were all the same age, and of course he would be interested in such a girl. That was why the boys were wrestling and making bathroom jokes. They all were interested in such a girl and didn't have a clue of what to do about it.

Alan's arms had grown longer than the sleeves of his sport coat. His teeth seemed big in a face that hadn't caught up with their growth. He was angular, both too big and too small, like a colt, with knobs and knuckles sticking out.

My heart ached at being absent for the preparation for today. I would have loved to help him buy a sport coat, select a shirt, anticipate, cajole, guide, nurture. To hear the whispers of which girl was stealing his pencil in social studies class so I could be on the lookout for her, to see how she looked in her finery. To help him get ready, staying at a distance but not too great a distance. A just-right distance. In a normal world, I trusted my instincts; I would have known how to find that just-right distance, that gray vague cloud where a mother was allowed to stand next to her growing, adolescent son. But I didn't know how to find the right distance when I was banned from the castle and had to swim the moat alone.

My need was exaggerated by my deprivation. The impedance principle: My need is too intense, too large to fit through the available pipeline. I counseled myself, *Hold back and pretend indifference.* I knew my intensity could act like a magnifying glass in the sunlight, focusing the sun's rays and burning a hole where I wanted wholeness.

I was anxious about Walter. I didn't see him anywhere, but I knew that if I dared to approach Alan, Alan would freeze in place, neither daring to acknowledge me nor daring not to. Making him paralyzed would not be a good thing to do, so I kept my distance, kept my cool, and looked at him surreptitiously, pretending he was someone else's kid.

There were 182 eighth graders graduating. Parents expectantly filled the folding chairs and slowly, order was created. The teachers managed to tame the boys into a line. "Pomp and Circumstance" began on the loudspeaker. The boys begrudgingly processed in, each paired with a girl who was poised, while each boy shuffled uncomfortably next to her.

After the small ceremony, there were refreshments, congratulations, and photos. I knew no one, and I was grateful to have Roy to talk to. I hoped Alan would appear organically, so we could take pictures without making a big deal of it.

Suddenly Walt, quite accidentally, was right next to Roy and me. It was the opening I'd been hoping for. I turned to Walter, smiled, and reintroduced him to Roy. "Hi. You remember Roy."

Walt froze. Roy smiled and said hello. Walter did not smile; he did not look at me, he did not look at Roy, so I forged ahead, trying to make this a civil moment. "Alan looks so handsome and all dressed up. I thought it would be nice if we could get a picture with all of us."

With that invitation, Walt's face contorted; he silently walked away without saying a word. It was chilling. Roy was flabbergasted.

"He was actually rude to me, too. You've told me how bad it is with Walter, but I had no idea how truly awful."

I nodded, my eyes filling with tears. Roy experienced it once; I experienced it repetitively.

"It's much worse than I imagined."

I was grateful to have a witness.

It took me years to see the truth: there was *nothing* I could have done to soften Walter toward me. My very existence caused trouble for my sons.

After graduation, visitation disintegrated to almost nothing. Accommodation didn't work, so I tried imposing structure. I wrote, "Walter, in trying to accommodate the boys' plans and activities this past year, I've seen them less and less, and it has become less and less satisfactory. I want to see them a minimum of one weekend a month (to me, a weekend is two nights)."[1]

Walter responded, "I do not think that the solution to the problem of how you can spend more time with the boys is to fix upon a certain weekend each month any more than it was or is to insist upon alternate weekends. I don't think it fair to Alan to ask that he forgo some school activity on a Friday evening, for example, because it turns out to be the third weekend of the month. I don't think that there is a formula which will provide a facile solution to your problem."[2]

He was right, of course. But it was the the only solution I had.

In the fall, I was successful at getting a full weekend. The boys and I were happily together on a Sunday morning in Cayucos, visiting Arthur and Rosie. We were reading the paper, cleaning up after a big breakfast, enjoying our companionable silence.

Sunday in Cayucos meant the beginning of the end of a piece of peace, the weekend coming to a close. A weekend of being fed and loved, a weekend of walks and talks on the beach. Love from others—along with absence of venom from the enemy—allowed us to unwind and be natural with each other, just another divorced mom and her kids. Walt and Nora were safely 250 miles away.

Then Daniel, now thirteen, started asking unusual questions. At 11 a.m., "Mom, when are we going home?"

"I don't know, probably around four, like we always do." Daniel knew the routine; we had done it dozens of times.

At 1 p.m. "If we leave at four, what time will we get home?"

"It's a four-hour drive, so probably around eight if we don't stop to eat. Why?" I asked.

"Nothing. Just wondering."

At 2:00 p.m., "Are there fairies in San Francisco?"

I was startled. Being out and proud was a not yet a cultural phenomenon, but San Francisco was the gay mecca of the United States. My body recoiled at the brashness of the word. I wondered what words they used in their Belvedere household, what prejudices they were being taught.

I was so caught off guard I wasn't sure how to answer. Should I take him to task for his ignorance, ask where he learned the word "fairies," explain the development of sexuality and gender preference? I punted. "What do you mean?"

"Are there ferries from San Francisco to Tiburon?"

Relieved I had misunderstood the question, I said I was pretty sure there were. "Why?"

"Nothing. Just wondered."

It seemed strange, this sudden interest in ferries. There was no context for the question, but I knew better than to push a thirteen-year-old boy. I let it go, but I didn't forget it.

We packed up and left at 4 p.m. Then, at 5 p.m., "What time does the last ferry leave San Francisco?"

"I have no idea. Why do you care?"

"Just wondered."

At 6:00 p.m., "What time does the last ferry arrive in Tiburon?"

By now, I knew something was wrong. I pushed harder to find out what.

He finally confessed, "You're not allowed to drop us off at the market. You have to drop us off at the highway, and we have to take the bus home. Or we could take the ferry and take the bus home. You're not supposed to drive us closer than the highway."

I was aghast. "That's crazy. I'm not going to do that. I'm going to take you home or let you off at the shopping center. It's already crazy not to take you all the way home."

"But she said we have to take the bus." He was clearly worried he would get in trouble.

"I'm not going to do that."

"Do you know what time the last bus leaves San Francisco?"

"I don't, and it doesn't matter. I'm taking you to Belvedere. I'm not letting you off at the freeway." I got busy talking about something else to hide how upset I was.

I was furious that Daniel had to contort himself to meet bizarre ultimatums. I realized Daniel's anxiety had been a background drumbeat the whole weekend, inaudible to the rest of us. Preoccupied, alone, his anxiety leaked out in small questions all day long. I thought we were enjoying the beach and each other, but he wasn't. He was trying to figure out how to maneuver in a crazy world where he could please no one.

We drove on in silence. We had been divorced eleven years! Why a new rule now? Alan said nothing, allowing his brother to do the dirty deed. I turned east off 101 North to Belvedere. As we pulled into the town center, Daniel's sigh from the back seat was palpable, physical, and enveloped the front. I started to turn around to inquire when I saw a bus pulling out. The gods were providing him with a cover story. He might have to lie, but at least he had a story that fit the bus schedule.

CHAPTER 45

....

September–November 1981

The following weekend, my old friend Susie, whose sons were in Alan's Boy Scout troop, called me. "You're coming to Court of Honor next Thursday, aren't you?"

"No," I reply. "I don't know anything about it."

"Hasn't Alan told you? He's being inducted as an Eagle Scout of Troop 23. I'm surprised you don't know."

Court of Honor! Boy Scouts? I had no idea. And there's a ceremony? Parents were invited? It was a blow to my belly to know that another mother—a relative stranger to Alan—knew more about Alan than I did.

I didn't let myself cry. I modulated my voice, erasing tears from its timbre, and calmly answered, "No, he doesn't tell me much of anything. I'd love to know anything you could tell me because I won't hear it from him." I felt humiliated begging a stranger to tell me news of my own child, making public how excluded I was.

"Well, he's a real leader in the troop. He's doing well in scouts, and the other boys really respect him."

Any tiny drop about my son made me conscious of the vastness of the missing ocean.

"You really should come. It's Thursday night at seven."

"Susie. I'd love nothing more than to come, but Walt and Nora wouldn't allow it. I can't."

"What do you mean, 'Wouldn't allow it?' You're his mother!"

"I know, but things are so awful between us that they would just get upset. Trust me, it wouldn't work."

"You should be there. Come as my guest. They can't tell me who I can bring and who I can't."

"Susie . . . it would be wonderful to be there, but I don't know. . . ." I desperately wanted to accept her invitation but knew it would mean trouble. For a moment, I indulged the sweet pleasure of imagining I could maneuver through their rules and actually be present at an important ceremony in my son's life, like an untraced airplane, covertly coming in below their radar screen.

"Of course, you can come," she said definitively. "There will be no more questions about it. You'll be my guest."

"Well . . ." I wanted to be convinced it could work. My mind went into overdrive. How to pull it off? If I just showed up unannounced, that would be unfair to Alan. If I let him know I planned to come, it would open many possibilities for torment. I had to be impeccable in my dealings with my sons so that ultimately, they could figure out that the complaints against me were groundless. I reached the obvious conclusion, even though I wanted to avoid it.

"I'd have to call Alan and let him know I'm coming, so that my presence there would not a surprise to him."

"Just call and tell him that I've invited you. I think he has to give a little speech. I was really impressed with him last June at the previous ceremony."

I knew it was an uphill battle, but I decided to enter the fray. I hung up and drew in a deep breath. I already knew it would take me days to recover; I worried how long it would take Alan to regain his equilibrium.

I called Alan. Unlike other times, he answered. "I talked to Sam's mom today, and she told me about your Court of Honor coming up next Thursday."

"Yeah."

I forged ahead. I hadn't really expected any help from the other end of the line. "She invited me to come as her guest, and I just wanted to let you know that she'd done that, and I'd accepted. I didn't want my presence there to be a surprise to you, so I'm letting you know."

Silence.

I talked a bit more; Alan responded with monosyllables. He sounded tight and uncertain. Finally, we hung up.

I breathed a sigh of relief that the deed was done. I'd announced it; Alan knew I was going. For Alan, however, the deed had just begun; he now needed to inform his dad. He was trapped—a mother who announced she was going to be a mother and a father who insisted she was not.

Three days later, my phone rang.

"Kay?" There was a strangled, small voice at the other end of the line.

"Yes," I answered hesitantly. I had no idea who was calling.

With difficulty, she said, "It's Susie." I realized she was crying. "I know I invited you to the Court of Honor as my guest, but . . ." She began crying again, and it took a minute for her to continue. "I'm going to have to withdraw the invitation."

I felt myself go cold. "Susie, what happened?"

"I hate to do this, but Walt called me, furious. He said Alan did not want you to come, and Alan had made that very clear to you, but you were intrusive and pushy and did not pay attention to Alan's desires. Alan wants nothing to do with you, but you won't listen."

I almost started crying from frustration. I felt impotent. It was so untrue! Alan had to fully support his father at his house, but Alan was different when he was with me. Mostly, he liked me, he touched me, he talked to me. We baked cookies, went to the movies, read stories. He was a normal kid who sometimes got mad at his mom and sometimes loved her. There was no way he would not want me at his Court of Honor except that his own survival was at stake. Now, in addition to hurting his sons, Walt was hurting my innocent friend.

"Walt said you had an affair, and he questioned your mental balance, said that you couldn't be allowed at a Boy Scout meeting. He was so intimidating."

"Oh, Susie, I'm so sorry. I didn't mean for this to happen."

"Then two hours later, Nora called and just started yelling at me, asking me how dare I invite you. You were dangerous to the children and how could I be so irresponsible as to invite you to a Court of Honor. You were not welcome there, and I should know that."

She paused to catch her breath. "I was being given lists of what you did wrong," she continued. "They were the stable parents doing well by the kids, and you weren't part of the picture. You were mentally unbalanced."

"Oh Susie, I'm sorry. I'm mortified. I didn't mean for you to be caught in this maelstrom."

"I'm sorry to withdraw my invitation, but I can't do it." She breaks down crying again. "They scared me."

It was new information to me that they said I was "dangerous" and "mentally unbalanced," but I wasn't surprised. I felt like a leper, bringing destruction on those who were kind to me.

I sent Susie flowers. Maybe I *should* just step out of my sons' lives, so they wouldn't be forced to deny me, and then carry the guilt of doing so. Maybe I should just give up and see them when they're eighteen.

CHAPTER 46

....

March 1982

After this incident, Walter pivoted again. For years, he had insisted I deal only with him about visitation. Suddenly, with Daniel and Alan at ages thirteen and fifteen, Walt told me I should deal directly with them, and I should never call either Walt or Nora again.

The boys said, "They say that after we're eighteen, luckily, they'll never have to deal with you."

But even when the boys agreed to see me, Walt helped them change their minds. They were enthusiastic about a Backpackers weekend we had planned together, but after a weekend with Walter, they no longer wanted to go. Walt canceled our visitation weekend because Alan had an event that required dress-up clothes, and I could not be trusted with his good clothing because of incidents years ago.

I encouraged Alan to bring their visiting German high school friend on visitation weekend so the two of them could explore Berkeley. Nope. Walt canceled my visitation. He wrote me, "Her parents are close personal friends. I won't risk the embarrassment of your pulling stunts in front of an outsider as you did earlier, like when you said, 'All I want is fifteen fucking minutes of your time.'"[1]

242

For any given weekend, it wasn't worth the money, time, aggravation, and escalation to start legal action to enforce my visitation arrangements. At best, I would end up with a piece of paper that was as toothless as the paper I had now.

Visitation degenerated to almost nothing. In 130 days, almost five months (from January to mid-May 1982), I saw the boys a total of six days and two school-night dinners.

Finally, *finally*, a scheduled visitation weekend with the boys actually came to pass, and we spent the weekend with our college-age cousins, Abby and Sam.

Luckily, when the cousins proposed the Yosemite trip, it fell on a weekend already planned for visitation. I could accept without creating an uproar. I convinced Alan and Dan that spending time in Yosemite with cousins was worth not accepting fancier alternatives from their father.

After seven hours of driving, we arrived around midnight at Yosemite Lodge. To pick up the boys, I had driven for an hour in rush hour traffic away from Yosemite. Once I collected the boys, I fought rush hour traffic back to where I had started, and then onward another five hours. I had accepted that Walt would never make things easy for me.

When we arrived, I released myself gingerly, forcing every creaking joint to move, one limb at a time. Abby and Sam, who'd already checked into their rooms, greeted us, and then we all headed for bed and sleep.

Saturday was crisp, sunny, and gorgeous. Always a mother, I'd brought bags of food and a cooler with milk, orange juice, and enough cereal and snacks for everybody. None of us had extra money, so we ate a breakfast of Cheerios and milk in our Sierra Club cups in our motel room. Then the day awaited us, with all of Yosemite before us. We obtained trail maps, and figured out our plan. We decided to conquer Bridal Veil Falls first.

What a relief to be a five-some. Abby and Sam were normal people and treated Alan and Dan like normal people, too. They asked Alan and Daniel questions about school, sports, and friends. Alan and Dan answered, as if they had tongues and lives. Abby and Sam treated me as a normal person, too. They knew how to laugh, and they were young, gorgeous, and exuberant. No freighted, hidden agendas, just interest in each other with good-natured teasing, leg-pulling, and fun. Balm for my soul.

We figured out where to hike, packed a lunch, and made decisions together. We didn't talk about who should live where, why I should be forced to use the back door, or the punishment meted out to Alan and Daniel if I was ten minutes early or five minutes late for pickup. My sons and I fell from our strained lives into an oasis of comfortable, banal normalcy. It was as if we'd dropped onto a foreign planet.

We hiked all day long. By evening, we were pooped. We ate in the cafeteria and then hung out in our motel room together, playing games. Alan and Daniel, newcomers to backgammon, learned to play under the tutelage of the college coed experts. I had brought Monopoly; we built hotels on Park Place and charged beaucoup bucks for landing on the Reading Railroad. Of course, we accused the banker of cheating. How sweet it was to simply be with my thirteen- and fifteen-year-old sons. I might as well have tried to fly as to have created such an evening on my own. I sent a silent prayer of thanks to my father for having such a terrific family, two generations removed from these cousins. Finally, we all said good night and fell into bed.

Sunday morning, while Alan and Daniel still slept, I savored reading in bed. I was in no hurry to start the day. Last night, we had agreed we would meet up whenever we all awakened. No one had knocked. It was nice to have Daniel and Alan sleeping on the bed next to me, snoring gently, feeling the unselfconscious intimacy of a family. I would have been happy to stay sequestered all morning.

Even though there was emotional tension in the triangle with my sons, we had an easy physicality. We were able to maneuver dressing, undressing, and brushing our teeth with fluidity and no embarrassment. Maybe I still carried the practical outlook bred into the farmers of my father's generation; maybe it was because they grew up backpacking with all of us sleeping together.

My reverie inside the cocoon of our room in Yosemite Village came to an abrupt end with a knock on the door. Dan and Alan had begun to stir, but no coherent English had flowed among us. I grabbed my robe and answered the door.

I let Abby and Sam into the room.

"Have you looked outside?" Abby asked.

"No," I answered.

Alan and Dan, fully awake now, were slowly becoming human. I pulled aside the curtain and was astonished to see nothing but white. It was snowing—wet, obese flakes.

"Good heavens! Come look!" I called to Alan and Daniel.

They came to the window; we all looked out, dumbfounded. It was hard to integrate what had happened while we slept, with no forewarning other than the temperature turning colder last night. In a few short hours, the outlook of the world had changed. The snow was deep and growing deeper by the minute.

The white wonderland of Sunday morning surrounded us.

Our plan had been a short morning hike, but, within minutes, it was clear no one would be hiking today. We dressed, ate some breakfast, and went to find out what was possible in this beauty of white. We dawdled on the wooden bridge nearby, and then erupted into a joyous snowball fight.

Then, my apprehension set in. It was clear our plan to leave after lunch was unlikely to work. We went to the ranger station to find out about road conditions. All the roads in and out of Yosemite were closed until further notice and would probably be closed all day. There would be another report at 2 p.m., but the likelihood of them opening today was small, and they might not even open tomorrow. It depended on the storm.

Boom. The guillotine dropped its axe. No alternatives, no questions, just reality. Just straight facts. We were stranded. Not a bad place to be stranded, and great people to be stranded with, but it meant we had to change plans. Walt and Nora did not like changes. An unexpected snowstorm was not going to be well received.

The frivolity of the day was gone. I tensed up. With civil people, it would have been a simple task. A phone call to say we were snowed in, and we would be in touch as our plans developed. With Walt and Nora, it would be a battle. Their tendrils were already creeping in to spoil this day. No matter what we did, no matter how careful we were, no matter what we said or how we said it, we would not have done it right.

"We're going to have to call your dad and Nora to tell them that we're snowed in, and you guys won't be home at six."

It was like a corpse—a smelly, awful corpse—had just plopped itself into the room.

They were somber. I was somber. Silence.

Abby and Sam were puzzled. Sam, a rational engineer, said, "Well, just call and say we were snowed in, and you can't get them home today." That seemed simple.

None of us responded.

"What's the big deal? You can miss a day of school and survive. Do you have any important tests?"

How to explain? They hadn't yet seen this bizarre labyrinth of rules that we negotiated every day, rules that created invisible barriers like the one we just smashed into headlong and with force.

"That would make sense, but it won't work." I was suddenly weary, knowing there was no hope of explaining because there *was* no explanation. Only Alan, Daniel, and I understood what we faced. Abby and Sam, like anthropologists coming into a foreign culture, were trying to make sense of rituals created to appease invisible forces, forces that stimulated animal fear and paralyzed bodies.

Daniel, Alan, and I had become frozen, like mummies.

CHAPTER 47

....

March 1982

I turned to Alan and Dan. "I think I should be the one to call. There's going to be trouble, and I'm the one they should get mad at. You shouldn't have to deal with their anger." As the adult, part of my job was to protect my children. I was ready to take the punches.

Silence.

We all knew that I had been told never to have contact with Walter and Nora again.

We were now physically in Yosemite, but emotionally in the Twilight Zone of living with Walt and Nora's Kafkaesque rules.

If Alan made the call, he was in trouble. If Daniel called, he was in trouble. If I called, both Alan and Daniel were in trouble. It was a constant gamble. In which direction did the least harm lie? Who should call?

They both convinced me their lives would be worse if I called. They agreed one of them should do it. I hesitated. They pleaded with me. Their fear was palpable. A routine phone call turned into a bomb threat. I was paralyzed with indecision because there *was* no good answer, no way to protect my boys from this fear.

Our cousin Sam chimed in. "I'll make the call." We all laughed in relief at the ludicrous suggestion.

Why the hell not? Give him the hot potato!

Dan got nervous that Sam might actually do it. "Sam can't call. They don't know who he is."

Daniel liked things to be safe, and a stranger calling wasn't safe. "Then I'll call," I said.

"No, one of us has to call," Daniel declared.

I capitulated.

Now it was the same fear, but a different question. Which boy should call? Alan or Daniel? Alan, the point person in this battle for existence, dialed their number, and we all stopped breathing.

"Dad? It's Alan."

We're all relieved that Walt answered the phone and not Nora. "We're in Yosemite, and there was a big snowstorm. The roads are all closed, and we probably won't be able to get home today."

I whispered loudly to Alan, "Tell him we'll call as soon as we have any news."

"We'll call as soon as we have any news." I, too, put words into his mouth.

After a short interchange, Alan hung up. I was flooded with relief. It wasn't too bad. Just a short, informational call. No hanging bodies.

We whiled away the afternoon. We tried another short walk, but there was more snow and no spirit. Abby and Sam found relief away from us for a while. We were not a fun gang anymore.

When Abby and Sam returned, we went over to the ranger station again. The verdict: No chance of leaving today. The cars that had attempted to leave were returning. Many cars were stuck on the highway. We were there for the night.

Whose turn now? Daniel got to step out of the shadows and into the spotlight. It was not fair to make Alan do it all the time.

We dialed and waited again. "Hi. This is Daniel."

We held our breath while we figured out who was at the other end of the line. Somehow, we knew it was Nora.

"All the roads are closed, and we can't leave." He stated the facts, just the facts, ma'am. He was quiet and listened. I had prepped him on his lines. "We'll call again as soon as we know when we can leave."

He listened. "Okay. Bye."

He turned to us, covering his anxiety with a semi-smirk. "She said I am to tell you we have to be home tomorrow night at 6:30 p.m." I never knew about her next instruction: I was to have fed them dinner.

I'm startled. "We don't know if we can even leave tomorrow. What do you mean?"

Dan said, "How do I know? I'm just telling you what she said."

There was no point in pushing Daniel. He was trying to quiet two beasts with one hand. I backed off. I knew that with California storms, the worst was likely over and it should be clear tomorrow. I was sure we could get chains, but we still didn't know the conditions of the highways, or if we would even be able to leave. I thought about calling back to clarify that we didn't know what was possible for tomorrow.

"We have no idea if we can get out at all. Should we call her back?" The question hung in the air. Obviously, no one wanted to call back. And to say what? What we've already said?

"There's nothing more to say. Let's wait." I answered my own question. They both had brought some books and homework and retreated to the safety and isolation of schoolwork. I tried to read. We listened to the local highway patrol bulletins on the radio. They reported that driving conditions were not safe: a bus was across the road, a tree fell on a VW, three of the four roads were closed entirely, cars were piled up, and people who had been on the road for four hours were returning to Yosemite.

The five of us ate whatever leftover scraps we could find for dinner. We desultorily played more cards. Alan sat glumly on the bed and tried paying attention. Daniel withdrew and wouldn't talk to anybody. What could have been a fun day of hooky, an unplanned interlude reveling in found time ended in involuted irritation and withdrawal.

Monday dawned cloudy but clear. The storm was over, and we could leave. I found a place to buy chains and paid to have them put on the car. We bid our farewells and drove headlong into our isolation and fear.

Having a clear task provided traction for my brain to come online. I realized I couldn't deliver the boys at 6:30 p.m.! As part of my job, I had scheduled dinner tonight with sixteen resident hall assistants. I couldn't cancel it. I didn't want to cancel it. I wouldn't cancel it.

How in the hell were we going to tell Nora? One more hurdle to negotiate. I took a deep breath and started to explain. "Boys, remember that I'm working with the resident hall assistants?" I asked.

"Yeah."

"I have a dinner with all of the Unit II RAs tonight. I hadn't thought about it until now. You've met some of them when they were at the house last fall after my class. Remember?"

They grunted assent. We were back to our unstable triangle— mom of good cheer and teenage sons of sullen autonomy.

"I can't stand up the whole group, so I can take you home before the dinner, which would mean getting you home around three or four. Or you could go to the dorms with me for dinner. Or you could stay home and watch TV while I go to the dorms and I could take you to Belvedere after the dinner and probably have you home by 8:30. What do you think?"

Alan responded, "I'm tired. I want to go straight to Belvedere from here."

"Either way is okay with me. What do you think, Dan?"

Daniel generally followed his older brother's lead. "Yeah. Me, too," Daniel answered.

They had been cooped up in a hotel room, and then a car, and I understood their need to get home and settled.

"Well, then, we have to let them know. Daniel called last time; Alan, it's your turn this time. We'll call from Escalante. My guess is that we'll have you home sometime around three. Does that sound okay?"

Sullen grunts of assent.

"I don't know about traffic, so it's hard to be more specific. I know they will want an exact time. If we say between three and four, do you think that will be okay?"

Grunts.

"Does that mean yes or no?"

"It's okay," they each mumbled.

"Alan, do you think you can say between three and four?"

With a defeated sigh, Alan said, "I guess so."

CHAPTER 48

....

March–May 1982

We were trapped once again between normal life and an Alice-in-Wonderland reality. Driving from Escalante to Belvedere, Alan knew that I couldn't predict an exact arrival time, yet violating their expectation of precision would give them one more chance to yell at Alan about how irresponsible I was. He would hang his head and hear it because speaking up would not be a good strategy. Alan's effort to live within both realities was making him less and less eager to expand into possibilities.

We stopped in Escalante. He made the call. He came back to the car and said that Nora wasn't home, but he left a message with a workman. I suddenly got worried that no one would be home when we arrived. It wasn't an issue of safety. They could take care of themselves. But what if they couldn't get in and had to wait outside? They were tired, dirty, and restless. I knew Alan had track practice after school and normally didn't get home till later. I wasn't sure about Daniel.

"Dan, what time do you normally get home from school?"

"Around three fifteen."

"So, you don't think it will be a problem if you get home around three, since that's the time you usually get home?"

"I don't know." He suddenly had no brains when it came to making a decision involving Nora.

"Since she said 6:30, she probably won't like it, but it should be all right since that's when you usually get home. If she's not there, is there a way to get in? Do you have a key?"

"I usually have a key, but I didn't bring it with me. But there's a hidden key we can use. Nora just doesn't like us to use it because we might set off the alarm."

"Well, if she's not home, I guess you'll just have to use it and hope you don't set off the alarm. There's not much we can do about it now."

Silence.

From Escalante onward, there was nothing but glum quiet. They didn't even argue over what music station to listen to. I would have preferred a little rebellion. I was ready and willing to tolerate KROK if it would have revived some life in the car. I tried to get a conversation going—any conversation would do.

I tried.

No luck.

I joined the doleful quiet. I chose the station, and we listened to classical music.

Finally, we arrived in Belvedere. They assured me they were okay and could get into the house. Breaking the rule, I left them at the gate instead of the market. They walked down the steps into oblivion.

I had no idea if they got in the house, how they got into the house, if Nora was there, or how much of an explosion there was. My only option was the one I took. I drove off to the dinner with the RAs.

Two days later, a letter from Walt arrived. Almost as soon as I started reading it, my brain stopped working. I let it fall to my lap and slumped in the chair.

"You may not see the boys in April. Two aspects of the way in which you conducted your visit with Alan and Daniel this past weekend is unacceptable: the lack of chains resulted in your not being able to bring the boys home on time. As you know, they both missed a day of school. Perhaps your negligence or oversight regarding the chains can be overlooked. Your unilaterally changing the time of their return cannot be overlooked. Dan told you that we expected them home after having dinner and at 6:30 p.m., Monday."[1]

I was weary, numb, and outraged by the preemptive tone, the assumption of my motives, and the projected, erroneous rationales for my decisions.

He concluded, "As a result of your performance this weekend, and in the hope that this action will cause you to think in the future and mutually consult, you will not be able to see the boys in April."

My stomach tightened at the thought, but I knew I had to fight this. I could not allow Walt to obliterate my legal visitation rights, ignore the court order, and treat me as if I were his adolescent child who missed curfew so he got to withhold my privileges. I must stand up for myself and for my sons' right to have a mother, even if my sons hated me for it, and even if it cost me money I didn't have.

I went for broke and filed for custody on April 29, 1982.[2] A hearing was scheduled for July 12. The opening legal salvo alone ate up two-thirds of a month's income, with no guarantee of success.

I had no way to talk to my sons before I filed, so I used what was available to me. I wrote them a letter of explanation (uncertain Walt and Nora would even show it to them), and told them I counted on seeing them in a month on Memorial Day with the Backpackers. Perhaps in that loving environment, I could talk to them about what was going on.

In my filing, I stated my bald truth. I believed it was in my children's best interests that I had custody of them, "so that the children can have a healthy, close relationship with both of their parents. I am willing to try to mediate this with either the conciliation court or mutually acceptable private mediation."

I knew my sons didn't want to live with me. I knew it was a losing battle, almost as foolish as Don Quixote and his windmills. I knew their lives and friends were in Belvedere. Alan was a sophomore in high school, Daniel a freshman. Moving to live with me would be disruptive and unlikely to happen.

Walt responded, saying it was I, not he, who was causing the problems. I was alienating them by going to school open house, swearing at them, and threatening court action if they didn't do what I wanted. He admonished me. "If you force them to do what they don't want to do, [it] will only cause your relationship to deteriorate further."[3]

Once the boys knew I'd started a court hearing, they refused to come on the Backpackers trip. They protested.

"I feel tricked," said Alan.

"I feel tricked," said Daniel.

Two boys, one response.

"You've ruined the summer."

"I won't see you till this is over."

"I don't want to see you just because the court says I have to."

"I'm furious at the way you did it." (As if there were a "right" way.)

I despaired. I feared I'd alienated them forever. There was nowhere to turn, no solace, no reassurance. Only their refusal to deal with me remained.

Walter's mid-March temper tantrum hijacked my life and my money. My lawyer had repeated contact with Walt, me, or opposing counsel, and I paid for each interaction. My lawyer billed me for eleven contacts in March, fourteen in April, and twenty in May. Some days had multiple legal interactions within a single day.

No amount of money, no legal document, no court hearing seemed to be able to offer a sane solution.

In June, I paid my lawyer my total monthly income less $58.

CHAPTER 49

·······················

June–September 1982

My mother was hospitalized in Arizona. There was no real diagnosis—neuropathy in her legs, mini-strokes, old age. My oldest sister, Laurel, had been estranged from my mother for six years, and my middle sister, Sarah, lived in Costa Rica.[1] My mother needed help, and I was it.

In April, I had just filed for custody. In the middle of lawyer appointments, I flew to Arizona in June. Our court date wasn't until July. When I arrived at the hospital and announced myself to the attending physician, he asked, "Are you Kay Morgan?"

I was startled at the use of my married name, which I hadn't used for sixteen years. Clearly, my mother was still holding onto it. I stammered a bit, then decided it was not worth correcting him.

"Yes. I wanted to check on how she's doing."

"She's ready for discharge if adequate accommodations can be made for her."

This was not the first time I had gone to her rescue. When she moved from Ft. Worth to San Antonio, I drove her. A few years later, when she had worn out her welcome in San Antonio, I drove her to Tucson. My mother found something wrong with wherever she was—the food, the people, the location, the weather. After she had alienated all her friends, her escape valve was to move.

After I got my mother out of the hospital—and between multiple calls to my lawyer to prepare for the impending court date—I spent three days arranging home care and getting her safely settled. When I left, her best friend of ten years drove me to the airport.

"I knew she had two daughters. I never knew about you."

I was stunned. I had no response. I stared at the highway while his words rolled around in my brain. How could he not know mom had a third daughter? How could she erase my existence so casually?

I was the ghost child to my mother.

I was the ghost mother to my sons.

For four months, I had had almost no contact with my children. At least my legal motion propelled us into conciliation court, where Walter was forced into mediation with me.

Walt's lawyer confirmed that Walt would meet with the social worker but used the communication to assert Walt's lie. "Mr. Morgan is not influencing his sons in their desire or lack of desire to see their mother. Mr. Morgan has never attempted to intervene or subvert Ms. Harrington's visitation with her sons."[2]

In June, in individual appointments, each of us—Walter, Nora, Alan, Daniel, and I—met with Linda Corcoran, our social worker.

Subsequently, Walter and I met with her together.

The judge could force Walt to be in the same room with me, but the judge could not make him look at me nor make him talk directly to me. Walt did neither, doing his best to make me invisible.

Ms. Corcoran had our history. She knew Walter was trying to eliminate me from my sons' lives. After much discussion and many examples, she asked Walt, "How do you plan to make sure the children maintain a relationship with their mother?"

With his characteristic smirk, he answered, "It may be heresy to say, but some children have a parent die, and they do just fine. I'm not sure the boys need a relationship with Kay."

I was stunned. I realized Walter would be his own worst witness without me saying a word.

I looked at her.

She looked at me.

Both of us were speechless in this drama. Walt seemed able to deny the reality that a child needed his mother, that a child would be harmed by her absence.

The social worker's report to the court stated, "The head of Family Court Services, Linda Corcoran, was unable to suggest a solution, and Respondent (Walter Morgan) was unwilling to participate in further mediation with Petitioner (Kay Harrington)."[3]

From my lawyer, I heard hand-me-down words from the social worker's report.

"Kay should back off. Those kids really don't want to see her."

The words rang in my ears, ping-ponging around my brain. Now what? Where was there to turn?

Even the social worker confirmed I was in the wrong. If that was what she said, maybe I *should* give up. Let them live their happy lives without me. I'd show up again when they were eighteen—or maybe not. It was not worth it anymore, this constant fighting to try to make a place for myself. If they didn't care, I didn't care, either. Let them eat dirt.

The social worker's notes, as told to me by my lawyer, stated the following. "She says she wants time, but then she brings a friend. She wants to talk about their problems, but they don't do anything with her. With their father, they go fishing, skiing, and sailing. They are not enthused. They complain about *having* to go. They want input."

I didn't like to fish, I didn't know how to sail, and I didn't have the money to ski. I brought a friend to help lighten the heaviness and help make conversation happen. A friend was a witness and helped me know I was not crazy. I talked about our problems because I wanted them to see it didn't have to be this way.

The social worker said the situation had gone on so long that the only thing to do was let the boys have time to grow up.

And then, at least there was a touch of frosting. In the second-hand recounting, my lawyer added some first-hand words. "The social worker hinted that she didn't like Nora."

I comforted myself with the thought that maybe the social worker didn't actually think I was in the wrong; maybe she knew that me pushing Walter just brought forth fire and fury. And maybe she knew that me pushing adolescent boys was counterproductive.

However, I refused to slink away.

I had played my ace-in-the-hole and came up with nothing. I had to do *something*.

Late June, even though she had "no active role in the matter," Mrs. Corcoran offered to meet with our lawyers in an effort to keep us out of court. We let go of the July court date.

They all met. Mrs. Corcoran was unable to find a solution, and Walt was unwilling to participate in further mediation.

Back to the court system. Walt filed his proposal with the court. His solution was to lessen my visitation to once a month and to keep the standing custody order of 1978.

Neither my lawyer nor I was happy with Walt's proposal. Not only had he violated the 1978 order multiple times, I did not want to lessen my visitation. My lawyer advised me to seek a change of venue, to get us into Alameda County so we could have access to the renowned family court counselor, Elizabeth Crocker, who had a reputation for solving tangled, unsolvable problems in custody cases. It was a slender thread, but it was all I had.

On August 6, I filed for a change of venue and got a Sept. 7 court date. I made the argument that neither of us had lived or worked in Contra Costa County for many years. We were likely to need ongoing mediation, and Alameda County was where Walt worked, where I lived, and where both our lawyers practiced.

Walt responded. "This motion to change venue appears to be a thinly disguised attempt to forum shop. For this reason alone, I believe it to be meritless. This is an abuse of the judicial system and a misuse of taxpayers' money."

If a change of venue were to be made, he requested it be to Marin County. We each had to include a list of witnesses—people who could vouch for our good parenting. It rattled my nerves to ask my friends to be on such a list; it rattled my nerves to read his list and wonder who these people were and what would they say.

Our court hearing was scheduled Sept. 7, 1982. Only our lawyers appeared to make the argument for change of venue.

On September 15, the judge ruled for Marin County.

Foiled again. But still costly in money and time. My lawyer billed me for calls to and from the social worker, conciliation court, opposing counsel, and me. Fifteen contacts in June, ten in July, and some were multiple contacts on the same day.

Because the case was transferring jurisdictions, my lawyer advised I would be better represented by a Marin County lawyer who knew the ins and outs of the local judges. After nearly ten years of working with a lawyer whom I trusted and who knew my case, another loss.

To secure the new lawyer's services, I paid a $3,000 retainer. Two months of my income in order—*maybe*—to have access to my sons.

I no longer felt like dying, but I was defeated and tired. I was tired of having a body with cravings and weight issues, and I was tired of fighting. I couldn't give up, but I didn't see a path to peace.

Since weekend visitations had evaporated, I pushed for my legally sanctioned, twice-a-month, mid-week dinners. In four months, I managed to get only two dinners.

I honked. They came up and got in the car.

"Where do you want to go?" I knew it would be pizza, but I asked anyway. I tried starting a conversation. I asked about their lives. I struck out, so I talked about mine. That went nowhere.

Silence. It was painful wanting to connect, not knowing how to make it happen, having all of us sit in silence. I knew almost nothing of their worlds. I was eager—no, I was *needy* to know more. Even though I felt left out, I didn't want to appear as needy as I felt. Their indifference increased my neediness. I knew it was not their job to take care of me, but I couldn't stop myself from asking questions. I defended myself to myself. *Isn't it the mother's job to go the extra mile, extend herself, and make conversation?* They had to have felt my pleading subtext, *Please include me in your lives!*

Part of the trouble was that I didn't know what my job was anymore. It had become a vague line. Were they sullen because they were teenagers? Were they sullen because I was forcing them to see me when I knew they didn't want to? Had they simply become unavailable, sour people, so different from the open-hearted boys I'd raised? It was hard to know.

They were holed up in their safety. *Talk about nothing, reveal nothing, stay out of trouble.*

When was it my job to take the burden? When could I expect them to be responsible for their own behavior? Age fourteen? Fifteen? Maybe thirty?

It made me sick how perky I tried being. I didn't want to break down in tears in front of them at Milano's. Then I *would* embarrass them and be giving them evidence to support Nora's claim that I was unstable.

I hated these pizza dinners. I hated the driving. I hated the forced conversation. I hated their withholding. I hated them. I hated me. I hated my false self.

But I knew I had to keep forcing them to see me. If I allowed them not to see me, I would lose them forever. Better to insist on face time, no matter how awful, than to give up. I knew a court order meant nothing; my only leverage was my courage and perseverance. I had heard of many men who had given up in such circumstances and said, "I'll see you when you're eighteen." Many men seemed capable of drawing a line; most mothers seemed to move the line to benefit the child.

Over the pepperoni, yet again, I considered giving up. As much as I wanted to, I knew I couldn't. I knew I wouldn't.

But I longed to.

Just. Give. Up.

I wanted to run away.

CHAPTER 50

....

June 1982–June 1991

During the summer of the custody proceedings, a new job fell in my lap—an offer to work for an executive search firm. With no risk, I could take a three-month summer leave from the counseling center to test drive the new job. I was intrigued. I could meet new people, travel all over the United States, yet be home on weekends to be available to my children, *if* they were available to me. It sounded glamorous, exciting, and like a good antidote to my children's absence.

I accepted and stuck my toe into the waters of the corporate world.

In the fall, I left the security of a civil service job at the counseling center, closed my private psychotherapy practice of ten years, and opted for a new adventure.

I became the secret sauce for the executive search firm. They used my PhD-validated psychological profiles of C-Suite job candidates to distinguish their firm from other head-hunting firms. In the early 80s, I met and helped populate the early movers and shakers of Silicon Valley. Only hindsight helped me recognize the history-making epoch I was part of.

I wore high heels. I wore makeup. I traveled at least every other week, sometimes hitting two or three cities in one day. I met high-powered, interesting men, and a smattering of women.

I routinely had breakfast at Rickey's in Palo Alto, except when I was interviewing candidates who did not want to be seen in public with a recognizable headhunter, especially people from Apple. I met with people on Sand Hill Road. I met the scientist who developed the first optical scanning technology, I met the man who first commercialized fiber optics, I met CEOs of Fortune 100 companies. I met the up-and-comers, and those who had arrived. I asked about their work histories, personal lives, goals, management styles. I got tired of hearing, "I'm tough, but fair."

I did not shrink from power showdowns. One evening over drinks, I asked a particularly slippery man, "Tell me about your weaknesses."

"I can't really say. I'm tough but fair."

"What do you mean? Can you give me an example?"

"Oh . . . I don't know. I'd have to think about that."

I stayed silent, staring him down, not rescuing him.

He fumbled. "You'd have to ask others."

"If I were to ask others, what do you think they'd say?"

"That would take me some time . . . "

"I have time."

I looked at him expectantly, slowly eating one peanut at a time, while I waited for an answer. Only I knew that whatever he said now no longer mattered; he had lost me by the first peanut.

The airline loyalty programs were new. I earned miles I could use personally. My salary had not increased significantly, but suddenly I felt rich with possibilities. I flew to the Caribbean to get certified to scuba dive. It was a lonely trip. I spent days waiting out bad weather, but finally I got to dive—and had an exhilarating ride on a fast, underwater current, careening through a tunnel. It was a new life to be able to have fun, to pursue what I wanted, and not constantly be responding to others' needs. It was heady to be in the power position with big-deal men instead of on the losing end in court with one big-deal man.

I flew first class, stayed in first class hotels, and met first class people. I had started piano lessons and managed to find darkened ballrooms where I could practice. At the Carlyle Hotel in New York City, an employee helped me find a piano in an unused ballroom. Industriously, I practiced my scales, my chord progressions, and my nascent tune.

As I found my way out, making a U-turn through rooms, I exited through a filigreed room filled with ladies who lunched. I was mortified to realize the French doors next to their shrimp salads were the same, porous French doors next to my scale-practicing piano.

At the Waldorf-Astoria, I enjoyed a drink while listening to the pianist, when a uniformed waiter, silver tray and napkin in hand, discreetly approached me.

"Are you Dr. Harrington?"

"Yes."

"There is a call for you. May I show you where you may take it?"

Sought out at the Waldorf! I felt like a movie star. I had arrived!

Men came on to me, and it perked my depleted soul. I indulged in some flirtations but nothing serious. In the nearly ten years I did this job, one man (married, of course) avidly pursued me. I accepted a lunch date. He sent flowers. And then another lunch date. I accepted multiple lunch dates. I was vulnerable enough to succumb to his attentions, and ultimately, we fell in love. Chaste (I had learned something!), we dreamed of being together. On one of my trips, we met in Washington, DC. After months of a growing friendship and intensifying chemistry, we allowed ourselves to make love for the first time. He moved out from his wife. I was hopeful, but he couldn't sustain it. We ended it, both of us heartbroken.

I had made progress. He was not controlling, nor did I allow the fantasy to linger and eat up months and years of my life on a man who wasn't available.

CHAPTER 51

....

August 1983

When Alan was a junior in high school and Daniel, a sophomore, I managed to snag them for a week vacation together. I nabbed a space for three to join a commercial group rafting the Colorado River in the Grand Canyon.

Suddenly, I found myself out of the boat. Thrown every way by the churning water, with the breath knocked out of me, I was scared. Underwater and unable to surface, I started panicking but stopped myself. I could not allow myself to indulge in the luxury of panic. I focused.

The safety drills came back to me. I knew I had to get oriented, figure out which way was down river, and get my feet pointed in that direction to protect my head from hitting rocks. *Don't fight, and the air in your lungs will help you float.*

I had been thrown from the boat in a Class IV rapids. Although scared, I was surprised and thrilled. As we had approached the rapids, the guide had warned us to hold on. I held as tightly as I could, till I was suddenly underwater, fighting for breath.

Having managed to get myself feet first with the current, I finally surfaced. Once floating, I almost relaxed and enjoyed the ride. I was not safe yet, but I didn't think I was going to die, and the frisson of danger was exhilarating. As a water baby, I felt at home.

I floated a long way down river till I washed up into an eddy at the side. The guide maneuvered his raft to fetch me. I was embarrassed and awkward, trying to hoist my uncooperative blubber into the inflatable raft. Alan, sixteen, and Daniel, fourteen, were relieved I was rescued. I was, too. Once safe, my major disappointment was that, with the impact of the rapids, my book went overboard, and I wanted to know how the story ended.

Our group consisted of thirteen people: a young couple without their children, an older couple who weren't in very good shape, two women who had signed up as a lark, the guides, and the father of one of the guides. Everyone got along.

Accustomed to the demanding need to use each minute, I had been restless the first day of the trip, but by the second, I joined the river's indolent pace. I watched the passing scenery, I read *Leaven of Malice* by Robertson Davies, and I paddled hard when we hit small rapids. The biggest luxury was having my meals cooked for me.

At night, we camped out. Since Alan and Dan were skilled backpackers, the camping was easy for us. The three of us made a campsite together, as did the other small groups. We were a unit within a larger group. I liked being a unit with my sons. No one harassed us, no one questioned whether we should be together, no one tried to steal one of them from me, and no one taunted me.

No one knew us except by how we showed up in the present. No past, no future. I liked my kids. I respected their skills. They liked me. I wanted what was best for them. In the Grand Canyon, I was simply their mom. As the thirteen of us got to know each other, we slowly became a larger group.

The last night of the trip, the whole group played charades. All in good humor, we mixed up ages, genders, and family constellations.

"Will you be on my team?" someone called out to me.

I caught a glimpse of Daniel looking at me, wide-eyed, surprised that his mom was chosen . . . was wanted.

Maybe she's not crazy.

I accepted the invitation and shooed Alan and Daniel over to the other team. Alan watched me as the guide made a joke about something, and we all burst out laughing.

People like her!

I hadn't played charades for years, but the energy of the group helped all of us get into the spirit. We wrote clues, put them in a bowl, and then picked randomly at our turn.

After a couple of rounds I heard, "Your turn, Daniel!"

Daniel took the scrap of paper with the phrase he had to act out. He shyly moved his body forward but left his confidence behind. Hesitantly, he stepped before our team and held up two fingers for two syllables. He put his arms up in the air, looking a little awkward.

"Surrender," someone called out.

He lowered his arms a bit.

"Catch."

He bent his forearms in a little, making a circle. Then he moved his body back and forth.

Silence.

He switched it up. He pulled his earlobe for "sounds like." He held his arms in front of him, as if he were on a horse, and lifted up his knees, one after another, each one higher than the last. He moved forward.

Right away. "Prancing."

Big grin. Another ear pull. Now he was back to swaying with his arms at chest height, a dreamy look on his face, shuffling his feet a bit.

"Dancing."

Big smile.

"Yes!"

Daniel's uncertainty disappeared, and his mischievousness grew before our very eyes. He held up one finger. One syllable. He glanced at me with a sly smile, blushing—both embarrassed and excited. He tapped his right buttock.

"Pants."

He tapped his bum again.

"Wallet."

He shook his head and repeated his motion.

"Bottom."

He looked encouragingly toward the guesser.

"Bottoms up?"

Frustrated, he shakes his head. He tapped his tuchus again, motioning to everyone to guess.

He then raised his hand to his face, tapped under his eyes, followed by another tap on his tush.

"Cheek!" Three people called out in unison.

"Dancing cheek to cheek!"

He was triumphant.

At my next turn, my clue was written in Daniel's handwriting. *Leaven of Malice.* What a surprise to find he'd paid any attention at all to my lost book! I acted it out, and Daniel guessed the right answer.

The next—and last—day of the trip, Dan triumphantly found my soggy, wet book in the river, damaged but legible.

The Grand Canyon trip changed the course of our own river. For five years they had been told I was unstable, mean, unreliable, and even dangerous. As they began seeing me through others' eyes, our good-natured boating community helped them reassess "truth."

Books dried out; bonds got rewoven. I learned the end of Robertson Davies's story. I felt hope for our own story.

The ease of the Grand Canyon trip couldn't last. The next time I saw them was another gloomy pizza dinner. Alan and Daniel said, "Dad says you spent our money without asking us."

I assumed Walt needed to dredge up another complaint because he had felt the shift in the boys, or sensed we had a good time on the Grand Canyon trip.

"I did use your money," I answered.

Silence. They didn't know where to go from there. They expected me to be defensive and deny it. Instead, I decided it was time for some truth to be spoken. "I'll tell you how I spent it." Now I had their full attention. No more playing with the napkin or forks.

"Your first year living there, two days before the deposit was due at Sequoia Camp, your dad said that he wouldn't pay for it unless I promised to give him custody of Daniel. I refused. I didn't want Daniel to miss out on camp, so I used some of Daniel's money from my parents to pay for camp. I also used some of your money to pay for our river-rafting trip in the Grand Canyon."

The facts shut them up. Silence.

Money was always on Walt's mind. What I didn't say was the only power Walt understood was money; he believed if he could drain me of money, he could drain me of power.

Two years after our Grand Canyon trip, using Alan as the messenger, Walt demanded I turn over to him the money my parents gave to the boys when they were born. I told Alan that made no sense. His dad had nothing to do with that money.

"I know it makes no sense. But Dad insists."

Alan would be in trouble if I refused. It was not worth fighting, not worth putting Alan in the middle of a fight he understood was about power, not money. I handed over the money that was left.

CHAPTER 52

....

August 1984–May 1985

In the fall of 1984, because Walt had declined their invitation, the Backpackers invited me to their outing on Angel Island. Alan, age seventeen, made heroic efforts to join us. He couldn't drive because his leg was in a cast, caused by shin splints from cross-country running. Using a friend's boat, he arrived like a conquering hero, delighting everybody with his resourcefulness.

Incrementally the shackles were loosening. By slow degrees, Alan let me into his world.

As a junior, he had his first girlfriend—a gem of a girl who helped convince him to give me the book *Fup,* the first Mother's Day present he'd given me since he moved seven years ago.

He included me in the party her family hosted before the Junior Ball. I was ecstatic to meet his friends and see them gorgeous, fluffed up, pleased, awkward, and shy. I was a proud parent with a camera.

Until later.

"Nora found the pictures you took at the party," Alan said when I called about pickup time.

"Yeah?" My anxiety quickly traveled to my nerves. Unconsciously, I white-knuckled the phone, knowing they had hurt him because I was there. I was a leper. Once again.

"She was really upset."

"What did she say?"

"She went to her room crying."

I deliberately loosened my grip on the phone. I was silent, waiting for more.

"She kept saying, 'How could you do this to me, after all I've done for you?'"

It was the line I often heard from my mother. How dare I not make my life revolve around her open wounds? My heart broke for my son. "I'm so sorry. But you know, you did nothing wrong by inviting me to the party."

He was silent. He was the one who had to live with Nora. "She was crying all day and wouldn't talk to me, except to say, 'I don't know how you could have done this. Wait till your father hears about this.'"

"I'm sorry she was trying to make you feel guilty, but you did nothing wrong."

More silence. I was glad he felt safe enough to tell me this secret from their house, but I couldn't embrace him over the phone. I couldn't make it go away. I couldn't be there with him when Walter twisted the knife in further.

"Thank you for telling me. Just remember that no matter what they say, you had a right to invite me to the party. You did nothing wrong." Maybe if I said it dozens of times, he might begin believing it. Maybe a thousand times.

I tried, but I knew nothing penetrated his misery.

They seemed to have struck a bargain in their own minds: If we feed and clothe you, we get to punish you for having a mother.

I faced the forever question: *Is my presence helpful or harmful to my sons? Should I turn down future invitations? After Nora's reaction, will Alan even risk extending a future invitation?*

Another reprieve, with the help of frequent flier miles. The boys and I spent Christmas 1984 together in Milan, Italy, where my sister, Sarah, lived with her two daughters. With no intrusions from Walter or Nora, we were able to have fun.

One day, while my sister worked, my boys, her girls, and I took a day train to Venice and hung around St. Mark's Square. We drank espresso. We walked through the narrow streets. A gondolier pushed us through the Great Canal. All of us bought hats, then posed at the Bridge of Sighs, snapping photos in our new finery. The next day, we all went to Chamonix, France, for a few days of skiing.

Next, we repatriated to our second home: Totana, Spain. Alan was ten when first there; he was now eighteen and off to college in a few months. Our old friends organized parties for us. We sang, we danced, we drank Rioja wine. Alan, blushing, was dragged to the dance floor by a pretty young girl to do a paso doble. Later, it was Dan's turn.

On New Year's Eve, we ate one grape at each stroke of midnight to bring good luck for the upcoming year. We were immersed with each other, survived minor irritations of travel, and returned home happy.

That June, Alan risked extending another invitation to me when he invited me to his regional track meet. I knew he was a star on the team, but I had never been to one of his races before. Not knowing anyone there, I felt awkward, but that didn't dampen my pleasure. Minimal as they were, I savored when the boys allowed the shards of their lives to intersect mine.

Alan led in the mile. The second time around the track, he maintained the lead. He kept it the third time. I yelled for him from the sidelines.

He came in for the home stretch. He was sweating. His face was concentrated. His will was visible in his body, focused on pushing forward. He crossed the finish line, sweat dripping from his face. I snapped a picture as he finished first.

I looked at his face. It had changed. The bones were reshaping themselves, becoming more angular, turning him into a man instead of a boy. I saw him with new eyes. No longer was he a child. He was strong, running, and determined. He was alive. When he was in the incubator, scarcely having the energy to move his four-and-a-half-pound body, I feared he would die. Yet here he was, winning, breathing deeply into those previously-undeveloped lungs, grabbing the high school regional title for the mile.

Alan had the courage to invite me. I belonged. I was his mother.

Both sons went to the East Coast for college, partially to get away from the impossible tug-of-war at home. Traveling for work as I did, I saw them periodically, and they welcomed my visits. By habit, I waited for the inevitable to come. Mothering might be snatched from me any minute, so I didn't sink into a cozy hammock, trusting I would still get to be their mother tomorrow.

Dan's passion for crew was the deciding factor in his choice to attend the University of Pennsylvania. Penn had a nationally ranked team. Dan inherited my father's athletic grace and was singled out for his technique and coordination. He was able to enter and exit his oar with skill and finesse, an essential quality for a good oarsman.

Twenty-five boys competed for eight spots. As a port rower, Daniel was eligible to be the stroke. The stroke was like the quarterback, setting the strategy and the pace for the boat. To evaluate individual rowers, the coach had them "row pairs," keeping one man constant and rotating the other.

One day, Dan called me with happiness in his voice. "I made the freshman boat! Coach Branner selected the boat, and then had us row pairs. The last race was a killer. I gave it my all and was almost sick at the end of it. But I'm stroke of the freshman boat!"

I got teary and swelled with happiness for him. During Dan's first year rowing at Penn, the freshmen men's crew was undefeated.

The routine repeated his sophomore year. I felt like an anxious stage mother. The coach was looking for technique, strength, and endurance, but he was also putting together an ensemble. The competition for the seating of the boat was daily and went on for three weeks. I called Daniel often during that time, invested that he make the varsity boat because it meant so much to him.

Finally, Dan called me with happiness in his voice. I was relieved, even before he told me the news.

"I made varsity!"

"Congratulations!" I exulted.

"Not only that. Coach made me stroke of the varsity boat!"

"Good heavens. Isn't that unusual for a sophomore to be stroke of the varsity boat?"

"Yeah. The last time this happened was fifteen years ago. He said he likes my coordination and technique. And I think he saw how I kind of keep people cool and from going off the handle. I get along with everybody, and I think that helped."

"You can be proud of yourself." My heart rested a bit. In spite of the turmoil of his childhood, he was excelling.

CHAPTER 53

························

September 1987–April 1989

Alan's back slowly disappeared as he walked over the bridge, past the yacht club, and into the night. Still not allowed on their street, I continued dropping him off at the market. He was leaving for a junior semester in Germany, a continent away.

I couldn't take my eyes off him. I didn't know when I would see him again. I wished we were marsupials so I could put him in my pouch to keep him safe. I didn't yet have the reassuring experience of him calling me in a few months, wanting the gingerbread house patterns and recipe, so he could make our traditional gingerbread houses for his Christmas in Germany.

Sunshine and milling people filled the plaza at Redwood Shores in nearby Foster City, California. In Daniel's junior year, Penn and Stanford were competing in the semifinals for the Adams Cup. A buzz of anticipation charged through the crowd as the two eight-man boats lined up for the starting shot. The gun went off.

Three weeks previously, when I learned the Penn crew was racing in the Bay Area, I knew I wanted to be there. I also knew there would be an issue with Walt, which would make Daniel nervous. I was angry that, sixteen years after our divorce, being together at a public event was still an issue.

"Which day do you want me to come?" I asked.

The question inherently announced that I was coming, no matter what his father said. I wanted to invite the families and friends he had known since childhood. I wanted a whole gang there, cheering him on.

"I think Sunday would be better. I'm not sure when Dad's coming, but he's more likely to come on Saturday."

"Okay, I'll make the party for Sunday. I'd also like to come Saturday, just to see you row, but I'll take a back seat if your father's there."

"I don't think he knows yet what he's doing."

Dan didn't give me explicit permission, but neither did he say no. I didn't push it.

Saturday, I scoped out the scene, figured out where to position the party for Sunday, but lingered around the edges in case Walt was there. I stationed myself toward the end of the course so I could see the finish.

Dan took the varsity boat out at forty-two strokes-per-minute, surging a half-length ahead in the first seconds of the race. I heard an audible gasp from the three people next to me. Maybe this wasn't going to be as close a race as Daniel had led me to believe. Even though he was rowing against my alma mater, I was rooting for Penn.

I knew he would have to lower the stroke count for the crew to sustain the 2,000 meters of water still facing them—choppy water with the wind coming from the south—but they now had the psychological advantage of being ahead. Penn stayed only a fraction ahead for the first half of the race, then neck-in-neck the last half. As they approached the finish line, both boats started their sprints and Stanford edged up. But Penn kept ahead and was first over the finish line! My heart leapt, and I cheered loudly. Penn won!

The Stanford rowers handed over their shirts; the Penn rowers, wearing the Stanford shirts like Superman capes, slowly rowed back to the dock. I walked in that direction, hoping to find Daniel for a hug and congratulations. The crew were happy, chatting in small clumps as they put away the rigging and oars.

I found Daniel and, careful not to embarrass him in front of his buddies, gave him a quick hug. "That was great! I got a bit nervous, but you pulled it off!"

"I know. We came out fast, but when we couldn't seem to pull ahead at the end, I was worried they might take it at the final sprint." He was pleased and smiling about their triumph. He was a shy person, not boastful, but he couldn't keep the grin from squiggling out around his lips.

I looked up at him adoringly from my five-foot-four frame, this six-foot-two golden Adonis, well-muscled and handsome. Where did he come from? How did I get blessed with such a beautiful son?

"After twenty strokes, I slowed us to a thirty-seven but that's faster than what we usually do. I was worried we couldn't—"

Suddenly, Daniel froze. His gaze was above me, focused in the distance. It was the terror in his eyes that made me turn around.

I saw a stranger aggressively walking toward us, looking directly at Daniel and making a beeline for him, ignoring everybody in his path. I wondered who he was. Then I saw Walter following in his wake. I, too, froze, suddenly immobile.

The man started talking to Daniel from a great distance. Mr. X kept up his demanding monologue as he approached. Daniel, mute and helpless, looked at me, turned back to look at this man, and didn't dare to look at me again. Dan had one arm on the oar, the other in mid-air, as if freeze-dried in action. I waited for him to finish his sentence, but drained of vitality, the sentence evaporated.

I had no more than a second until this man was upon us, interrupting, creating a triangle with Daniel and me, with Walt trailing behind, a fourth soon to join us. I was invisible to this stranger, nothing more than a breath of wind. He cleared the way for Walt, napalming any bodies in his way.

Daniel, unable to stay connected to me, was also unable to maintain any social graces. He didn't introduce me to the man. There was no place to put my words, no place to put my body. This man had created an airtight seal that excluded me. I was invisible again.

"You slowed the boat down to a thirty-seven . . ." I tried continuing the conversation, but my words bounced back, mocking me. My body contracted.

Daniel, mute, glanced at me, eyes pleading. "Please don't make this worse."

I decided the best way to save him was to melt away into the crowd. I felt like a holograph, talking but making no sound, as if I were in a dream. I weakly dribbled out a few more words, trying to finish a sentence and maintain some dignity. I ended by saying, "I'll see you tomorrow." I forced the words into the space between us, even though I knew Daniel was beyond hearing.

Daniel looked at me helplessly and slightly shrugged his shoulders, unable to do more. I hated Daniel for being paralyzed. I hated Walt for putting that fear in Daniel's eyes, that paralyzing fear of a haunted, trapped animal. I faded away, humiliated and enraged.

As I walked to the car, I burst into tears. I tried to keep the crying quiet, holding back the sobs, but they rose up, making my attempts at decorum as flimsy as rice paper. I scolded the sobs down, only to be swamped a few steps later. I felt as if St. Peter had denied knowing me three times before the cock crowed, except Jesus handled it better than I.

I hated myself for leaving. Daniel was almost twenty. When would my sons be able to stand up for me?

I reached the car. Unable to manage any executive action like turning on the ignition, I slumped down. *Just drive home. Go to bed. Go swimming. Call someone. Just keep it together.*

I made it to the freeway safely. There was not much traffic on a Saturday afternoon, but my head wouldn't leave me alone. Should I talk to Daniel about what just happened? Or should I let it go? If I broached the subject, I risked driving him further away; if I ignored it, I had condoned his ignoring me.

I got home, crawled in bed, and wept, but for a limited time only. I needed to function. I needed to barbeque chicken and make potato salad for the picnic tomorrow. Slowly, I pulled myself together. Thank God I had shopped and didn't have to be out around people, pretending to be okay. I decided I would cook tomorrow morning.

Needing the soothing comfort of water, I went for a swim. I sat in the dark and womb-like sauna. I avoided eye contact. I pretended I wasn't there, and others gave me a wide berth. Tears leaked out at unknown moments. I talked to no one. With a brutal push from the present, I regressed to the suppurating wounds of the past. Mired in their tenacious pull, I sought to be invisible once again.

Sunday was another beautiful day. I got up early, cooked, and got ready for the day. I had organized a group of ten—the same family troops who surrounded us at holidays as the boys were growing up. They were troupers. They were *our* troupers.

Penn raced Navy in the finals. We were the loudest cheering section of the whole scene. We hooted and hollered, and Penn pulled ahead. They won! Penn won the Adams Cup!

Our group was so large—complete with a Penn pennant— that some people came to join us, assuming we were the official alumni delegation. I had told Dan to invite his fellow crew to our picnic and made sure we had enough food for all. Dan found us after the race, bringing along some buddies. We ate, we talked, and the jovial group helped paper over the pain of yesterday.

Walt had come only on Saturday. Sunday, unabashedly, Daniel was free to be my son.

CHAPTER 54

....

May 1989

My mother savored her preparation for death. Every few years, she wrote us three daughters a letter about her postmortem wishes. Maybe she used this behavior as a substitute for threatening suicide. I had come to her rescue and helped her move many times. But she upset me when she wrote instructions for the disposition of her personal possessions—disposition to everyone but to me.

She hadn't spoken to my oldest sister, Laurel, in years, yet she stated, "Laurel should get the opal ring. Sarah should get the very old tea chest. Ted [Laurel's son] should get my wedding and engagement rings. Pat Trevor [a friend] should get 'anything she desires of my personal and household possessions.'"

She was silent about me, as if I didn't exist.

When I next talked to her, I dared to bring it up. "Mom, when you sent the letter distributing your personal items to Laurel, Sarah, and even Pat Trevor, you left me out. It hurt my feelings."

She was genuinely surprised that I'd be hurt. "Oh, I'm sorry. I didn't mean anything by that. What do you want?"

"It's not about the property or what I want. It's about being left out, not even being mentioned."

"I don't know why you're upset. Just name what you want, and you can have it."

"There's not anything special I want."

"Well, have it your way. But you can have something, if that will make you feel better. What about the miniature statue of the Chinese man on the bamboo mat, the one we kept on the sideboard in the dining room?"

She reduced my overtures the way Walter used to, by blaming me—"I don't know why you're upset"—and being dense—"I don't understand." I couldn't recognize those dynamics when I was married, but they shone in bas-relief now.

By now, I knew better than to pursue it further. "Yes, I'd like the Chinese man on the mat."

Years later, a homeopath prescribed a remedy—dissolvable pellets—to help me heal my "mother wound." Because "like heals like," the remedy contained the essence of what needed to be healed. My remedy was derived from a type of Brazilian rattlesnake, an adversarial animal that was cunning, twisted, manipulative, malicious, vindictive, and jealous.

Only months after Daniel's regatta, Alan's graduation from Tufts University approached. I had been continuously traveling for work, changing time zones and living in hotels. A good night's sleep was a scarce luxury. My exhaustion pulled me to stay home. And not dealing with Walter also made me want to stay home. I assumed I would not go.

But Alan called me a few weeks before graduation.

We chatted, and then he said, "My graduation is May 21st. Can you come?"

I was dumbfounded. "Are you sure?" I didn't want him to struggle with warring parents. Although I would have liked to be there, I didn't want him to be punished for including me again. "I don't want to make it hard on you with your father.

Why don't we keep it simple and create a celebration for you when you get home?"

He hesitated. "I'd kinda like to have you here."

I was thrilled. My decision was instant. "Say no more. I'll be there."

It didn't matter if I was tired, if I didn't want to travel more, if I didn't want to deal with Walter. If Alan wanted me there, I'd be there!

I marveled. He invited me. Of his own free will. *He* made the choice. A milestone. No longer was *I* the one who had to decide on forcing my way in or agree to retreat. Not till later did I learn that he invited me first, then invited Walt and Nora, saying I would be there. I was astounded.

The miracle had happened. Knowing the risk, he chose to include me. His father might walk out of his life and disinherit him from a family that had substantial money. The timing might have been unconscious, but it was smart. Using the trusts left for Alan by Walt's parents (but controlled by Walt), Alan secured his college education before demonstrating his guts, stature, and independence.

Alan did not waver. The invitation was real.

I attended.

Walter and Nora chose to be absent.

I wanted to make Alan's graduation more of a celebration than just me, and my frequent flier miles gave me options. Alan's cousins from Colorado—Nate and Bonnie, our Santa Cruz crew, were going to live with me for the summer and get a taste of Berkeley. I asked if they could come a few days early and go with me.

Our timing was tight. To be safe, we needed to leave by 6 a.m. for the airport. Because they worked, Bonnie and Nate couldn't leave Colorado till the night before, but if they drove all night, they could get to Berkeley by 5:30 a.m.

When they hadn't arrived by 6 a.m., I was in a tizzy, already calculating later flights and how to arrive in time for the graduation ceremony. But they pulled in the driveway at 6:10 a.m., parked the car, transferred luggage, went to the bathroom, got in my car, and we left for the airport by 6:15 a.m. We flew over Colorado, where they'd been just twelve hours earlier, and then onto Boston.

We made it. We celebrated. And then we slept.

Three weeks after Alan's declaration of emancipation via his graduation invitation, he and I were at a Roy Hart Theatre[1] voice workshop in the Château de Malérargues in Anduze, France, sitting on century-old hand-hewn stone steps. I accidentally happened upon this theater-based work a year earlier and enjoyed it thoroughly. I got Alan in a weekend workshop in Boston before his graduation and offered him this trip as his graduation present. He accepted.

As part of our tuition, in addition to group work, everyone got three private voice lessons, and also a lesson in movement, ensemble voice, and acting. Alan had given me the go-ahead, so I requested that Alan and I combine our private lessons, thus having six lessons together.

Kaya, our teacher, was five feet tall, petite as a parsnip with a mischievous smile and an open heart. She could move her late '60s body like a twenty-year-old-dancer. She was alive, vibrant, sexy, wise, and kind.

With no words, the depth of her gaze scooped up my inner world and held me, frightening me a little. What might she see, unbidden? Could I keep any secrets from her? Fairly quickly I felt safe and decided I could trust her with our family trauma.

In our first joint private lesson, I explained our history. Both timid and urgent, I pushed facts on her. I wanted her to understand, I wanted her balm to seep into the raw crevices. After five minutes, she cut me off; she needed no more. The voice was her vehicle for healing, not the disembodied vehicle of words.

Although she started voice work with both Alan and me— using scales and expanding the range of pitches—she then focused on me, specifically on my head voice. It was too meek, too uncertain. With Alan observing, Kaya and I worked for about thirty minutes. She instructed me on breathing and how to put power into the voice. We were in an upstairs room with windows overlooking the countryside.

"Stronger," she demanded.

I tried creating a stronger sound.

She had me flop like a rag doll to loosen up; she touched my chest. She gave me a pitch from the piano, fairly low. I matched it.

"Open your throat."

I tried.

"Sing to the hillside over there, so anyone can hear you."

My sound was better, but it didn't carry far. As I was making these sounds, she touched my body again, to bring awareness to places that were tight. I was frustrated and wanted to give up. I wanted to flounce like a three-year-old having a tantrum. "I've done my best, and I can't do it!"

She lightly touched my back and shoulders. She looked impishly at Alan, and said, "There are a lot of things your mother has not said. For many years." She then looked at me. "Put all that rage, all those things you haven't said into your voice. Make people on the hillside hear you."

Suddenly, there was a power and clarity in my voice that I had not dared to know. Anyone within miles could have heard me. For that moment, I was not a scared, obsequious pleaser. I was a woman to be reckoned with. In my peripheral vision, I saw Alan's eyes go wide, uncertain what to do with such a mother.

"Yes." Kaya was pleased, experiencing the teacher's pleasure when the student breaks through. "Now more." She pushed again, had me repeat it to make certain I knew it was not a fluke. I produced a glorious, clear tone again.

She pushed me up the scale in this new voice. She pulled me down the scale. Seamlessly, she included Alan, and slowly focused her attention on him, letting me rest, swimming in my new-found vibrations.

Happenstance and scheduling determined the location of any particular lesson. Our next lesson was in a cellar with thick, stone walls like catacombs. In spite of it being early summer, the air was cold and damp. In three places on the long wall, the stones gave way to an indentation with a Gothic arch, as if for a relic or statue. The room was relatively narrow and not particularly large. It was well lit; it felt enclosed, safe.

In the second lesson, Kaya again worked with both of us and then took on my chest voice. She created a sound—a beautiful, resonant, fully textured sound from her chest and asked me to match it. Because I am an alto, this was not a hard pitch for me to produce, but when I tried opening the deep, resonant capacity of my lungs, I started weeping. She moved to work with Alan and his chest voice, and then returned to me. I could not go to that place in my body without weeping. There was too much grief held around my heart. A slight needle—a resonant sound—punctured my flimsy protection. I felt naked, vulnerable, miserable. The helplessness of years of being unheard and unseen, of being prevented from being a mother . . . the sound I produced touched my impotence and anguish.

I wanted to flee back to the powerful voice of the other lesson. That big voice was like a sword to protect me; this voice was an open wound that needed blood-clotting intervention to save me. I spent the whole lesson in and out of tears, aware that my son had never seen this part of me. He had often seen me cry, but he had never witnessed this raw, unvarnished grief, and I worried it scared him. All I could do was trust Kaya to lead both of us through to a place of safety.

She did. By the end of the lesson, I was exhausted but calm. We did not finish until 3 p.m. People were doing their own voice work down at the pool or taking a siesta. Alan and I didn't have to be anywhere for another two hours, when the whole group would meet for chorus practice.

The two of us sat together on the stairs outside the catacombs. He was below me, both of us cool in the shadow of the stone building built in the 1800s. The June sunlight was strong, shadows sharp. The afternoon lull gave us privacy and time. Ivy grew up the wall of the building, with an ivy refrain repeated on the wall of the outer edge of the steps. The stone felt cool and rough on my bottom.

I looked at Alan on the step below me, right next to my knees. His blond hair was wavy, escaping to curls on the nape of his neck. His eyes were startlingly blue, their hue somewhat softened by the shadows. His long face was angular, with high cheek bones. He looked like a blond version of his father—same nose and face structure. Even at twenty-two, his hair suggested a receding V would be appearing in short order; his hairline was also his father's.

We were in companionable silence, when Alan looked up at me. "Why did you give up custody?"

CHAPTER 55

····················

June 1989–December 2005

The question hung in the still, breezeless air. It was the question I'd wanted him to ask, longed to answer, longed to have him understand, longed to have him strong enough to want to know. How could he ever understand? Could we now bridge the chasm that his father's vengeance hurled in our path? Could we find an antidote to the poison his stepmother leaked into every interaction, day after day, night after night, year after year? By now, the years added up to sixteen since the divorce. Were there enough days remaining to undo the sins of commission and omission?

Even though unspoken between us, we both understood the enormous risks he had taken at graduation, only days ago, and we both knew those risks were not over. A demilitarized zone had existed between us for twelve years and—at twenty-two, a newly minted college graduate—my son dared to enter the DMZ. And I dared to meet him there.

I inhaled deeply and plunged in. My answers crept fearfully, resolutely into the terrain of no-man's land. I was comforted by the happenstance physical touch—my knee against his shoulder— that neither of us rearranged.

"When we divorced, you were not quite six, and Daniel was just barely four. I had full custody; your father was not interested in having custody. I don't know what changed, but after a few years, he started telling you that you could live with him. You and Daniel would come home after visiting him saying, 'I want to live with Dad. If we live with Dad, he'll get a sailboat.' I would always answer, 'You're too young to make that decision. Your father and I make that decision, and we've made it, and you're living with me.' I became a broken record."

I paused to see how he was taking in my summary of events. He had moved to lean against the wall of the stairs, his profile to me, looking at the ground. His knee was now against my knee. He was not coming closer, but neither was he fleeing.

I had waited twelve years for this moment. I didn't want to blow it. I felt like we were on the tippy-toppy point of an isosceles triangle: one side was the past, the other side was the future. If I didn't use this moment well, we could topple off like Humpty-Dumpty, both come tumbling down, never to be put back together again.

"You began saying you wanted to live with him, and you were getting old enough that it was touch-and-go regarding whether a court would listen to your desires. A judge, for sure, would have listened to a child of fourteen, and at eleven and twelve, it was likely. You were ten. I spent a lot of time with my lawyer trying to figure out how much weight a judge would give your testimony. I fought the idea of you moving; I protested to your dad. I said that I had no objections to you living with him at some point, but you were too young. He would hear none of it."

I paused again. He glanced at me to continue.

"The turning point for me came when I found out that, without my knowledge, your dad had already taken you to a lawyer to have you officially deposed. You were only ten years old, and you testified that you wanted to live with your father. My heart broke picturing you in some lawyer's office, answering questions while someone transcribed every word you said. At that point, with a lot of soul-searching and agonizing, and after talking with Arthur and Rosie, I surrendered. I knew it would not be good for you to have to testify against me in court, and I didn't want to put you through that. You said you wanted to live with him, and my hands were pretty well tied. I knew I could fight it, make you go through something awful, and probably still have the courts decide you could move to live with your father, since that's what you said you wanted. I decided it would be easier for you to recover from leaving me—and feeling abandoned, than to carry the guilt of testifying against me, with no ultimate gain."

A lull fell upon both of us.

As an afterthought, I said, "But you must realize, I didn't believe everything a ten-year-old boy said."

He suddenly pivoted and looked directly up at me. With a sigh of relief, he said, "Boy, am I glad you knew that!"

The following year, Daniel skipped his college graduation ceremony and went to Olympic training camp for sculling, where he discovered he wasn't tall enough to become an Olympic sculler. He left camp and, like his older brother, became gainfully employed.

My child-rearing years were over: Walter existed inside the minds and emotions of my sons, but he was no longer relevant in my life.

Twelve years after his college graduation, Alan married.

Twenty-nine years after our divorce, because I'd be there, Walter refused to come to Alan's wedding. Alan wanted him there; he wrote him letters, he pleaded with him. Walt finally relented, but with conditions. He would come, but only if he did not have to talk to me or be in pictures with me.

We pulled off the wedding without incident, but later I learned that Walter was upset with many things, two of which were my toast celebrating the presence of both of Alan's parents and also, the bride's photo collage, to which I had contributed photographs.

A year after Alan's wedding, Nora wrote to both Alan and Daniel, asking them for a favor. She requested that neither acknowledge her anymore on Mother's Day, as they had done regularly in the past. Her own mother had just died, and she wanted Mother's Day to be exclusively in memory of her own mother.

"Inasmuch as I've always wanted to be child-free, which I am now, I'd like to remember this day as a special day between my mother and me. With you boys grown, I no longer have to have children around, which I find blissful."[1]

Sixteen years after his college graduation, Daniel married. With no pleading, he invited Walt and Nora to his wedding, and said that he had invited me. With no hesitation, Walt immediately informed Daniel that he would not come.

Christmas, 2005, five months before Daniel's wedding.

"Schnapps?"

"Maybe a whiskey?"

"A coffee? Some water?"

We were all in disarray after Christmas Eve dinner—that breathing space between the meal and the opening of presents. A pleasant repose. Except for the Christmas carols from the stereo and the occasional crackling of the fire, we were mostly in companionable silence.

After twenty-six years of supporting myself, I had married Richard, seven years before this evening. Originally, we had met when our sons were in fourth grade together in The Academy; we met again years later through a mutual friend.

Richard was taking orders from the full-bellied adults whose bodies were strewn about our living room: one with a leg slung over the arm of a couch, another holding my infant grandson, while a fourth read a storybook to my three-year-old granddaughter.

In order to sit beside my son, whose head was in the newspaper, I kicked aside the wrapping-paper leftovers from the earlier opening of a present. The fireplace threw off heat that we, in chilly Northern California, were glad to have on this festive evening. Along with its flames, the fire brought intimacy and peace.

Tired after cooking, I looked around in contentment. Both sons were here, each with a receding V-hairline. My only daughter-in-law was here. Daniel's fiancée, who would become my new daughter-in-law in five months, was on the phone, getting a detailed description of our dinner and our Christmas tradition of eating Walt's Aunt Virginia's delicious persimmon pudding.

New grandchildren were here. My funny, smart, safe, husband was here. I didn't yet know—and didn't need to know—that our home would provide a safe landing place for years to come for Richard's daughter and her offspring as well as my sons, daughters-in-law, and grandchildren as they became adults.

"I'll have a schnapps, please."

"One schnapps coming—"

Look around. My contentment was interrupted by a voice, seemingly from God.

I felt impatient with His instructions, since I was already looking around.

Can't you see I'm already . . .

But one does not admonish God, whose advice rarely comes so clearly.

I slowed down. I breathed. I looked around. I looked more quietly. I looked more deeply. I asked my eyes to focus differently. I looked again to make sure.

Both sons. I counted my toes, I counted my fingers, I counted my children. Ten, ten, and two. Yes, my body was here, and I was in my body.

I checked again. The thought form of "Walt" was not even in the room. No one was afraid of him. No one was strategizing how not to anger him. No one was surreptitiously trying to forge a relationship with me while keeping it secret from him.

I blinked. I swallowed. I asked for a schnapps, and looked around some more. Walter was no longer a threat. Walt had made himself irrelevant.

My eyes expanded to see this tableau as part of a bigger field. This wasn't just Christmas Eve. This wasn't just about my sons. This was about my husband, my sons, my family, my home. This was about family, the most important thing I lost in the divorce. I saw the people I loved most together. Here in our home. My family.

Viscerally, for the first time in thirty-three years, I knew I could breathe easily and drop my vigilance. I did not have to be on high alert, ready for the next blow, ready to muster up yet again.

I dared to think the thought.

I'm safe. I let my body relax. *My sons and I are safe.*

I inhaled. I exhaled. I inhaled again, a little more deeply. I kept breathing . . . in and out . . . in and out . . . in and out. Finally, I got God's message. Walter no longer had the power to make me a forbidden mother.

The war was over. The war was over.

Love, along with a lot of grit, had held us together.

EPILOGUE

....

When Alan is in his fifties, and we're finally safe enough to talk about the past, he tells me something I never knew.

"When we were in high school, I remember Dan and I would sneak around trying to find a way to see you."

What wounds would have healed if I had known then that they weren't lost to me?

In 2018, by serendipity, Alan learns that the old Morgan house in Santa Cruz had been sold and is now available for rent; I secure it for us for a week in August. My two sons and I return to our historical vacation spot, but this time, my sons bring their wives and two children each, and I bring my husband, the only grandfather the four grandchildren know. The grandchildren repeat the rhythms of their fathers. The four young cousins walk across the train trestle to the boardwalk, getting deliciously scared as they look at the big drop down to the river. They ride the Giant Dipper, bang into each other in the bumper cars, and get semi-sick on corn dogs.

As a grandmother, I look at the same view of the same beach as when I was a young mother, when I was filled with hopeful expectations for my marriage and my life. Forged of stronger steel now, the vacation brings me full circle. The house, the beach, the view, the sons, the wives, the children, and my husband provide a healing bookend to an arduous passage. We cook, eat, laugh, swim, ride the waves, read, and do jigsaw puzzles. We are all alive, whole, and together.

I enjoy watching the grandchildren grow—these four new souls who chose our family. We are all miracles of courage, love, and grit.

My sons are shocked when they receive an email from Walter telling them of Nora's death. She had been ill for three years, but Nora and Walt chose to keep it a secret. Both Alan and Daniel reach out to their father, arranging flights for a weekend trip together so they can be with him. I am proud they want to comfort their father.

Writing this memoir has allowed me to be at peace with the turmoil of the past and with the pain Walter and I inflicted on each other and on our sons. The passage of time, increasing wisdom, and a broader view of life have helped me find compassion and forgiveness for all of us, including myself. Together, Walter and I created two boys who have grown into fine men who are good sons, husbands, and fathers. They are tempered in the forge of their own fates and have created their own unique destinies.

I am content . . . and curious about the future.

AUTHOR'S NOTE

....

"Someone I loved once gave me a box full of darkness.
It took me years to understand that this, too, was a gift."
—MARY OLIVER[1]

I **hope this memoir** illustrates two beliefs which help me make sense of my life:

1. We all have energetic bodies that pull and repel other energetic bodies. We draw people into our lives who will provide us the lessons we signed up to learn. We may be open to learn . . . or not. Many people choose to stay closed, thus condemning themselves to recreate these same lessons again and again until they finally grow, either in this lifetime or another.

2. We co-create our lives with Spirit, and we always have choices. Our choices shape not only who we are, but who we become. We co-create the alchemy of biology, chemistry, and physics, which determines what is able to move from potential to matter.

Once we incarnate, our soul's work—and therefore our work—is to develop a relationship with ourselves, both individually, with our ancestral history, and as part of the great mystery of life. We are all born with a full connection to Spirit, but barriers develop that inhibit our direct access. Necessarily, we inherit and create belief systems, which protect us and help us make sense of the world. These belief systems generate stories, which we tell ourselves, but those stories seldom are true. To evolve, we need to dismantle this early scaffolding and peel away our false stories.

Increased consciousness requires us to sacrifice comforting but outgrown identities, and choose the difficult task of embodying the fruits of the spirit[2], such as compassion, love, and forgiveness. This path takes courage and fortitude. If we want to succeed, we must harness our time, energy, and strength to the task; only a dedicated focus can prepare us to receive the light and the love that is everywhere.

This memoir is the story of the fate I was born to and the destiny I created through choice, responsibility, and paying the high cost of consciousness. Carolyn Myss likens consciousness to living on a high floor of a building, where the view is more sweeping than the view on the first floor—but the apartment is more expensive.[3]

I was born to the perfect family for me, offering the perfect lessons my soul needed to learn. Both of my parents were responsible, good people but because of the limitations from their own ancestries, upbringings, and their historical times, neither had the skills nor interest in nurturing my itty-bitty baby consciousness with the care and love I needed. Feeling unseen and unsafe, I developed strategies to survive. These strategies were bottom-floor defenses of blame and victimhood.

I chose the perfect first husband for me; he, too, was a responsible, good person whose limitations fit hand-in-glove with my upbringing. With him, I could continue the pattern of feeling ignored and not seen, and make my pain his fault.

Touch woke me out of my trance. Instead of going through the motions of living, the motions of dutifully fulfilling my obligations (as my mother had done, and as I was trained to do), I wanted to live on a higher floor with a more spacious view. Paul was the perfect person to thrust me out of my first-floor programming and also the perfect person to help me clarify my real choices: I could continue the old programming in a different flavor or make the leap to the unknown, the leap to find and develop a relationship with myself, to become responsible for myself, and to create my own destiny. With much fear and at great risk, I chose the vibration of being vital and alive. I chose to move to the upper floors of the building but to do so, I had to sacrifice my historical protections of denial, blame, anger, and self-righteousness.

Choosing consciousness is one thing; living it is another.

Walter and Nora tested me, again and again. My mother taught me that my existence hurt others, especially her. Walter reinforced that belief in my adulthood; he believed I was damaging to my children, and he punished me (and them) when I dared to assert myself as their mother. Like all of us, Walter and Nora developed their own strategies to survive, and I became the screen onto which they projected their own fears and shadow selves.

In order not to lose my relationships with my sons, I had to take hold: I could no longer indulge in dissociation, or hide in addiction, or yearn to die. I had to get stronger, be less fearful and less worried about pleasing people. I had to integrate my fragmented parts and learn, over time, to care for my body with love and respect.

No matter what my parents had done or not done, no matter what Walter or Nora had done or had not done, it was my responsibility to create my own upper floors and live in an environment in which I could nurture my inner self and cultivate my relationship to Spirit.

I am grateful to all my teachers, especially my parents, sisters, Paul, Walter, and Nora, all of whom helped me change the trajectory of my life.

With decades of work and an evolving team of psychotherapists, bodyworkers, spiritual counselors, and, above all, grace, I have come through this demanding birth canal to find the sacred and to experience life as a gift instead of a burden. I am now able to view these events with neutrality, simply as what was and what is.

I no longer believe I damage those I love. I believe my life is a blessing to me and to others, and no part of me wishes I were dead. I embrace the beauty life offers. I hold this story as a gift of my destiny, and I offer it as a gift to the reader.

Because every day I am filled with new grace, new understanding, and new healing, this story will always be incomplete. I see myself (and all of us) as fragments of The Divine, who manifest in this world of Love, Light, and Law. My duty is to be as conscious as I can be, as aware as I can be, as present as I can be, and in my imperfect, humble way, do my best to bring heaven to earth.

LEGAL HISTORY APPENDIX

....

September 1, 1972
Walt and Kay separate. Kay files for divorce. Kay offers joint custody. Walt declines.

September 1972 to April 1973
Walt's initial financial proposal is no child support and alimony for one year only. Kay declines. Lawyers negotiate about finances for eight months. After nine months of negotiations, there is no agreement on financial support. Court hearing is scheduled for May 5, 1973. (Hearing #1)

May 5, 1973
Walt and Kay are in court to settle temporary financial support. (Hearing #1)

May 16, 1973
Judge rules on interim, temporary financial settlement. The decision of who pays attorney fees is postponed to final decree. (Hearing #1)

June-July 1973
Kay spends two months preparing for interrogatories and depositions for the hearing ion July 26. (Hearing #2)

July 26, 1973
Hearing for final divorce and financial settlement. (Hearing #2)

July 30, 1973
Final order is the same as interim order for financial settlement. Walt has to pay Kay's lawyer's fees.

October 4, 1973
The divorce is final.

October 5, 1973
Kay signs a legal waiver, allowing Walt and Nora to marry without waiting six months.

October 9, 1973
Walt marries Nora.

Fall 1975
Walt starts telling the boys (ages seven and nine) that they can choose where to live. He promises to buy a sailboat if they live with him. Kay tells the boys they cannot make that decision; she and Walt will make it.

March 31, 1976
Walt says he is concerned that the boys are not receiving proper care and training from their mother at home. Walt threatens to go to court to get custody, "if necessary."

April 9, 1976
Kay writes Walt that she will consider allowing the boys to move with him in a year *if* he will give her a year of cooperation and not undermine her. He interprets her letter as a promise with no change of behavior on his part.

June 3, 1976

Kay asks to take Alan to Spain to meet her sister and her family there for vacation. Walt files an Order to Show Cause to prevent Kay from taking Alan to Spain and to prevent Kay from sending Daniel to the camp of Daniel's choice. (Hearing #3)

June 10, 1976

Court hearing about Spain and summer camp occurs. (Hearing #3)

July 6, 1976

Judge rules in Kay's favor. She can take Alan to Spain and send Daniel to the camp of his choice. Walt has to pay her lawyer's fees. (Hearing #3)

September 8, 1976

The previous spring, Walt agreed to pay private school tuition for a year. When school opens, Walt makes his agreement conditional on a promise to give him custody at the end of the school year. Kay files an OSC for school tuition, and for his withholding of child support. Kay gets court date of Oct. 20, 1976. (Hearing #4)

September 17, 1976

Walt wants a custody review because he believes Kay is not capable of providing a good environment for the children. He wants the court to sanction Kay (by making her pay his attorney's fees) for acting in bad faith, and "other sanctions felt by the court to be appropriate."

October 1976

Kay gets a referral, and Walt and Nora agree to a joint meeting with a child psychiatrist to help them mediate visitation schedule, custody, and communication. Kay releases the court date of Oct. 20, 1976. (Hearing #4)

February 7, 14, 28, and March 10, 1977
Lawyers are needed to make summer arrangements. Walt and Kay sign binding documents about visitation and child support.

April 12, 1977
Kay gets May 26 court date, asking for school tuition, Cost of Living Adjustment increase in child support, and mediation. (Hearing #5)

April 15, 1977
Walt issues a deadline: Kay must sign Walt's stipulation for summer arrangements by April 20 or he will not participate in summer plans. (He will forgo having the boys for the summer and not pay for camps.) Kay signs in time.

April-May, 1977
Kay spends many hours preparing all the documents needed for court on May 26—school records, every financial document of the last two years, etc. (Hearing #5)

May 2, 1977
Walt's lawyer examines Kay's financial records in his office. Kay's lawyer examines Walt's financial records in her office.

May 16, 1977
Walt is deposed by the opposing lawyer. Kay is deposed by the opposing lawyer.

May 23, 1977
Walt offers to pay one year of tuition if Kay promises him custody at end of school year. He will withdraw the threat of suing for custody if Kay agrees. Kay declines Walt's offer, and risks Walt filing for custody immediately.

May 26, 1977
Both Walt and Kay appear in court to litigate tuition, child support, and court-ordered mediation. (Hearing #5)

June 6, 1977
Judge rules an increase in child support, no school tuition, is silent about mediation. Custody was not before the court, so custody is left undecided. Judge makes Walt pay Kay's attorney fees.

June 1977
Walt wants custody but has never had the boys more than two weeks at a time. Kay proposes a summer "experiment" for Walt to have the boys full-time. Lawyers outline the agreement.
Walt sends them to camp for July.

June 15, 1977
Kay's first visitation as noncustodial parent. She is not allowed at the front door.

June 1977
Walt uses Kay's absence to have Alan (age ten) legally deposed, testifying that he wants to live with Walt.

June 20, 1977
Walt gives Kay a deadline of June 30 to decide where the boys will live in the fall. He is poised to sue.

June 27, 1977
Kay meets Walt's June 30 deadline. Kay will allow Alan to move in September but wants two more months to decide about Daniel. Kay wants an evaluation procedure in place.

August 3, 1977
Walt threatens immediate custody proceeding if Kay insists on an evaluation procedure. She lets it go.

September 1977-February 1978
Alan is living with Walt. Walt and Kay have ongoing disagreements about pickup times, clothes, visitation, schedule, access, etc.

February 27, 1978
Given the history with Alan, Kay wants stronger legal agreements before she will allow Daniel to move. Even though they do not have a case pending, and therefore are not eligible to use the court's mediation services, Kay maneuvers to get an appointment with a social worker and invites Walter. Kay meets with social worker.

March 3, 1978
Walt meets with the social worker.

April 6, 1978
Walt and Kay meet with a social worker from conciliation court to map out agreements for Daniel's impending move. The agreements include visitation and pickup times. Walter refuses further mediation.

April 13, 1978
The social worker sends a written report, which outlines the agreements, including a pickup time on Saturday morning.

April 28, 1978
Walt unilaterally instructs his lawyer to change the pickup time to Friday evening. Kay doesn't sign it.

May 26, 1978
Kay asks Walter's permission to take both boys to North Carolina for the long weekend. She has accepted a job offer at the University of North Carolina, Wilmington. Walt agrees.

June 12, 1978
Walt files for custody and asks the court to prevent Kay from taking either boy out of state. (Hearing #6)

June 18, 1978
Kay files a response, asking the court to allow both boys to live with her in North Carolina. The court date is on June 28, 1978. (Hearing #6)

June 19, 1978
Court date postponed from June 28 to July 24. (Hearing #6)

June–July 1978
Kay spends six weeks preparing for court, getting statements from teachers, etc.

June 28, 1978
Walter refuses to pay Daniel's summer camp fee due July 1 and transfers Daniel's deposit to Alan, leaving Daniel high and dry. Walt explains Kay has not promised a transfer of Daniel's custody in the fall. Kay pays the deposit for Daniel so he can keep his place in the summer camp he loves.

July 14, 1978
Walt sends a proposal for change of custody. Kay agrees Alan will move to live with him but she will keep legal custody. Walt will allow Daniel to move with Kay for one year to North Carolina if she signs a legally binding change of custody for both of them,

starting in a year. She agrees and signs. They let go of the July 24 court date. (Hearing #6)

Kay creates a memorandum of agreement: Walt and Nora will encourage visitation with Kay, and all parties will be cooperative. Kay will have access to them by phone with no interference. Walt and Nora will not speak ill of Kay to the boys. Walt and Nora agree, but then say the agreement may never be used in any court proceeding.

March 16, 1982
Walt announces he will withhold Kay's legal visitation in April because she and the boys were snowed in at Yosemite the previous week.

March-April 1982
Lawyers get involved to settle visitation disagreements and summer plans. There are no solutions. Walt maintains he is not withholding visitation, but it is the boys who don't want to see Kay. Walt says it is Kay who is alienating them by such things as going to open house and saying "fucking" two years ago. He insists he does not plan competing events to her visitation. He will not force them to see her.

April 29, 1982
Kay files an OSC for full custody of both boys, using two-thirds of her monthly income just to pay a retainer and to file. Hearing scheduled for July 12, 1982. (Hearing #7)

June 1982
A social worker from conciliation court meets individually with Walt, Nora, Kay, and the children.

June 11, 1982

Walt will be traveling on July 12 and requests a change of date for the hearing. Kay accommodates his request. The custody hearing is moved from July 12 to July 7, 1982. (Hearing #7)

June 23, 1982

Walt files a proposal that Kay lessen her visitation to one weekend a month, and that Walt and Kay meet quarterly to make a three-month schedule. He forbids a mediator to be present at the scheduling meetings. (Hearing #7)

June 24, 1982

The social worker offers to meet with both lawyers to try resolving the issues without court. Walt and Kay let go of the court date of July 7, 1982. (Hearing #7)

July 1982

The social worker is unable to find a solution. Walt is unwilling to participate in further mediation. Because it is clear ongoing mediation services will be needed, and Contra Costa County does not have as good mediation services as Alameda County, Kay's lawyer advises her to seek change of venue to Alameda County. Alameda County is where Kay lives, where Walt works, and where both lawyers practice.

August 25, 1982

Kay files for change of venue to Alameda Count to have access to mediation in a good family services system. A court date is scheduled for Sept. 7, 1982. (Hearing #8)

August 29, 1982

Kay files for custody.

September 2, 1982

Walt says Kay's request for a change of venue is abuse of the judicial system and misuse of taxpayers' money. (Hearing #8)

September 7, 1982

A hearing is held about the request for a change of venue. (Hearing #8)

September 15, 1982

The judge rules for Marin County, not Alameda as Kay requested. (Hearing #8)

September 27, 1982

Kay hires a new lawyer in Marin County. Kay pays two months of her income for retainer fee. There is no guarantee she will gain access to her sons.

ENDNOTES

....

For All Chapters
Except for Kay/Catherine, names have been changed to protect the privacy of all individuals.

All letters were typed or handwritten and mailed via the US Postal Service unless otherwise specified.

Dialogue between Kay, Walter, or Nora are based on notes taken at the time of the interactions.

Chapter 2
1. Lucy Woodson Moore's Needlepoint, "To be a Virginian, either by birth, marriage, adoption, or even on one's mother's side, is an introduction to any state in the Union, a passport to any foreign country, and a benediction from the Almighty God." The admonition when growing up: Don't ask anyone if they're from Virginia, because if they are, you'll know. If they aren't, imagine how they'll feel.

Chapter 18
1. Gail Collins, *When Everything Changed: The Amazing Journey of American Women from 1960 to the Present* (New York, Boston,

and London: Back Bay Books, Little, Brown and Company, 2009.), 35.

"The vast majority [of girls in the 1960s] had no more confidence in their ability to earn a good living than did Jane [Austen's] heroines."

2. September 12, 1972. Walt writes a letter to Kay's grandmother.
3. October 20, 1971. Kay's father sends a note to Kay about her mother's angry letter.

Chapter 20

1. May 21, 1976. Walt writes to Kay, "Kay, I've let you walk all over me in regard to the boys for too long."
2. March 17, 1973. Walt's letter to Kay.
3. August 15, 1973. Walt's handwritten note to Kay regarding new alimony and child support structure.

Chapter 21

1. June 15, 1973. Kay's letter to Walt pleading for regular visitation, without last minute cancellation.
2. July 13, 1973. Letter from Walt's lawyer, stating the judge "in substance agreed that the solution to the Morgan family's financial problem would be for Mrs. Morgan to find employment."

Chapter 23

1. Gina Frangello, *Blow Your House Down*, (Berkeley, California: Counterpoint, 2021), 46.

"Still, no matter what you tell yourself consciously, you can't seem to shake your body's belief that somehow male cruelty has the power to make a girl important."

Chapter 24

1. January 20, 1975. Walt responds to Kay's inquiry to start to arrange for his court-approved weeks for spring and summer vacations.

2. Feb. 11, 1975. Kay writes to Walt informing him she will be responsible for the boys during spring vacation.

3. April 24, 1975. Walt writes to Kay stating Nora was mad at her for not liking Alan's haircut, and thus, Nora had more to add to her "mental little black book on Kay."

Chapter 25

1. November 14, 1975. Kay changes her last name back to her maiden name.

2. March 26, 1976. Walt's response to Kay's March 19 request to submit the insurance claims for her family therapy session with the children.

3. April 9, 1976. Verbal conversation between Kay and Daniel.

Chapter 27

1. April 9, 1976. Kay writes to Walt stating if she can have the boys one more year with his support and cooperation, she would give them a choice of where to live at the end of the year.

2. April 27, 1976. Walt thanks Kay in a letter but ignores her condition about cooperating, asserting the children will live with him the following year.

3. May 10, 1976. Kay's lawyer cautions her that if she wants to clarify Walt's misunderstanding, it may propel him to start litigation immediately.

4. May 12, 1976. Kay writes to Walt about taking Alan to Spain with her and Daniel returning to AdventurePlus camp.

5. May 21, 1976. Walt responds to Kay, threatening to go to court if Kay takes Alan to Spain.

6. June 3, 1976. Walt files OSC to prevent Kay from taking Alan to Spain and to prevent sending Daniel to AdventurePlus.

7. July 6, 1976. Judge rules in Kay's favor and allows her to take Alan to Spain and Daniel to AdventurePlus. Walt has to pay Kay's lawyer's fees.

Chapter 28
1. September 4, 1976. Kay cancels Backpackers' trip and admits her vindictiveness.
2. September 6, 1976. Phone conversation between Walt and Kay.
3. September 8, 1976. Phone conversation between Kay and Nora.

Chapter 29
1. September 8, 1976. Walt writes to Kay refusing an evaluation procedure at the end of the year. He sees the move as a "simple place in change of abode."
2. September 1976 and May 23, 1977. In September 1976, Kay insists on having a third party or tape recorder present during Kay and Walt's discussion to have a record of their agreements. On May 23, 1977, Walt responds to Kay's court filing for tuition and uses Kay's insistence of a third party or tape recorder as evidence of her insecurity.
3. September 27, 1976. Kay's lawyer writes to Walt's lawyer referring to a conversation on September 17, 1976, where she quotes Walt's lawyer as saying Walt wants custody as soon as possible.
4. September 29, 1976. Walt's lawyer writes to Kay's lawyer. Walt wants a custody review and a court sanction.
5. October 4, 1976. Walt asserts he can provide a better environment for the children than Kay can.
6. September 9, 1976. Kay asks Walt to meet with a therapist together and submit claims to his insurance.
7. September 9, 1976. Walt's lawyer writes that Walt refuses to submit insurance claims for family therapy.
8. October 31, 1976. Kay invites Walt to address custody issues with Dr. Friedman.
9. November 3, 1976. Walt agrees to see Dr. Friedman but a joint session is not scheduled until the new year.

Chapter 30
1. January 18, 1977. Walt, Nora, and Kay meet with Dr. Friedman

to discuss communication issues, the boys' living arrangements, and their summer plans.

2. Kay makes a mistake in seeking a referral for a child psychiatrist instead of looking for someone trained in managing interpersonal dynamics. A family therapist is needed, but family therapy is relatively new at the time.

Chapter 31

1. March 10, 1977. Walt's lawyer writes Kay's lawyer, refusing help from conciliation court because problems are Kay's alone.

2. April–May 1977. Kay prepares all documents for court scheduled for May 26. All figures are in court documents and in the public record.

3. May 23, 1977. Walt files in court, refusing to pay tuition, increased child support, or Kay's attorney fees. He questions whether child support payments are being spent on the children.

4. May 23, 1977. Walt responds to Kay's Order to Show Cause for an increase in child support, COLA, etc. It is filed in the court document.

5. March 1977. Lawyers are needed to make summer arrangements. Kay and Walt sign binding documents about visitation and child support.

6. April 15, 1977. Walt issues edict with April 20 deadline. Kay must sign Walt's stipulation for financial arrangements for summer plans or he will not have the boys for the summer.

Chapter 32

1. June 15, 1977. Kay's first time as a visiting parent.

2. June 1977. Walt has Alan legally deposed to testify he wants to live with Walt.

3. September 13, 1977. Personal verbal communication from Judith Wallerstein, Kay's professor, who was a senior lecturer at UC Berkeley 1966–1991. Wallerstein's career was centered around a twenty-five-year-long study, the "California Children of Divorce Study," investigating the effects divorce has on families,

resulting in her book *The Unexpected Legacy of Divorce: A 25-Year Landmark Study by Wallerstein, Lewis, and Blakeslee* (New York: Hyperion, 2001).

Chapter 34

1. June 27, 1977. Kay meets Walt's June 30 deadline.
2. July 7, 1977. Walt writes to Kay wanting to be generous with visitation. He will not press for legal custody at this time.
3. August 3, 1977. Walt writes to Kay about the boys' move. He is unwilling for any evaluation at the end of the year.
4. August 3, 1977. Walt threatens Kay with custody proceedings.

Chapter 35

1. August 28, 1977. Kay writes to Walt saying that Daniel will live with her for the upcoming year. She makes Daniel's two requests.
2. September 27, 1977. Ongoing communication between Walt and Kay.
3. December 17, 1977. Walt tells Kay via phone conversation he is canceling Alan's visitation.
4. September 1, 1977. Walt's writes Kay insisting Alan be neatly dressed for school when Walt picks him up.
5. January 8, 1978. Walt writes to Kay regarding no exchange of clothes between the houses.
6. September 6, 1977-September 24, 1977. Ongoing letters between Kay and Walt regarding open house at school.
7. September 27, 1977. Ongoing letters between Kay and Walt regarding Backpackers trip.

Chapter 36

1. September 8-September 27, 1977. Ongoing letters in response to Kay pleading to include Daniel in a mid-winter vacation. Walt denies the request multiple times.
2. December 27-January 8, 1978, Walt stops paying Daniel's out-of-pocket medical expenses because of head lice. Walt writes that

he has proved Kay was negligent because there is not an epidemic.

3. December 27-January 17, 1978. Walt writes Kay, unilaterally changing the Friday evening pickup time. Kay responds with a Saturday morning pickup time.

4. April 1978. Daniel tells Kay he is scared of being brainwashed like his brother.

5. January 24, 1978. Walt writes to Kay indicating he thinks Kay's efforts to get them into conciliation court are projecting her need for therapy onto him.

6. February 27, 1978. Kay writes the social worker and copies Walt, stating Nora has told the boys Kay is a mean mother who lies.

7. May 9, 1978. Daniel writes letter to Kay stating that Walt hates her.

8. April 6, 1978. Kay and Walt meet once with a social worker from conciliation court to map out the agreement for Daniel's impending move. Walt refuses further mediation.

Chapter 37
1. April 28, 1978. Walt unilaterally instructs his lawyer to change the agreement about pickup time. Kay does not sign.

2. May 2, 1978. Alan's letter to Kay declines her invitation to see Victor Borge.

3. May 22, 1978. Nora writes to Kay stating they never asked Alan to live with them.

4. April 24, 1978. Walter writes to Kay, informing her that Alan is upset about Kay coming to the open house.

Chapter 38
1. June 1978. Dan writes a pirate note to Kay, saying she can count on him going to North Carolina.

2. June 1978. Alan's note stating he would do anything to stay with Walt.

Chapter 39
1. June 12, 1978. Walt files for custody and asks the court to

prevent Kay from taking the boys out of state. Walt attempts to discredit Kay's mothering abilities.

2. June 28, 1978. Walt writes to Kay informing her he will not entrust her with Alan's slacks.

3. July 11, 1978. Kay obtains note from pediatrician, which stated there was epidemic proportions of head lice last winter.

4. June 28, 1978. Walt writes to Kay refusing to pay Daniel's summer camp fee.

5. July 28, 1978. Kay's lawyer writes to Kay, commending her on her "high level of parenting."

Chapter 40

1. April 19, 1979. Kay writes to Walt changing the date when she will send Daniel to California.

2. April 27, 1979. Walt writes to Kay, demanding her to live up to her responsibilities.

3. May 9, 1979. Kay writes to Walt, stating if the demands of the custodial parent didn't work when she had the role, they do not work now, either.

Chapter 42

1. May 22, 1978. Nora writes to Kay stating she believes Kay owes her thanks and monetary compensation.

Chapter 43

1. April 22, 1980. Kay documents Nora's slap and behavior in a letter to Walt.

2. May 14, 1980. Kay's lawyer writes to Kay, confirming entire situation is unhealthy, wondering if lawyers and judges are even relevant.

Chapter 44

1. July 13, 1981. Kay writes to Walt wanting a minimum of one weekend a month, scheduled around the boys' needs.

2. July 20, 1981. Walter writes to Kay stating there is not a formula to have a visitation schedule.

Chapter 46
1. April 14, 1982. Walt writes to Kay he does not want to risk allowing Alan and Alan's friend (a son of Walt's German colleague) to visit Kay because of the cursing incident two years ago.

Chapter 48
1. March 16, 1982. Walt writes to Kay stating she has been negligent in Yosemite and is not allowed visitation in April.
2. April 29, 1982. Kay files for custody.
3. April 14, 1982. Walt refuses to allow the German student to visit, continuing to bring up the cursing incident.

Chapter 49
1. Kay's mother ends their relationship over hurt feelings about gift-giving. Her mother writes to Laurel, Kay's sister, "My mental health is not stable enough to survive and tolerate the hurts you inflict in every letter. . . . Naturally, I am grieved and sad to lose a child and grandchildren, but this way is like a gangrenous arm that has to be amputated."
2. June 1, 1982. Walt's lawyer writes to Kay's lawyer, asserting Walt has never tried to subvert the boys' visitation with Kay.
3. August 25, 1982. Kay's lawyer files court document referring to Walt's unwillingness to participate in further mediation. This is filed as part of Kay's request to change venue.

Chapter 54
1. Roy Hart studied with Alfred Wolfsohn, a young German soldier in World War I who was tormented by his memories of the war and by the sounds he had heard. Wolfsohn started trying to replicate those sounds of horror, experimenting with his own

voice, pushing it to new places and discovering new emotions. Slowly, he began realizing he was healing his psyche through his voice, and found himself drawn back into the world of the living. He grew to believe the voice is the mirror of the soul and that people can heal themselves through voice work. When Wolfsohn died in 1962, Roy Hart continued both the therapeutic and artistic application of Wolfsohn's vocal technique by founding the Roy Hart Theatre.

Chapter 55
1. May 11, 2002. Nora writes a note to Alan and Daniel.

Author's Note
1. Taken from "The Uses of Sorrow" in *Thirst* by Mary Oliver. (Beacon Press, 2007).
2. *The Holy Bible*, Authorized King James Version, (Philadelphia, PENN: National Bible Press, 1944), Galatians 5:22–23. "The fruits of the spirit are love, joy, peace, forbearance, kindness, goodness, faithfulness, gentleness and self-control."
3. Taken from The Phenomenon of the Inner Self and the Power of Love, Light and Law Workshop in Paso Robles, January 2023. Given by Caroline Myss.

ACKNOWLEDGMENTS

·······················

My thanks go to:

Jane Anne Staw, who helped me give birth to the writing of this story, patiently making room for my tears and then, nearly twenty years later, helping me complete the writing process and creatively reorganize it.

Ellen Sussman and Elizabeth Stark, whose classes and workshops first gave me the structure, feedback, and courage to complete this project. A shoutout also goes to Sonoma County Writers Camp.

Brooke Warner, founder of She Writes Press, for caretaking and publishing my memoir.

Lorraine Fico-White and Kathleen Furin, editors with She Writes Press, who helped shape and refine the writing and the structure.

Richard, my husband. My relationship with him has allowed me to experience a love in which the boundary between giving and receiving is dissolved. Growing up in a family that kept score, this is a gift I could not have imagined was even possible.

My sons, both of whom make me proud; they are good men, husbands, fathers, providers, and sons.

My parents, who gave me a good education and demanded a good work ethic.

My two sisters, who survived alongside me. We were The Harrington Trio.

The bevy of Harrington cousins who took me in when I needed help, especially Denny and Barbie, and Di and Bill, and the next-generation cousins who grew up to become my friends. Thanks also to the farm cousins who made themselves available for our visits; they let us eat the freshly picked corn, milk the cows, and feed the baby lambs.

Paul, for giving me the opening I used to save my life.

Walter and Nora, for forcing me to find a deeper, stronger and more loving self.

All the teachers, practitioners, and bodyworkers who helped me to become more conscious, to integrate dissociated trauma, and to release deep, unconscious holding patterns. By training, these helpers were psychotherapists, couples' therapists, voice teachers, spiritual counselors, Rolfers, osteopaths, homeopaths, physical therapists, acupuncturists, Tai Chi practitioners, Chi Nei Tsang practitioners, Gyrotonic teachers, and fitness trainers. By name, these helpers were Janeece Dagen, Liz Duncanson, Karina Epperlein, Justine Fixel, Andrew Harvey, Joe Helms, Thomas Hüebl, Mana Jampa, Gilles Marin, Robert Leichtman, Diana Lion, Tina Long, Roger Morrison, Caroline Myss, John Nelson, Jak Noble, Lori Opal, Mark Rittenberg, Patricia Rochette, Michael Salveson, Yuan Tze, Mariano Wechsler, and Landry Wildwind.

My early morning swim friends—especially Susan Helmrich—and my swim team, the Streamliners.

ABOUT THE AUTHOR

Catherine Harrington grew up in Colorado, one generation removed from the family farm in Longmont. After graduating from Stanford University, she fell into teaching high school Spanish. At twenty-eight, married and with two pre-school children, she returned to school to become a psychotherapist. In the years that followed, she did career counseling and taught courses at UC Berkeley, supervised the clinical work of PhD candidates at the Wright Institute, and was an assistant professor at the University of North Carolina Wilmington. She subsequently worked in executive search for nine years and then spent ten years as an organizational consultant. Since finishing her PhD, she has had a private psychotherapy practice. Catherine and her husband of nearly thirty years live in the Bay Area. They have four adult children and six grandchildren. To celebrate her eightieth birthday, Catherine swam from the Golden Gate Bridge to Alcatraz.

Author photo © Reenie Raschke Photography

SELECTED TITLES FROM SHE WRITES PRESS

She Writes Press is an independent publishing company founded to serve women writers everywhere. Visit us at www.shewritespress.com.

You'll Never Find Us: A Memoir by Jeanne Baker Guy. $16.95, 978-1-64742-155-7. In the summer of 1977, an Episcopal priest delivers a letter to thirty-year-old Jeanne informing her that her German nationalist ex-husband has kidnapped their two young children and fled the United States. Unable to get the help she needs from the law, she makes a decision: she will search for and ultimately steal back her son and daughter.

Sophia's Return: Uncovering My Mother's Past by Sophia Kouidou-Giles. $16.95, 978-1-64742-171-7. Seven-year-old Sophia watches her mother leave their family home without a good-bye or explanation—a mysterious departure that becomes her worry stone. Decades later, when she returns to Greece from her adopted home in America, she uncovers a family story she had never been told.

Pieces of Me: Rescuing My Kidnapped Daughters by Lizbeth Meredith. $16.95, 978-1-63152-834-7. When her daughters are kidnapped and taken to Greece by their non-custodial father, single mom Lizbeth Meredith vows to bring them home—and give them a better childhood than her own.

The Buddha at My Table: How I Found Peace in Betrayal and Divorce by Tammy Letherer. $16.95, 978-1-63152-425-7. On a Tuesday night, just before Christmas, after he had put their three children in bed, Tammy Letherer's husband shattered her world and destroyed every assumption she'd ever made about love, friendship, and faithfulness. In the aftermath of this betrayal, however, she finds unexpected blessings—and, ultimately, the path to freedom.

Parent Deleted: A Mother's Fight for Her Right to Parent by Michelle Darné. $16.95, 978-1-63152-282-6. A gripping tale of one non-biological, lesbian mother's fight for shared custody of her children—an intimate, infuriating, and infectious story of perseverance, sacrifice, and hope in the face of debilitating adversity.